The News from Waterloo

Brian Cathcart is professor of journalism at Kingston University London and a founder of Hacked Off. He has been deputy editor of the *Independent on Sunday*, assistant editor of the *New Statesman* and specialist adviser to the Commons Select Committee on media, culture and sport. He is also a historian. His books include *The Fly in the Cathedral: How a small group of Cambridge scientists won the race to split the atom*; *Were You Still Up for Portillo?*; and *The Case of Stephen Lawrence*, the definitive account of the notorious racist murder, which won the Orwell Prize and the CWA Gold Dagger award.

www.thenewsfromwaterloo.com

A London newsboy selling papers, 1815.
The words on his hat say 'Second Edition News'.

The News from Waterloo

The Race to Tell Britain of Wellington's Victory

BRIAN CATHCART

FABER & FABER

First published in 2015
by Faber & Faber Ltd
Bloomsbury House
74–77 Great Russell Street
London WCIB 3DA
This paperback edition first published in 2016

Typeset by Faber & Faber Ltd
Printed and bound by CPI Group (UK) Ltd, Croydon CRO 4YY

The right of Brian Cathcart to be identified as author of this work
has been asserted in accordance with Section 77 of the
Copyright Designs and Patents Act 1988

Thanks are due to Sebastian Faulks for permission to quote
from his novel *A Week in December*

A CIP record for this book
is available from the British Library

ISBN 978-0-571-31526-0

FSC
www.fsc.org
MIX
Paper from
responsible sources
FSC® C101712

2 4 6 8 10 9 7 5 3 1

Contents

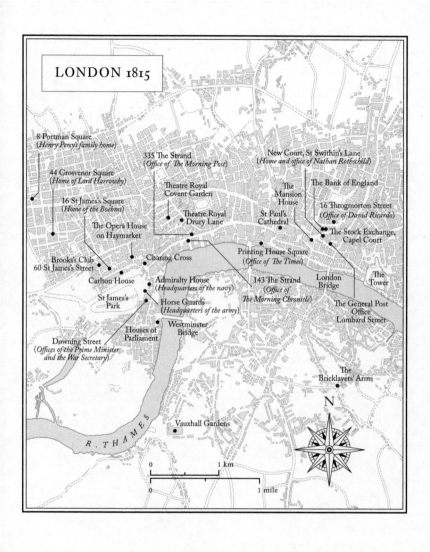

LONDON 1815

8 Portman Square
(Henry Percy's family home)

44 Grosvenor Square
(Home of Lord Harrowby)

16 St James's Square
(Home of the Boehms)

335 The Strand
(Office of The Morning Post)

New Court, St Swithin's Lane
(Home and office of Nathan Rothschild)

The Bank of England

Theatre Royal
Covent Garden

The
Mansion
House

16 Throgmorton Street
(Office of David Ricardo)

Theatre Royal
Drury Lane

St Paul's
Cathedral

The Opera House
on Haymarket

The Stock Exchange,
Capel Court

Brooks's Club
60 St James's Street

Charing Cross

Printing House Square
(Office of The Times)

Carlton House

Admiralty House
(Headquarters of the navy)

143 The Strand
*(Office of
The Morning Chronicle)*

London
Bridge

The
Tower

St James's
Park

Horse Guards
(Headquarters of the army)

The General Post
Office
Lombard Street

Downing Street
*(Offices of the Prime Minister
and the War Secretary)*

Houses of
Parliament

Westminster
Bridge

The
Bricklayers' Arms

R. THAMES

Vauxhall Gardens

N

0   1 km

0   1 mile

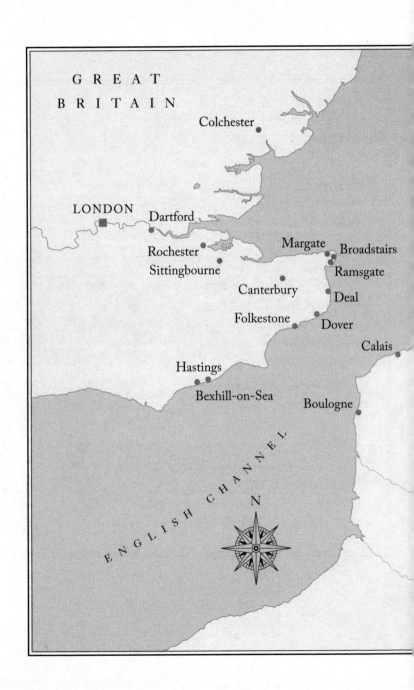

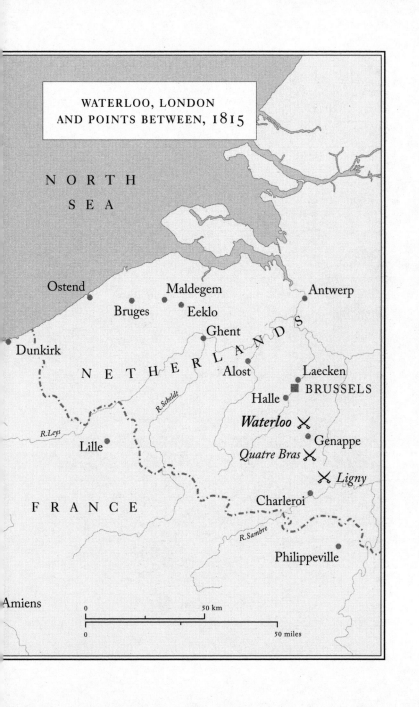

WATERLOO, LONDON
AND POINTS BETWEEN, 1815

NORTH
SEA

Ostend
Maldegem
Antwerp
Bruges
Eeklo
Ghent
Dunkirk
NETHERLANDS
Alost
Laecken
R.Scheldt
Halle
BRUSSELS
Waterloo ✕
R.Leys
Genappe
Lille
Quatre Bras ✕
✕ Ligny
FRANCE
Charleroi
R.Sambre
Philippeville
Amiens

0   50 km

0   50 miles

Foreword

The defeat of Napoleon Bonaparte at Waterloo was the most momentous news to reach Britain in the whole of the nineteenth century. To those living at the time it was a cause of heartfelt national celebration and to subsequent generations it was proof that nothing could rival British valour and generalship, while viewed from today it still stands out as an epoch, ushering in an age of unprecedented imperial and industrial power. Given such historical significance, there is something incongruous in the means by which the news travelled, with no steam power or electricity to hurry it along but propelled only by the muscle power of men and horses and by the wind in the sails of ships. Still more surprising is the discovery that, in the two centuries since then, the basic facts of what happened – who brought the first word of the victory and how long it took – have remained a mystery.

It is not that people didn't care. A great deal has been written on the subject, and there are even films about it, but this has only added layers of controversy and confusion. There is what might be called an official narrative in which word was rushed to London by an aide-de-camp to the Duke of Wellington, but others have told different and more colourful tales. A yachtsman cruising in the Channel was said to have picked up the news and dashed home with it; a young architect who had been travelling on the continent, it was claimed, turned up at the door of a Cabinet minister in London to announce the victory. There was also the man who came ashore on Hastings beach crying 'Hurrah! Wellington has thrashed Boney!', and the secretive figure who landed at Bexhill-on-Sea and paid a king's ransom to be rushed to the capital. Like all good urban legends, these accounts come with earnest bona fides – 'my father's memory was a good one', and 'I had the above statement from the gentleman's own lips.'[1]

More widely known, and repeated to this day, is a story that the victory signal was transmitted to London along a line of semaphores, with unfortunate consequences. Signallers atop Winchester Cathedral, it is said, had passed on only the first words of the message, 'Wellington defeated Napoleon at Waterloo', when a sudden fog descended. The next semaphore station in line faithfully relayed what it had received, and so ministers were given the wholly wrong bulletin: 'Wellington defeated.'[2] Another recurring story relates that the news was brought not by a man at all, but by a carrier pigeon. But most persistent of all is a tale retold in every decade, in every medium and in almost every language: that the first man in London to know the outcome of Waterloo was the banker Nathan Rothschild. Though it was given currency by a writer happy to sign himself 'Satan', and though it was later endorsed by Nazi propagandists, this tale has been repeated so frequently by historians, only some of whom have acknowledged a dearth of supporting evidence, that in the wider world it is often simply stated as fact.

What really happened, though obscured by myths and mischief, is happily not quite lost to us. It is still possible, notably with the help of newspapers of the time, to reconstruct the events of the midsummer days that followed the victory. And the fact proves no less exotic than the fiction. It turns out that over the roads and seas between Waterloo and London there was a race – a sometimes faltering, sometimes comical race in which truth could not always keep pace with nonsense, but a race all the same. And there are roles in the drama for an exotic Russian diplomat, a Regency dandy, a shady French courtier, a tearful young lady, at least one smuggler, a wild-eyed newspaper editor, a Green Knight, a forged diary, fast coaches, slow ships and a little boat with four stout sailors heaving at the oars. History being an untidy business, in the end some mysteries remain and a few new ones arise, but the solution to the whodunnit is, I hope, clear.

Many people helped me with my research, in many ways. Beth Brewster, David Rodgers, Martin McQuillan and other colleagues at Kingston University have been unstinting in their support, as has everyone at the Hacked Off campaign. Among librarians and archivists who have been generous with their time I would like, in particular, to thank Melanie Aspey of the Rothschild Archive London and Christopher Hunwick at the Archives of the Duke of Northumberland at Alnwick Castle. Others to whom I am grateful include Lavinia Griffiths, Alan Ford, 'Ton van Ijzendoorn, Lesley Haigh, Peter Durbin, Geert van Doorne, Howard Barrett, Herbert H. Kaplan, Sir William Mahon, John Griffiths, Graham Farmelo and David James Smith. I alone bear responsibility for errors and misjudgements. The chief debt I owe to my sons Tom and Patrick and most of all to my wife, Ruth, without whose help and generous support this book could not have been written.

Brian Cathcart, 2015

A Note on the Text

This book contains a good deal of quotation and for ease of reading I have taken some liberties with texts, notably by replacing some of the capital letters so liberally used by Regency writers with lower case, by adjusting some punctuation to a more modern style and by standardising some spellings (settling, for example, on 'dispatch' rather than 'despatch'). I hope I have not interfered with meanings, but anyone with concerns should consult the originals. Readers should also beware of times, which ought generally to be taken as approximate. Today people living on the Kent coast keep the same time as those in London, while Belgium is normally one hour ahead of Britain. It was not so, or at least not uniformly so, in 1815.

I

Sunday: The News is Made

In the early weeks of 1815 Europe was savouring an unfamiliar experience: peace. Napoleon Bonaparte, soldier and strategist of almost superhuman genius, had at long last been vanquished by a grand coalition of powers, bringing to an end, or so it seemed, a quarter of a century of bloodshed and turmoil. The defeated emperor was now in exile on the little island of Elba, off the coast of Italy, and the old order had been restored in France with the installation as king of Louis XVIII, brother to the monarch guillotined in the Revolution. As the victorious allied armies slowly made their way home, Europe's diplomats assembled at the Congress of Vienna, a marathon of dining, dancing, gambling and philandering punctuated here and there by haggling over plans for a grand new international order. The thoughts of an exhausted continent, in short, were slowly turning to life without war and revolution. Then, suddenly and astonishingly, the great nemesis resurfaced, his charisma and brilliance apparently undimmed. And, no less astonishingly, his country, or at least the mighty army that still dominated it, welcomed him back. Gone in an instant was that mood of relief and hope.

Bonaparte landed on the French Riviera on the first day of March with a thousand men. Three weeks later, with not a single shot fired, he was back in Paris and restored as emperor, the hapless Louis having fled in terror. The European powers, aghast at these developments, proclaimed Napoleon an outlaw and formed themselves into what would be called, with weary predictability, the Seventh Coalition. The Russian and Austrian empires, the kingdoms of Britain and Prussia and a handful of lesser states and statelets scrambled to reassemble the vast forces that had been required to overcome the French leader a year earlier. Great columns of soldiers still trudging homeward were turned on their heels and directed back towards France.

Logic suggested that an alliance on such a scale must triumph again, but history showed that Bonaparte had a knack of unstitching grand coalitions. Europe's greatest general since Alexander the Great was also a devilishly clever politician: as skilfully as he could outmanoeuvre his enemies on the battlefield he could also prey on their mutual jealousies, bewitching their leaders into trusting his promises and following his wishes. Who could tell whether the Seventh Coalition would endure like the sixth, or fail like the fifth, the fourth and the third? In Britain, which had itself once been induced to sign a peace treaty with the French emperor, there were doubts about a new war. Shedding British blood to force an unwanted Bourbon on to the throne of France for a second time was an unattractive prospect. The brief interlude of peace, moreover, had exposed alarming social divisions and economic difficulties at home, and these were weak foundations for struggle abroad. Another long war could barely be contemplated.

Napoleon, knowing it would be fatal to wait for his enemies to come to him, swiftly assembled an army in the north with a view to fighting the Prussians, British, Dutch and other lesser allies who were already gathering in Belgium. If he could win early victories there, before the Russians and Austrians could bring their far greater forces into the field, then he could sow doubt and fear among his adversaries. And if that happened, if there were any hesitation, any crack in the grand alliance, then everything might be possible. On 15 June 1815, therefore, he threw his forces across the frontier with Belgium and the next day, with characteristic bravado, fought two battles at once. The greater part of his army, under his own direction, confronted the Prussians at Ligny and sent them reeling northward. A smaller force, under Marshal Ney, took on the British, Dutch and assorted Germans just a few miles away at the crossroads of Quatre Bras. Ney came close to victory against enemies arriving late on the battlefield, but the Duke of Wellington rallied his men and the encounter ended with honours even. By Saturday 17 June, therefore, with the Prussians apparently *hors de combat*, a confident Napoleon was preparing to turn almost his whole force against Wellington. The duke, meanwhile, was falling back to a defensive position along a ridge straddling the road to Brussels, just south of the village of Waterloo.

*

Battle was joined there late next morning, and if the prologue had been theatrical – the escape in darkness from Elba, the triumphal advance on Paris, the humiliating flight of Louis XVIII, the furious denunciations of the allies, the about-face of the armies – then the climax was simply brutal.

Wellington had a word for it: 'pounding'. Never having faced Napoleon across a battlefield before, he was on the alert for tactical brilliance, but when he saw his adversary at work his verdict was sharp: 'Damn the fellow. He is a mere pounder after all.'[1] For hour after hour the French, numbering in all about 77,000 men, mounted frontal assault after frontal assault. There was little subtlety or science to it. Artillery blasted away at the closely bunched allied lines, pausing periodically to allow great masses of French soldiers to swarm up the muddy slope and assail their adversaries with musket and bayonet. Occasionally, heavy cavalry – the ultimate land weapon of the day – would charge thunderously, sabres slashing. And all the time Wellington's army of 73,000 men clung to their position on the ridge. The carnage was relentless and terrible. 'Hard pounding this, gentlemen,' remarked the duke as he watched his men fall, adding grimly: 'Let's see who will pound the longest.'[2] The smoke of 400 cannons darkened an already cloudy sky until a summer's afternoon was like foggy twilight. The few buildings on the battlefield became the scenes of desperate struggles, bodies piling up in every door and gateway. Sunken lanes ran with blood while out in the open the lines of men bludgeoned, bayoneted and shot each other, the living trampling over the dying in the effort to lock arms again. It began after 11 a.m., and as evening drew near the French were still pressing forward in great waves, forging uphill to cries of *Vive l'Empereur!*, only to be repulsed at the top with further slaughter. Wellington used the same term again in a later reflection: 'Never did I see such a pounding match. Both were what boxers call gluttons.'[3]

Napoleon had roused his soldiers that morning with the

promise that they would be in Brussels by nightfall, but as evening came on he could see that time was against him. His men were tiring and his artillery was running short of ammunition, and night would bring more respite to his adversaries, with their shorter lines of supply, than it would to him. Worse, he knew that he could not hold off the Prussians, for Blücher had managed to gather his forces and direct them west across country towards Waterloo. As the hours passed, Prussian men and guns in ever greater numbers engaged the French on their right flank and it was plain to Napoleon that he must break through very soon or his army would be squeezed in a vice. So at about 7.30 p.m. he gambled all. Riding his white Arab stallion Marengo and with his military band playing patriotic tunes, he personally led the Imperial Guard to the start line for a new assault. Held in reserve thus far, these were the finest fighting men in Europe: everyone knew that when they fought they won. And as they drew level and then passed their emperor on the way towards the allied guns, the rest of the battered French army, its pride and confidence refreshed, girded and followed. Wellington, seeing them coming, re-ordered his line.

One last time, the armies collided. For perhaps half an hour more there was carnage and confusion. The cannon fire on both sides was merciless. The advancing French line shuddered and in places gave way, but so too did the allied line. Still the gluttons went at each other, but now there were flashes of something more than mere attrition. French infantry nearing the crest of what seemed a thinly defended part of the ridge suddenly found lines of British guardsmen leaping to their feet and pouring volley after volley on them at short range. Near by, a British commander took the unorthodox step of wheeling his whole force side-on to the French and raining fire from the flank. Witnesses spoke of ranks of soldiers falling like corn to a scythe. And all the time, on the other side of the battlefield, more Prussians were joining in. A British officer recalled:

> the field was so enveloped in smoke that nothing was discernible. The firing ceased on both sides, and we on the left knew that one party or the other was beaten. This was the most anxious moment of my life. In a few seconds we saw the redcoats in the centre, as stiff as rocks, and the French columns retiring rapidly, and there was such a British shout as rent the air.[4]

Even the Imperial Guard were recoiling. All day Wellington had shepherded and manoeuvred his motley army with one objective in mind: to cling on to the ridge. No longer. 'Go on! Go on!' he cried, waving his men down the slope and into the attack. 'Now!' he called to an officer. 'Now is your time!' Catching sight of soldiers celebrating, he told them: 'No cheering my lads, but forward and complete your victory!'[5] Napoleon, watching through a telescope from the other side of the valley, declared to his staff: 'It's over now. We must go.'[6]

Within minutes the French retreat was a rout. Not only were Wellington's men rushing forward, but the Prussians had also broken through on the French right. The chase was on, first to the village of Genappe and after that southward in the darkness towards Charleroi on the River Sambre, beyond which lay the French frontier. Most of Wellington's army, however, soon slowed and halted, leaving the Prussians to lead the pursuit. Exhausted and hungry, they made camp for the night, counted their losses and picked over fields littered with the minor spoils of war. Before long Wellington himself, having ridden out to assure himself of the enemy's complete disorder and to see the many captured French cannon, turned back towards his headquarters. By chance, some time after 9 p.m. he met Blücher on the road. '*Mein lieber Kamarad!*' exclaimed the Prussian after an awkward embrace. '*Quelle affaire!*'[7]

Military historians will argue forever over which moment, which order, which manoeuvre and which set of soldiers were decisive at Waterloo, but as a symbolic conclusion to the day's action the encounter between Wellington and Blücher has no rival. It was there, in a few words, that the two commanders acknowledged their victory to each other. The most ardent hopes of the morning had been realised and they must have glimpsed, even if they did not fully grasp, the implications of what had been achieved. This was not merely the end of a hundred anxious days since the escape from Elba, but it was the end for Napoleon Bonaparte, whose mystique was shattered and whose army was broken. It was the end, too, of the historic cycle of upheaval that had begun with the storming of the Bastille in 1789. The great gamble that was the emperor's second coming had failed; swords could soon be sheathed; trade and travel could resume; bloodshed and uncertainty could end. Though Wellington and Blücher knew they must march all the way to Paris to secure their advantage, both surely realised that on the field of Waterloo that day a long chapter of history had closed. What they had achieved would be a matter of importance and astonishment to a whole continent, and indeed to many people even farther afield. In other words, it would be *news*; indeed, there has rarely been news like it.

Sunday–Monday: The Waterloo Dispatch

As twilight turned to darkness in Belgium, the Duke of
Wellington had other things on his mind besides telling the
world about his victory. Parting from Blücher, he turned his
famous horse Copenhagen towards Waterloo village and the
inn where he had slept the previous night. Generals are rarely
alone on campaign, and accompanying the duke now was a
trusted entourage of senior officers, aides-de-camp and diplomats representing the allied powers. By some accounts they
dismounted and walked part of the way. It was at least four
miles to the inn, and the road took them back through the
scenes of some of the day's most murderous action. An officer
who passed that way soon afterwards described the spectacle:

> The dead were innumerable, French and English inter-
> mixed. Those who had fallen in the road had been
> trampled on by horses and wheels of artillery into a mass
> of blood, flesh and clothes, hardly to be distinguished
> one from the other. In the hollow between the two armies
> on each side of the road there lay piles of dead French-
> men and horses, among whom were many of the Imperial
> Guard.[1]

It was a charnel house, a hellish scene illuminated by a thousand camp fires. The corpses, many already stripped naked,

were heaped highest in those places where the fighting had been fiercest. Here and there Wellington returned the greetings of his soldiers and acknowledged the occasional cheer, but the mood was more funereal than triumphant. And once they were past the worst of the battlefield they found themselves among the pathetic columns of the wounded, some walking and some borne in carts, all heading rearwards in the hope of relief.

It was past 11 p.m. when they reached the inn, and there Wellington found a young officer from his staff fighting for his life. Sir Alexander Gordon was an aide-de-camp who had campaigned with the duke for six years and of whom he was especially fond. In the final phase of the battle Gordon was struck in the thigh by a musket ball – by one account, at a moment when he was begging his commander to take cover. The shattered leg was amputated, but Gordon had lost too much blood and by the time Wellington reached his bedside he was weak and, despite doses of laudanum and wine, in pain and distress. He could barely speak, but the duke was able to tell him that the battle had ended in victory.

Waterloo had taken a toll on both sides that shocked even the most experienced campaigners. Almost a quarter of the allied army, it would later be calculated, had been killed or wounded or had gone missing. There is barely a memoir or a letter by any survivor that does not reflect horror, and it has been said that, measured in casualties per square mile, the carnage bears comparison with the first day of the Somme in 1916. For Wellington this came very close. Although miraculously he himself had escaped injury, of his personal staff of half a dozen men – a little group known as his 'family' – one was dead, another was dying and a third had been rushed to Brussels after losing an arm. Some of his most senior officers had been killed or gravely wounded, and the list was growing alarmingly. His most seasoned infantry general was dead. His cavalry commander had lost a leg. His Guards commander had lost an arm. His quartermaster was dying.[2] And, as he had been reminded so vividly on his homeward trudge, the toll of other ranks had been terrible. So it was in depleted and subdued company that the duke sat down to supper.

The inn was small, and since the dining room was given over to the wounded the table was set in the duke's bedroom upstairs, where the party numbered eight or ten, among them some of the diplomats. Military dinners at this time often entailed prodigious feats of alcohol consumption, but on this occasion just one toast was proposed and that was not to victory but to the memory of the Peninsular War, which had first brought most of them together. Years later one of those present recalled: 'The Duke said very little, ate hastily and heartily, but every time the door opened he gave a searching look, evidently in the hope of some of his valuable staff approaching.'[3] As they talked, a question arose. Should something be done that night to get the news to the king of France? Louis XVIII had been staying in the city of Ghent, on the far side of Brussels, and was poised, anxiously, to retreat northward in the event of an allied defeat. Wellington declared himself too tired to write, and it was agreed instead that the job would be done by one of the diplomats at the table. The duke instructed him to inform the king that the most complete victory he had ever gained had been gained that day and that the French army was in complete rout; that he himself [Wellington] had followed them several miles and had seen sixty pieces of cannon taken, and that they were now closely pursued by the Prussians and could not possibly halt again on this side of the frontier.[4]

Soon after this the guests departed, and Wellington retired to bed.

By now it must have been nearly 1 a.m. What had been done to spread the word? Wellington, who as allied commander had a unique authority to pronounce on the outcome, had made no effort even to get the news to Brussels, let alone transmit it to his government in London or, for that matter, to his own family there. The only communication he had authorised was that letter to the king of France, and even that may not have been his idea. Nor, for that matter, was he assuming that his subordinates were doing the job for him: there is no record of any other senior officer taking responsibility for the task that night, and no one afterwards expressed the view that this had been an oversight. This may seem strange, but British military convention of the time held that significant events should be reported to London in formal dispatches written by the commanding officer at the scene. That was both his duty and his prerogative. And such dispatches were rarely brief since they were not only a medium of news but an official record and even a first draft of history (so that to be 'mentioned in dispatches' was a lasting badge of honour). Trouble and time must be spent getting this right. Wellington had sent many dispatches from his campaigns in India, Portugal, Spain and southern France, and it had never been his habit to write them immediately after battle. Of course, in those earlier cases the lines of communication were longer, and when it took weeks or even months for a dispatch to reach London a delay of a few hours in the writing, or even of a couple of days, counted for little. Waterloo was much closer to London than, say, Salamanca or Badajoz, but Wellington would not be hurried. He saw the priorities clearly: what mattered was whether Napoleon was beaten, not when ministers learned about it. It is likely, however, that on the night of Waterloo he barely considered such matters, for whatever the protocol was, and whatever his personal habits, he simply did not feel equal to the task. This was not a man brimming with pride in a great achievement and eager to share it with others. Instead, he was weary to the bone and, as he would write the next day, 'quite broken down' by the losses sustained by his army.[5] When the idea of writing to the king of France came up that night, we are told, 'the Duke said no, that he had won the battle for him but that he was so exhausted that he could not write a letter that night but must go to bed'.[6]

•

He did not sleep long. At 3.30 a.m., just as dawn was breaking, Gordon died of his wounds, and the surgeon, John Hume, was hesitating over whether to tell Wellington when his mind was made up for him by a senior officer seeking orders from the duke for troop movements. Hume later painted a vivid picture of the scene:

On this I decided to see if he was awake, and going upstairs to his room I tapped gently at the door, when he told me to come in. He had, as usual, taken off all of his clothes, but had not washed himself; and as I entered the room he sat up in his bed, his face covered with the dust and sweat of the previous day, and extended his hand to me, which I took and held in mine whilst I told him of Gordon's death and related such of the casualties as had come to my knowledge. He was much affected. I felt tears dropping fast upon my hands, and looking towards him, saw them chasing one another in furrows over his dusty cheeks. He brushed them suddenly away with his left hand and said to me, in a voice tremulous with emotion, 'Well! Thank God I don't know what it is to lose a battle, but certainly nothing can be more painful than to gain one with the loss of so many of one's friends.'[7]

Now at last Wellington turned his thoughts to his dispatch. He dressed and ate some toast, and by the time he took up his pen the sun was coming up to light the work. To this day in the inn at Waterloo (now a museum) are preserved a chair and folding table he is said to have used, and an artist later painted the scene.[8] On the face of it his job was straightforward: he had to give an account of the fighting, identify officers and regiments who had distinguished themselves, provide a first estimate of casualties and indicate what his next moves might be. But he must have known that this was a dispatch unlike any other he had written. So sensational was the victory, so decisive and significant the battle, that every household in Britain would soon know about it and speak of it. And for every reader in the English language the dispatch would be the essential document and might remain so for years. In short, Wellington was composing a historic text.

Addressing himself to the Secretary for War, Lord Bathurst, he began:

> Bonaparte, having collected the 1st, 2nd, 3rd, 4th, and 6th corps of the French army and the Imperial Guards and nearly all the cavalry on the Sambre and between that river and the Meuse between the 10th and 14th of the month, advanced on the 15th, and attacked the Prussian posts at Thuin and Lobbes on the Sambre at daylight in the morning.
>
> I did not hear of these events till in the evening of the 15th and I immediately ordered the troops to prepare to march; and afterwards to march to their left as soon as I had intelligence from other quarters to prove that the enemy's movement upon Charleroi was the real attack.*

This was, it is clear, no news bulletin; it did not open with the most important fact, that the French had been comprehensively defeated. Instead, in conventional dispatch style, it was a narrative. Though Wellington had fought two battles since the 15th and the Prussians a third, this was his first official

---

* The full text of the dispatch is given in Appendix 1, p. 299.

report to London since the fighting began, and he started carefully and clearly at the beginning. The Prussian outposts, he explained, had fallen back before this first French advance, and the following day saw two battles. To the east, at Ligny, the Prussians were engaged, while in the west the French were halted by his army at Quatre Bras. In keeping with dispatch style, Wellington named those who did well in this first encounter: 'His Royal Highness the Prince of Orange, the Duke of Brunswick, and Lieut. General Sir Thomas Picton, and Major Generals Sir James Kempt and Sir Denis Pack, who were engaged from the commencement of the enemy's attack, highly distinguished themselves.' And he did not reserve his praise for senior officers alone: 'The troops of the 5th division, and those of the Brunswick corps, were long and severely engaged, and conducted themselves with the utmost gallantry.' We don't know how much of this he wrote before he was forced to break off, but day had dawned and Brussels beckoned: there were jobs to be done and orders to be given. His polyglot army must be rallied, provisioned and set on the road to France in support of the Prussians. Moreover, with so many senior colleagues dead and wounded he had to make decisions that others would normally have made, and he had to consider how to fill the vacancies. So the draft dispatch was tucked away, the field trappings were packed up and Copenhagen was saddled again. Soon the duke and what remained of his staff were making their way along the chaotically cluttered road through the forest of Soignes to the Belgian capital.

*

By his own account the first words that greeted him on his arrival were: 'What news?'[9] It was early, and the city, or at least its large community of assorted expatriates, was still emerging from a period of terrifying uncertainty. Since their experience of the news from Waterloo will help shape London's experience it is worth reviewing what had happened to them.

That spring and early summer, as the allies mustered their northern armies in Belgium, Brussels had enjoyed a giddy spell as the social capital of Europe. In particular, it had become an unlikely second home for London's high society, with officers and their wives and mistresses, aristocratic camp followers, politicians and well-heeled tourists of all kinds taking up residence. They and their many servants laid on balls, promenades, dinners, theatre, racing, hunting, cricket and everything else that was required to keep the British upper classes happy. Also enjoying the fun, if not the cricket, were exiled French royalists, representatives of the Prussian and other German forces, diplomats of all nations and – in some numbers – Dutch officials. These last were in town because the great powers, having liberated Belgium from Napoleonic rule in 1814, had decided in their wisdom to place it under Dutch rule instead, as part of a new Kingdom of the Netherlands.

For this colourful community the climactic moment of the season would be the famous ball given by the Duchess of Richmond at her residence on the Rue de la Blanchisserie on the evening of 15 June. More than two hundred were invited, and dancing was accommodated in an adjacent coach shed, lavishly fitted up for the night. The duke was seen to flirt outrageously with the woman who was the apple of his eye at that time, the married and very pregnant Lady Frances Wedderburn Webster. Precisely when he learned that the French had attacked that morning, or at least at what time he was satisfied this was not merely 'an affair of outposts', is a matter of controversy, but there is no doubt that he was distracted from the pleasures of the ball and eventually forced to abandon them by the need to organise the military response. From that moment Brussels ceased to be a place of enjoyment for expatriates and became frightening instead.

Most of the civilians had expected to observe from a comfortable distance as the allied armies rolled into France and humbled Bonaparte on his own soil, so the discovery that the fighting was moving rapidly in the opposite direction, and that they risked being taken prisoner, or worse, came as a great shock. Brussels was an open city, its ancient walls only surviving in parts, and it could not be defended against a French army. Nor did it help that many native *bruxellois* were thought to have no stomach for a fight: some saw little to choose between rule by the French and rule by the Dutch. So it was that, once the expatriates had seen the allied army march out in haste to confront the advancing enemy, panic took hold. A scramble for horses, carriages and places on passenger barges turned into an unseemly frenzy, with most people desperate to reach Antwerp, a walled city to the north that could be defended and from which, if necessary, they might escape to England by sea. On Saturday morning, after the first muddled news arrived from Ligny and Quatre Bras, followed swiftly by the first casualties, the panic was renewed and a further wave fled by whatever means they could find along the roads and canals. Even so, some expatriate civilians remained. The writer Fanny Burney had left it too late. As an Englishwoman married to a senior French royalist army officer she was doubly an enemy of Bonaparte, but when on Sunday morning she tried to find a place on a barge to Antwerp – no carriages were available by then – she discovered that all vessels had been requisitioned to move military stores and the wounded. Among others stranded was Thomas Creevey, an MP of the Whig opposition who had settled in Brussels the previous autumn in the expectation that it would be a quiet, cheap and comfortable place in which to nurse his invalid wife. By now Mrs Creevey was too ill to be moved, so he and his plucky stepdaughters, Ann and Elizabeth Ord, stayed on to share her fate. Elizabeth would later write: 'I think Sunday was the most miserable day I ever spent in my life and one I could never forget if I was to live 1,000 years.'[10]

They were all desperate for news from the battlefront. 'All of which we seemed capable was to inquire or to relate, to speak or to hear,' wrote Burney.

All the people of Brussels lived in the streets. Doors seemed of no use, for they were never shut. The individuals, when they re-entered their houses, only resided at the windows, so that the whole population of the city seemed constantly in public view.[11]

Given that even Wellington himself could not have been sure of the outcome of the battle until after 8 p.m. at the earliest, and given also the nature of the fighting, it is hardly surprising that in the course of Sunday no clear or accurate picture reached the city a dozen miles away. Instead Burney, Creevey and the rest endured something much more distressing than ignorance, for events in the afternoon repeatedly conspired to suggest that the very worst was happening. The darkest moment was the dramatic passage through the town of an allied cavalry regiment in full flight and giving every impression that French dragoons were at their heels. These were the Cumberland Hussars, a regiment of aristocratic German volunteers who were held in reserve at Waterloo in the early part of the fighting and failed to follow the example of others by dismounting to take cover from the cannon fire. After watching their mounted comrades fall like ninepins for an hour or so they lost their nerve, and when they were eventually ordered into action they turned and fled. Reaching Brussels in great disorder, they clattered spectacularly up the Rue de Namur and crossed the Place Royale without a pause before continuing northward in the direction of Antwerp. This was probably the first of the several occasions on which word flashed around Brussels that 'The French are in the town!' It happened again a little later, Burney records. A 'violent, loud, affrighting' howl went up, she wrote, 'issuing from many voices', but it turned out that this was a troop of captured French cavalrymen being paraded through the streets. By contrast, a fleeting moment of hope came when someone burst into Burney's room shouting: *'Bonaparte est pris! Le voilà! Le voilà!'* She looked out of the window in excitement to see that, indeed, a senior French officer was being led into town on horseback, his hands tied, but her heart sank when she made out his face. This was not the emperor.

As afternoon turned to evening, it was British witnesses who were spreading alarm. Around 4 p.m. Creevey met a fellow MP, Thomas Legh, who informed him that 'everything looked as bad as possible', and he soon found Legh's view endorsed by a Guards officer just in from the battlefield: 'Why sir, I don't like the appearance of things at all. The French are getting on in such a manner that I don't see what's to stop them.'[12] Burney, too, found retreat and defeat on every lip. 'The dearth of any positive news from the field of battle', she wrote, was 'nearly distracting in its torturing suspense to the wrung nerves'. Looking back on these hours, she lamented the inadequacy of official communication: 'At certain houses, as well as at public offices, news, I doubt not, arrived; but no means were taken to promulgate it; no gazettes, as in London, no bulletins, as in Paris, were cried about the streets; we were all left at once with our conjectures and our destinies.' She was right: at 'certain offices' there was indeed news, for the Dutch government had begun issuing bulletins in the name of its most senior official in the city, Baron Godert van der Capellen. His early reports presented a rosy interpretation of the events at Quatre Bras and Ligny, and his fourth bulletin, issued on Sunday at 8 a.m., gave the impression that the armies of Wellington and Blücher were preparing to attack the French. Dutch officials in Brussels were keen to sustain morale in the city by showing optimism, but they were poorly informed themselves and manifestly bad at spreading the word.

Around the town, the unofficial news seemed only to grow worse. At 10.30 p.m. Creevey, his wife and his stepdaughters received a visit from Major Andrew Hamilton, a family

friend, who had just come from the battlefield accompanying a wounded general. Weary and depressed, he told his
friends that, although the allies had fought heroically, it was
his opinion when he left the field that the battle was lost,
and he urged Creevey to take his family and escape in the
hours that remained before the French arrived. Friends of
Fanny Burney, meanwhile, were giving her a similarly bleak
message: Bonaparte, having at first been driven back by Wellington, had executed a turning manoeuvre. Now the duke
himself was in danger of capture, and Brussels would fall in
the morning.

Creevey and his household went to bed fully dressed,
fearing the worst. Burney, however, records that last thing at
night 'an officer burst into the room with assurances that the
enemy was flying in all directions'. This was more accurate,
but the difficulty by now, after so many different accounts,
was that there was no more reason to believe him than anyone else. In fact, an official announcement was made in Brussels at 3 a.m. – a formal, printed bulletin from Baron van der
Capellen declaring on behalf of the Dutch government that
the allies had been victorious – but it does not appear to have
been effectively disseminated, even after daybreak. Creevey,
rising at 6 a.m., heard nothing of it. Instead he made his
way to the home of a friendly Belgian aristocrat in search
of news and there received a surprise: 'The first person I saw
was Madame de Jaurenais, walking about in *déshabillé* amidst
a great bivouac of horses. She told me immediately that the
French were defeated and had fled in great confusion.' A
doubting Creevey tracked this information to its source, a
senior British officer, who confirmed that he had received the

welcome news by messenger from the battlefield in the early hours. With that Creevey was convinced, but his stepdaughter Elizabeth, after all the confusion of Sunday, took longer to satisfy. 'Though the good news was more confirmed every minute,' she wrote, 'we hardly knew how to believe it.' As for Fanny Burney, she did not conquer her doubts for another whole day: 'It was not till Tuesday the 20th I had certain and satisfactory assurances how complete was the victory.'

*

So it was into a dazed and almost disbelieving city, not yet ready for general jubilation, that Wellington rode around 8 a.m. It was Creevey who called out to him, 'What news?' and the duke replied: 'Why, I think we've done for 'em this time.' Briskly he made his way to his Brussels residence overlooking the park and after conducting some urgent business sought the quiet of an upstairs room. There he would complete the official dispatch, but not before dashing off this note:

My dear Lady Frances,

Lord Mountnorris may remain in Brussels in perfect security. I yesterday, after a most severe and bloody contest, gained a complete victory, and pursued the French till after dark. They are in complete confusion and I have, I believe, 150 pieces of cannon; and Blücher, who continued the pursuit all night, my soldiers being tired to death, sent me word this morning that he had got 60 more.

My loss is immense. Lord Uxbridge, Lord FitzRoy Somerset, General Cooke, General Barnes and Colonel Berkeley are wounded; Colonel de Lancey, Canning, Gordon, General Picton killed. The finger of Providence was upon me, and I escaped unhurt.

Believe me, etc.,

Wellington[13]

This was timed at 8.30 a.m. That he should have given priority to putting at rest the mind of Lady Frances Wedderburn Webster tells us a good deal about the duke's feelings for her, but no less striking is the style of the note: in a hundred words he summed up the story of a bloody contest and a 'complete victory'. This simple, urgent and direct approach he set aside when he returned to his official account.

Although the Waterloo dispatch is a narrative punctuated with those vital 'mentions' of distinguished conduct, it is not without artifice. Wellington had found during the Peninsular War that any hint of weakness, indecision or error was likely to be exploited by what were called 'croakers' in London – those in politics and the press eager to criticise the government and its conduct of the war. So he had learned to take precautions – to the point where, on one occasion in Spain when a subordinate drafted a dispatch he considered too circumspect, he declared: 'This won't do. Write me down a victory.'[14] After Waterloo he could have had few worries about the croakers, but his dispatch none the less shows signs of presentational care. He avoids any suggestion that Napoleon's advance into Belgium on 15 June might have taken him by surprise, or that Quatre Bras was, in the circumstances, a

fortunate escape. And he is so discreet about the undoubted
Prussian defeat the same day that the reader is left to deduce
what happened from their subsequent retreat.

The overriding characteristic of the dispatch, however, is
its restraint, and not for nothing did the American ambassador in London later remark that it read more like a defeat
than a victory.[15] The build-up is slow – the whole document
runs to about 2,350 words and 1,000 of those have passed
before the fighting at Waterloo even begins. Nowhere does
the word 'victory' appear, even though Wellington had used
it in his note to Lady Frances, nor 'triumph', and the only
mention of 'glory' relates to the conduct of an individual
officer. Sunday's action itself flies by in just 400 words. Wellington wrote that the battle began with 'a furious attack' on
his right wing, followed by 'a very heavy cannonade' and
'repeated attacks of cavalry and infantry' all along the line.
Then in just ten words he wrapped up a sustained frenzy
of military activity – those hours of pounding – to which
thousands of pages of historical analysis have since been
devoted: 'These attacks were repeated till about seven in
the evening.' The account of the decisive period, the 'cri-
sis', as it would be known, is scarcely less economical: 'the
enemy made a desperate effort with cavalry and infantry
supported by the fire of artillery to force our left centre
near the farm of La Haye Sainte, which after a severe contest was defeated'. With this, and noting that the Prussians
were now on the battlefield in force,

I determined to attack the enemy and immediately advanced the whole line of infantry supported by the cavalry

and artillery. The attack succeeded in every point. The enemy was forced from his positions on the heights and fled in the utmost confusion, leaving behind him as far as I could judge 150 pieces of cannon with their ammunition, which fell into our hands.

If all of this is bare of emotion, the same cannot be said for what follows a few lines later:

Your lordship [the War Secretary] will observe that such a desperate action could not be fought and such advantages could not be gained without great loss, and I am sorry to add that ours has been immense.

Not for the first time in his career, Wellington freely showed his grief and shock, and though he went on to name twenty-one British generals and nine colonels who had distinguished themselves in battle, and to praise various divisions, brigades, corps and regiments, his compliments were mingled with tributes to the dead and wounded in a way that might have been calculated to sink the reader's heart. The final paragraph was this:

Since writing the above, I have received a report that Major General Sir Wm. Ponsonby is killed, and in announcing this intelligence to your Lordship, I have to add the expression of my grief for the fate of an officer who had already rendered very brilliant and important services and was an ornament to his profession.

There followed a preliminary count of the British casualties, with totals of 2,432 killed, 9,528 wounded and 1,875 missing. As Wellington knew, these would prove to be underestimates.

It is a remarkable document. Three-fifths of it have passed before the reader learns that the French are beaten, and what remains after that is largely anguished solemnity. In a short time this dispatch would reach an astonishingly wide readership and would attract great praise for its modesty but also criticism for failing to spread its compliments more widely. To that charge the duke would plead guilty, though he must have known that he could never have satisfied everyone. It is worth remembering, however, that it is a lengthy piece of work, written in the teeth of many distractions, in a single morning, in a state of some distress and after a night of very little sleep. Perfection could hardly be expected.

The writing was complete around noon, and Wellington then gave the manuscript to his staff to make at least one corrected fair copy, and probably two. One of these, we know, was destined for the War Secretary, Lord Bathurst, but in the duke's correspondence of that day there is also a short note to the Duke of York, who was commander-in-chief of the British army, saying: 'I have the honour to enclose to your Royal Highness the copy of my dispatch of this date to the Secretary of State, reporting the military operations to this day.'[16] It seems likely that this second copy was sent at the same time. Wellington also wrote short personal notes of sympathy to Alexander Gordon's brother and to the brother of his military secretary, Lord FitzRoy Somerset, who had lost an arm. When all was in order these papers were placed in the hands of Wellington's chosen messenger, Major the Hon. Henry Percy. The time was now 1 p.m. on Monday or a little later. Some sixteen hours after the outcome of the battle of Waterloo had been known beyond doubt, the news, in the form of the dispatch, was at last on its way to London.

3

Monday: London

Etched by R.B.Peake

As Wellington composed his dispatch in Brussels, two hundred miles away in London readers of the *Morning Chronicle* were contemplating and discussing a short item that was given prominence in their paper:

> Paris, June 14 – It was by the barrier of La Villette that the Emperor left Paris. He stopped a few minutes at Bourget, and was to pass the night at Soissons. Marshal Bertrand and General Drouet accompanied his Majesty.

It was no more than a crumb lifted from a French newspaper, but it was the nearest thing to news of the conflict that the *Chronicle* was able to provide that morning. On the activities of the allied forces in Belgium it could only say: 'Brussels papers to the 14th instant make no mention of the armies.' And what did that little paragraph from Paris mean? Most readers probably saw its significance: Bonaparte was on the move. Those who knew the geography understood more, for La Villette was the northern exit from Paris, and Le Bourget and Soissons lie on the road to the Belgian frontier – if Napoleon had left in that direction, it was surely to take command of his army in the north. But the *Chronicle* did not explain these points, nor did it offer any general review of the likelihood of war. That subject had been discussed in the London press for days, and the *Chronicle*'s editor, apparently considering further speculation useless, limited himself to the blunt observation: 'We see no prospect of avoiding the fatal extremity of war.' He had the comfort of knowing that his rivals in the newspaper market had no more to offer than he did. The *Times* gave that same paragraph, word for word – 'It was by the barrier of La Villette that the Emperor left Paris' – and again no news from the armies in Flanders. The *Morning Post* had the same, and so did the *Morning Herald* and the *Public Ledger*. It is thus a straightforward matter to calculate how far the London press lagged behind events on the continent. Napoleon's departure from Paris had occurred not on 14 June, the date given to the paragraph, nor even on 13 June, but early in the morning of Monday 12 June, which means that in London on the morning of Monday 19 June the most up-to-date information about the European conflict was a week old. Four days after Napoleon had invaded Belgium, and one day after his defeat at Waterloo, Londoners could not even be sure that hostilities had begun.

The age of steam transport had not yet dawned, and electrical communication – telegrams and telephones – was still decades off, so it is tempting to conclude that the people of 1815 were simply stuck in an ancient rut. Limited as they were to horse and sail, they may seem to have been no better equipped to get news from place to place than the Anglo-Saxons or the Romans were. And yet by the year of Waterloo a revolution in communications and transport had been under way for a generation and more, and it was not a subtle revolution of the kind that can be detected only in retrospect but one of which the people of the time were fully aware. Indeed, rather like us today, they were proud to be living in an age of communication so rapid and lively that it would have befuddled their grandparents.

The most exciting expression of this revolution was a technology that made possible the transmission of information over distances of hundreds of miles, not in days or hours but in minutes. Every educated person knew about it and it was regarded as one of the wonders of the age. It was known as the telegraph, though today, if we remember it at all, we distinguish it from its electrical successor by calling it the mechanical or optical telegraph.[1] It worked by relaying signals between high vantage points with the assistance of telescopes, and it was developed in France, where the first chain of purpose-built telegraph stations entered service in 1793. So successful was it that soon a network stretched out across the country and, as the French conquered their neighbours, reached as far as Amsterdam and Venice. And so well did it work that they used it to transmit not only important official information but also winning lottery numbers.

A technology this useful could not remain exclusive for long, especially in wartime, and sure enough the British Admiralty quickly copied it. England's first two telegraph lines opened in 1796, linking naval headquarters in London with Portsmouth to the south, the navy's home port, and with Deal to the east, next to the Channel anchorage of the Downs. Other lines followed, to Plymouth in the west and Great Yarmouth on the North Sea coast. The British system relied on large frames holding eight shutters that were opened or closed according to the navy's code. These combinations were read from distance with the aid of high-quality telescopes and then relayed to the next station down the line. Signallers became quick, so that a simple message might leave the roof of the Admiralty and pass – by way of stations at Lambeth, Nunhead, Shooter's Hill, Swanscombe, Gad's Hill, Callum Hill, Beacon Hill, Shottenden Hill, Barham Downs and Betteshanger – to the navy yard at Deal, in less than half an hour. Given that it would normally take eight hours to deliver a message over the same distance on horseback it is little wonder that the telegraph was seen by the public as almost miraculous. In practice, however, the Admiralty tended to restrict its telegraph activity to its own administrative business, and the glowing public reputation of the new technology depended largely on its exploits in France, where the authorities liked to show it off. French newspapers frequently presented important news under the heading 'telegraphic dispatches', and these reports, with the same exciting label, would often be reproduced in the British press. Soon the word 'telegraph' became a popular shorthand for speed and modernity: fast ships and sleek models of carriage were named after it, as were stagecoach services and newspapers ambitious to impress the public with their swiftness.

The telegraph was not, however, something to which the public had access, so for all its novelty and brilliance it did not change lives. The revolution on the roads, by contrast, did precisely that. As late as the middle of the eighteenth century it could reasonably be asserted that road travel in Britain was slower and more troublesome than it had been in the time of the Romans. The roads themselves were often in a dreadful state, and the conveyances passing along them were mostly crude and lumbering. But commerce, politics and society increasingly demanded something better, and though the change when it came may seem slow in retrospect, it was real enough. The new network of canals, while making possible a dramatic expansion in the movement of goods, also removed from the roads some of the heavy traffic that was most responsible for wrecking surfaces, breaking bridges, gouging out potholes and generally blocking the way. The Turnpike Acts of 1766 and 1773, though they worked no sudden miracles, set in motion a gradual improvement in road maintenance. And the increasing vigour and esteem of science and engineering encouraged the idea that it was possible to rise above the past, that routes could be straightened, surfaces made more robust, new bridges built and natural obstructions overcome. In 1815 the best was still to come. John Loudon McAdam had published his landmark work, *The Present System of Road Making*, just four years earlier and was only beginning to put into practice his techniques for creating better surfaces. And Thomas Telford, though he had already accomplished great feats of engineering, had just recently received approval to start his transformation of the road from London to Holyhead. But the sense of progress was already powerful. In Jane Austen's *Pride and Prejudice*, published in 1813, Elizabeth Bennet expresses surprise on hearing Mr Darcy refer to fifty miles as an easy distance, only for him to reply: 'And what is fifty miles of good road? Little more than half a day's journey. Yes, I call it a very easy distance.'[2]

For the traveller the greatest improvements had begun in 1784, when the Bristol entrepreneur John Palmer proved to a sceptical government that well-made and well-managed horse-drawn coaches could convey the mail from town to town more reliably and rapidly than men on horseback – and could carry paying passengers to boot. Thus began the mail coach services that set new standards for personal travel, and they were soon the pride of the country. Existing commercial stagecoaches, though usually cheaper, were challenged and usually outclassed by these liveried official carriages, whose drivers kept to time and had a welcome tendency to remain sober. The mail coaches in their turn forced improvements in the service of 'posting' – a matter of horses, not letters. On any journey over distance horses inevitably wearied, so every ten or fifteen miles it was normal to 'post', or exchange tired horses for fresh ones, usually at an inn with stables. The steady increase in passenger traffic and the discipline and high standards required by the mail services infused a new professionalism into this business. Inns became quicker at their work and kept larger stocks of better horses. And as standards rose, journey times fell. Average carriage speeds edged up past seven miles per hour to eight and even nine. On rare occasions ten miles per hour could be achieved on the best roads. So novel was this that people worried about the effects on passengers. When a young Edinburgh man, John Campbell, announced to family and friends that he proposed to take the fast mail coach to London, he caused great alarm. The rapid movement of these coaches 'was thought to be highly dangerous to the head, independently of all the perils of an overturn, and stories were told of men and women who, having reached London with such celerity, died suddenly of an affection of the brain'.[3] Campbell's acquaintances begged him at the very least to halt for a day at York to recover his equilibrium – advice he ignored, with no ill effect.

Swifter movement of people inevitably meant improved communication of news, and not only in the letters that were carried in the mail coaches. By 1815 every decent-sized town in the country had a newspaper, and London, it has been estimated, had no fewer than fifty-six – 'of which eight were published every morning, seven every evening, seven every other evening, sixteen every Sunday and eighteen on other days, weekly'.[4] At least twice every day, therefore, the London public had access to fresh news, and the industry that provided it was not only busy and competitive but also well established. Daily morning papers, in some respects the most recent arrivals on the scene, had been operating successfully for a generation and knew their business well. Titles had loyal followings and the best of them were familiar parts of the city's life – and not just the city's, for London newspapers, rushed out across the country every day by mail coach, were also an important means of informing the provinces.

The means existed in 1815, therefore, not only to move news from place to place more swiftly than ever before but also to disseminate it more rapidly. Given all this, how quickly could news travel from Brussels to London? The mechanical telegraph, sadly, was unable to help. Exciting as it was, it was also inflexible, useless at night, unreliable in bad weather and, worst of all from the point of view of government, expensive, requiring as it did land, buildings, staff and equipment. It should be little surprise, therefore, that in 1814, as soon as Napoleon had been defeated and exiled, the Royal Navy's telegraph system was shut down.[5] No one complained at the time, but when in the following March Bonaparte returned from Elba and his advance northward was reported to Paris day by day along the French signal lines, at least one London paper could not resist noting primly that 'in France they have not [been], as we have been, so penny wise as to destroy the telegraphs'.[6] With war again in prospect the Admiralty took out of mothballs the telegraph lines to Portsmouth and to Plymouth, but there is no evidence that the London-to-Deal line, which pointed east and might have carried news arriving from Belgium, was reactivated. As for the telegraph routes in Belgium that had been built by the French, they had also ceased to function. The mechanical telegraph, therefore, was not available that June to convey news between Brussels and London.[7] And we can also set aside any idea that London received news from Belgium by pigeon post. In the 1870s no less an authority than William Tegetmeier, who advised Charles Darwin on the subject of pigeons, claimed that this was how word of Waterloo arrived, and when Hollywood made a film of the story in 1934 it showed pigeons delivering the news, but there is no evidence that the idea was even considered at the time.[8] Isolated instances of the transmission of messages using pigeons in Britain can be found in the eighteenth century, but it was not until years after Waterloo that the birds were put to use by news organisations, stock market traders and bookmakers.

There is no escaping it: the fastest way to move information between Brussels and London in 1815 was by the use of horsepower on land and wind power at sea, and the usual route for this had three stages that were almost equal in length. The first crossed northern Belgium to the port of Ostend, a distance of roughly seventy-five miles, and at optimum speed a carriage could cover it in nine hours. The next stage was the North Sea crossing, usually to Ramsgate or Margate on the Kent coast, a distance of about seventy miles. A good ship, in favourable conditions, might sail this in eight hours. The final stage, over land to London, was again about seventy-five miles, taking another nine hours or so. Adding the stages together, therefore, it should in principle have been possible for news to travel from Brussels to London in around twenty-six hours. In practice, however, anyone who completed the journey in so short a time would probably have been the talk of London for weeks.

The revolution in road transport, real though it was, still had some way to go, and the traveller still had to reckon with turnpikes and river ferries, broken wheels and broken bridges, arguments over bills and taxes, lame horses, quagmires in the road, highwaymen and bandits and the need to eat and sleep along the way. An average speed of eight miles per hour could not be counted upon, still less nine or ten. And far greater uncertainty attended the sea crossing, for though it was no great distance and though the waters were well charted and not especially treacherous, this passage over the North Sea was remarkably unpredictable. The winds and the weather were capricious, the tides and currents often unhelpful, and Ostend harbour, which had a sand bar across its mouth, often added to the difficulties. So when the ferry companies boasted in advertisements of crossings that took eight hours and even less, this was the experience of the lucky few. Among the records of those who travelled to Belgium in the two or three months before Waterloo are many examples of sea crossings alone that lasted more than twenty-four hours and some of more than forty-eight hours – that is, two whole days and nights at sea. So while the fastest time possible for the journey from Brussels to London may have been around twenty-six hours, in practice thirty-six hours would still have been considered quick and forty-eight hours, or two days from city to city, was a good time if not a remarkable one.

On Monday 19 June 1815, however, the London papers were not two days behind events in Belgium, nor even three. They were a week behind. And this was not the result of some freak storm that had cut Britain off from the continent, for the weather was nothing out of the ordinary. It follows that there was more to the delay than the practical difficulty of getting word from one place to another. Other factors were at work, and chief among them was something that seems strange to us today and that can be illustrated by a single fact. Although London may have had fifty-six newspapers, all competing more or less vigorously for readers, not one editor had sent a journalist to Belgium with a brief to observe events there and send timely reports home. No British newspaper reporter, in other words, was present at the battle of Quatre Bras or the battle of Waterloo, nor were there reporters in Brussels picking up information at Wellington's headquarters. The world of news was very different then.

*

A newspaper in 1815 was normally a single, large sheet of paper, folded once, to make four pages that were a little bigger than a modern tabloid. The two outer pages, front and back, were given over in their entirety to hosts of small advertisements, each a paragraph long. Here are a few examples from the papers of that Monday morning:

> Payne's Waltzing and Cotillion Academy . . . Mr P. respectfully informs the nobility and gentry that his morning academy for the above elegant and fashionable dances is now open . . .

> A married clergyman, graduate of Oxford, resident seven miles from town in a most healthy and beautiful part of Kent, undertakes to instruct ten pupils in the classics and in the different branches of the mathematics . . .

> Instant command of money: Messrs Richardson and Co. have the unlimited command of money for good securities of every description . . .

> Mr Hawkins, no. 20 Old Bond Street, and Mr Duncome, no. 199 Fleet Street, beg leave to inform the public that they have been appointed by the proprietor of the Sand Rock spring sole agents for the sale of the Aluminous Chalybeate Water . . .

> Wanted, by a laundress: a few families' wash-
> ing; having an undeniable airy situation, she
> has followed the above employment for many
> years . . .

> To families leaving town: a genteel, domesti-
> cated couple of high respectability but limited
> income, that are totally unencumbered, with
> only one servant, would undertake the charge
> of a house at the West End of town during the
> summer months . . .

> Wanted, at an academy where the most liberal
> salary is given: a writing master.

There were also advertisements for the sale of houses, farms, shops, horses, carriages, domestic libraries, pianos, lottery tickets, exotic cloths, snuff boxes, wines and much more, as well as notices for plays, concerts and spectacles of various kinds and announcements of meetings of companies, societies and religious bodies. Out of these items rises the hum of everyday life in Regency London, and that hum was the first thing that greeted the buyer of the paper, before he or she had even opened it. News, meaning topical information and commentary, came second to advertisements and was restricted to the inside pages, 2 and 3. Even that space was not sacrosanct: if more advertisements were sold than could fit on pages 1 and 4, the surplus would often displace editorial matter inside. When one editor declared that 'it is only by advertisements that a newspaper can be printed', he was stat-

ing nothing more than the truth.[9] Some papers even made
a virtue of the primacy of commercial matter by including
the word 'Advertiser' in their titles, while others were explic-
itly established as vehicles for advertisements in particular
trades, such as books, shipping and the pub business.

If advertisements came first, then second in importance
was the reporting of Parliament. An American diplomat
giving his views on the British and their habits shortly after
these events declared that 'one of the things that strikes me
most is their press', and he explained:

> I live north of Portman Square, nearly three miles from
> the House of Commons. By nine in the morning the news-
> papers are on my breakfast-table, containing the debate
> of the preceding night. This is the case though it may
> have lasted until one, two or three in the morning. There
> is no disappointment; hardly a typographical error.[10]

The background to this marvel was that a generation earlier
a struggle had been waged and won by newspapers for the
right to report speeches in the two Houses, in the teeth of
objections from MPs and peers who felt that their discus-
sions should be confidential. That right to publish was now
exercised with great vigour, and among both journalists and
readers it was widely regarded as the true *raison d'être* of
a newspaper. Normally ten columns of space were available on the two inside pages combined, and it was common,
when Parliament was sitting, for half of this to be devoted
to verbatim accounts of debates and speeches. Most of the
full-time reporting staff of most of the leading papers were

involved, in relays, in observing, noting and writing these, and they believed that by doing this work alone they were discharging the best part of their duty to inform their readers. To many, in other words, what was discussed in Parliament, and the manner in which it was discussed, *was* the news.

As for the remaining editorial columns, they were filled from a variety of sources. One staple was extracts from the government publication the *London Gazette*, providing official announcements and regular lists of bankrupts that were important to the world of commerce. Another was the court circular, offering such snippets as:

> The Prince Regent intends to make an extensive excursion this summer through the midland counties, and has received various invitations from several noble families to honour them with his visit on this occasion.

There were also reports from the London law courts, many supplied by magistrates' clerks, though if there was a conspicuous case papers would provide fuller coverage. They also carried lists and accounts of society events, interesting clippings lifted from provincial or rival papers, stock prices, ship movements, births, marriages and deaths and theatre listings. Here and there might be short paragraphs of gossip and the occasional joke, usually a pun, of which the best that can be said is that they rarely stand the test of time. Here is one of the better examples:

> The King of France, in alluding to the treach-
> ery of Marshal Ney, pleasantly observed that
> he was the *ne plus ultra* of traitors.

More typical is a play on the family name of the Earl of Harrowby, which was Ryder:

> Lord Harrowby congratulating the Duke of
> York on the excellence of his winning horse
> at Ascot, the Duke replied: 'My Lord, this is
> not the first King's Plate to be won by a good
> *Ryder*.'[11]

If a newspaper operating along these lines were to appear today it might be called an aggregator, meaning that, rather than generating its own original content, it tended, as some modern online publishers do, to assemble and publish information that was already available from other sources. Even where the words were written by a paper's staff, such as in the parliamentary or the longer court reports, it was an attempt to give a direct account of public proceedings, in other words to capture and pass on data. Relatively little of what newspapers did involved what today we think of as their primary role: reporting, in the sense of finding out new factual information and announcing it to readers in dedicated original articles. This did occur – there was prob-ably a small amount of it in most editions of most papers – but it was not a priority, for the job of reporting as we know it had not evolved.

This does not mean that the pages of 1815 newspapers were

bare of original material. Often a paper would publish an item of opinion on a political or cultural matter, sometimes in the form of a poem, and frequently signed with a pseudonym. This might be significant and high-minded, or it might be mischievous within the narrow bounds permitted by the libel laws. The key to a paper's character, however, and the home of its views, was the leading article. Usually written by the editor, this appeared in a prominent position in larger and better-spaced type than most of the rest – it was designed, in other words, to catch the reader's eye. It was the editor's opportunity to guide the reader through the most significant material published in the adjacent columns that day, placing events in context and weaving them into one or more arguments reflecting the paper's point of view.

And what about foreign news? In a time of war such as this, with Bonaparte on the loose, it was obviously important and interesting to readers, but here editors confronted the power of the state in a more direct way than in any other of their activities. Governments liked to keep the press under their thumb, and in general they relied on two instruments. The first was the law, and particularly the libel law: the courts all too readily accepted that anything in a newspaper to which the government took exception amounted to a libel, with the result that a number of leading editors at work in 1815 had spent time behind bars. The second was tax: both the paper on which the newspapers were published and the advertisements which provided most of their revenue were subject to such heavy taxes that it is likely most titles were only marginally viable. More than half of the 6½d that a reader paid for a daily paper went straight to the government in the form of stamp duty, and this was about to get worse, for in that same month of June 1815 an increase in the duty had just been announced. From the government's point of view these taxes, besides raising revenue and keeping editors under financial pressure, had the additional merit of placing newspapers beyond the means of most people and so restricting the circulation of potentially dangerous political information and ideas. All of this may seem amply restrictive, but when it came to foreign news official involvement went an important step further, for in practice the government asserted control of the news itself.

A handbook of 1811 by James Savage entitled *An Account of the London Daily Newspapers, and the Manner in Which They Are Conducted* describes how papers acquired most of their foreign news: 'The editors of each of the daily papers are furnished by the foreign department of the Post Office with the principal contents of the continental newspapers, translated into the English language, for which the proprietors of the paper pay a weekly or annual sum.'[12]

Remarkable as it may seem, this was correct. The progress of the Napoleonic Wars had been reported by British newspapers largely in the words of newspapers such as the *Journal de Paris*, the Brussels *Oracle*, the *Haarlem Courant* and titles in Hamburg, Stuttgart, Naples, Vienna, Stockholm and other European cities. And as Savage explained, in the first instance the contents of those papers were usually sifted, translated and summarised, and issued in a standard form to all papers that were prepared to pay, by officials of the Post Office – a department of the government. Only on the day after these summaries had been distributed were the foreign newspapers on which they were based released to the press, upon which, Savage explained, 'the editors cull from them any further articles, which possess sufficient interest, and insert them generally with an observation of this sort: "We this day resume our extracts from the French (German, or Dutch) papers," as the case may be.'[13]

How this came to be normal practice is a nice illustration of how life in Britain worked in the *ancien régime*. Editors wanting to be first with the war news had long employed agents in cities across Europe to send to London copies of their local newspapers as often as they appeared. By law, however, all newspapers entering the country from abroad had to be delivered first to the General Post Office at Lombard Street in London, where they were sorted and prepared for delivery. Frustratingly, and despite frequent complaints, only one delivery of foreign papers went out from the Post Office per day, at 2 p.m., and London newspapers were not permitted to collect them at other times. Worse, there was an understanding that ministries and foreign embassies by right should see papers before the press. In consequence, batches of newspapers ordered and paid for by London editors might languish in Lombard Street for days. This could scarcely be borne, and corruption had provided a kind of remedy. First, Post Office staff found it in their interest to browse the quarantined newspapers and discreetly leak interesting highlights for money. Then, when this provoked complaints in Parliament, the Post Office simply placed the process on a formal footing, appointing official translators who prepared the standard press digests referred to by Savage, which were offered to all London papers at a guinea a time. Editors could hardly refuse without yielding a competitive advantage to their rivals, so they paid up. Thus it was that the first draft of most foreign news read by the London public was written by government officials and released to the press at a time chosen by the government. More than that, favoured newspapers would sometimes receive the summaries ahead of opposition ones.

Editors naturally chafed at these arrangements and sought ways around them, for example by resorting to the black market. One editor recalled years later:

> Frequently a single French newspaper, smuggled over in spite of the continental non-intercourse policy [Napoleon's trade ban], would be brought for sale, about three or four o'clock, and ten, twenty, a hundred guineas paid for it if the date was recent and it contained any fresh accounts or bulletins of Bonaparte's German campaigns.[14]

Papers also encouraged people going overseas to write them letters giving news, and they were happy to publish extracts from interesting letters received by anyone else in London. But Post Office officials made this difficult too. They controlled the delivery of letters from abroad just as they did that of foreign newspapers, and they would delay or even destroy them if they suspected their position of power over the press was being undermined. A decade earlier the *Times* had fought a battle over this and lost, finding that, even when it took the precaution of having letters from abroad addressed to a third party, they would be opened by the Post Office and the interesting pages removed.[15] The control extended to correspondence carried outside the official mail system, so that a week before Waterloo customs officers were reminded that they must search all vessels leaving or arriving in ports 'for letters said to be illegally brought and carried from and to Ostend'.[16] Any they found were to be confiscated and forwarded immediately to Post Office headquarters in London.

Take these factors together – notably, the Post Office stranglehold, high taxes and the absence of a strong tradition of professional reporting – and the failure of newspapers to send journalists to Belgium is less of a surprise. The idea was probably never even discussed by editors because it was outside the normal frame of newspaper activity, but if it was, it would have been rejected as expensive and as a hopeless challenge to government power. On the few occasions when newspaper employees are known to have ventured into the field of conflict, moreover, the outcomes had not been encouraging. In 1809 Henry Crabb Robinson of the *Times* found himself in Corunna, in northern Spain, when Sir John Moore's army retreated to that city. At dinner he learned that the French had arrived on their heels and that fighting had begun. 'I walked with some acquaintances a mile or more out of town, and remained there till dark – long enough to know that the enemy was driven back; for the firing evidently came from a greater distance.'[17] He then boarded a ship and sailed for England. Had he waited just a little longer and asked a few questions, he could have brought home, exclusively, firm news of Moore's victory and also of the general's death, but that did not occur to him. Nor did his editor reproach him for this. A few months later a parliamentary reporter for the *Morning Chronicle*, Peter Finnerty, sailed with a British invasion force to Walcheren in the Netherlands. His main aim was not to report the campaign day by day but to write a book about it, but as the expedition rapidly became a disaster the *Chronicle* published a number of dispatches from him, including first-hand descriptions of fighting. Finnerty's experience did not, however, inspire others to follow his example, not least because he was arrested in Walcheren on the orders of the War Department and not long after his return was thrown in jail for libel.

*

Seen against this background, the seven-day gap between Napoleon's departure from Paris and the appearance of that news in the London papers begins to make sense. Moreover, France and Britain were at war, and Bonaparte had imposed an embargo on cross-Channel shipping with the deliberate intention of keeping the British government in the dark. The French newspaper that carried the line about the emperor leaving for the north was the *Journal de Paris,* and a single copy of this had come ashore at Deal, probably acquired by the navy from a neutral ship or a smuggler. From Deal it was sent to the Admiralty in London, where no doubt their lordships perused it before passing it on to the Post Office. There, in due course, a lengthy digest was prepared which was issued to the daily newspaper offices some time on Sunday evening. This explains why all the newspapers had that paragraph in exactly the same terms: 'It was by the barrier of La Villette that the Emperor left Paris.' In practice a delay of seven days in reporting continental news, though it can be explained in this instance, was probably unusually long. Four days, allowing two for travel and two for bureaucracy, was nearer the norm, and less was possible when the government saw the need to hurry. That Monday afternoon London began to make up time.

The city's evening press was just as lively as its morning counterpart and had developed a practice of appearing in several editions through the afternoon. The first editions were published around noon and distributed by 'newsboys' who hawked them around the streets, blowing horns, swinging rattles and shouting out headlines to gain attention. As in the morning papers that Monday, there was one significant item of news, and once again every paper had it in exactly the same terms, doubtless carefully crafted at a desk in the Post Office. This time, however, it gave the newsboys something to shout about:

> Brussels, June 16: Hostilities began yesterday. The French began first. They entered Charleroi, a little frontier town, from which they seem to have retired this morning, for the post is come this morning, but four hours later than usual. The Belgians conducted themselves very well. The brave Lord Wellington set off this morning at seven o'clock. In the course of the night and till noon today, all the troops have passed through Brussels that were at three or four leagues' distance. They all advance, and within two days will have passed the frontiers. We have good hopes that all will go well.

This was just three days old, written on the afternoon of the previous Friday. From selling unusually stale news, the papers now had something unusually fresh, if a little mis-leading. Presented to readers as 'Flanders Mail', the report began accurately – the French did indeed attack by way of Charleroi, and Wellington did lead his army out of Brus-sels to meet them – but it was mistaken when it claimed that Charleroi was recaptured and that the allies intended to invade France. Still, for the reader in London one thing mattered above all: war with France had resumed.

In a second edition timed at 1 p.m. the *Courier* was able to add this:

> An officer is just arrived [in Brussels] from the Duke of Wellington. On the 16th Bon-aparte put his army in motion, calculated at about 130,000 men, and attacked the Prus-sian outposts at Givet. In the night of the 16th a Prussian officer communicated the above intelligence to the Duke of Wellington, who immediately put his army in motion. His Grace proceeded to Nivelle, where the mass of his army was collecting. The accounts do not state that an immediate battle was expected, but it is most probable.

An hour later the *Sun*, a rival to the *Courier*, announced:

> The two armies are front to front, and before this time a battle may have been fought. If

Bonaparte can bring only 120,000 fighting
men into the field – and we very much doubt
if he can do more – we may hope for a speedy
termination of the contest and of the tyrant's
cause.

By Monday evening, therefore, London knew not only that
hostilities had begun, but also that an important battle might
already have taken place.

4

Monday: News on the Move

The officer chosen by Wellington to carry his dispatch to London, Major the Hon. Henry Percy, was the fifth son of the Earl of Beverley and a grandson of the Duke of Northumberland. Aged twenty-nine, he was single, handsome and blessed with the build and curly black hair of an Adonis. More than that, he was a charmer – Creevey would write that he was 'by far the best hand at conversation of the duke's young men'. Already before 1815 he had played his part in one event that is etched both in Britain's history and in its literature: the burial of Sir John Moore at Corunna.

> Not a drum was heard, not a funeral note,
> As his corse to the rampart we hurried.

Four officers carried that corpse, and one of them was Percy. Moore, an unusually popular and well-respected general, fell in the 1809 battle from which the *Times*'s Henry Crabb Robinson had walked away. It was the final action of a campaign against the French in northern Spain, and it was fought to give the British force time to evacuate the port city and escape to England. Percy had by then been aide-de-camp to Moore for two years, and when his chief was knocked from his horse by a cannon-ball in the heat of the battle, it was he who lifted him and propped him against a bank of earth, and he who rode to fetch the surgeon. Later that night, with victory assured and the army safe from capture, Percy wept at the bedside as Moore breathed his last. The troops were already boarding the ships when he and three comrades lowered the general's corpse – wrapped only in a coat because there was no time to make a coffin – into a hastily dug grave on the Corunna ramparts.

> Slowly and sadly we laid him down,
> From the field of his fame fresh and gory;
> We carved not a line, and we raised not a stone –
> But we left him alone with his glory![1]

Moore had given Percy his opportunity. An earl's fifth son may have many advantages – among them, in his case, an Eton education – but with the bloodline so secure he had no obvious purpose in life and was obliged to find one. His oldest brother, George, who would eventually inherit their grandfather's dukedom in 1865 at the age of eighty-six, was making his way in politics, while another brother was on the way to becoming a bishop and two more were doing well in the navy. Henry, big and strong, chose the army. Before he was eighteen his family bought him a lieutenancy in the 7th Regiment of Foot, and then Moore, almost certainly responding to string-pulling, offered to try him out as an aide-de-camp. It was a curious job, high-flying and in many ways unmilitary. A general would usually have several aides, and they would be his secretaries and messengers, drafting, correcting and copying orders and dispatches, and, when appropriate, delivering and explaining them and gathering the responses. They had to be personable and diplomatic so that they could represent their chief in the company of senior officers and government officials, but they also had to be brave, for in battle they carried orders whatever the risks, and brought back the replies. Percy, it seems, was good at all of this and served Moore in Sicily and London before following him in 1808 to Portugal and then into Spain. Moore's death at Corunna was thus not only a personal, emotional blow to him – he would carry a lock of the general's hair with him for the rest of his life – but also a professional set-back. He automatically lost his staff position and returned to his infantry regiment, with which, it seems, he fought in Wellington's hard-won victory at Talavera. In 1810 he switched to the cavalry, becoming a captain in the 14th Light Dragoons and playing his part in a string of military actions that summer. Then in September, as Wellington's army withdrew westward towards Lisbon with the French in pursuit, his luck once again deserted him. The *Leeds Intelligencer*, among other British papers, reported:

> The Hon. H. Percy of 14th Dragoons (brother
> to Lord Lovaine), it is said, was taken prisoner
> lately in Portugal. He had the command of the
> piquets, and his horse becoming restive at the
> approach of the French party he was in conse-
> quence surrounded by them.[2]

By this stage Percy must have caught Wellington's eye, for the duke wrote immediately to Marshal Masséna, the commander of the French forces: 'Captain Percy, whose fate concerns me greatly, was wounded and captured or killed yesterday near Celorico, and I would be much obliged if you would allow news of him to be given to my aide de camp.'[3]

As it turned out, though Percy's military career had once again been set back, his well-being was not a cause for concern, for he appears to have spent the remaining three and a half years of the war living in comfort and relative freedom with his father in the heart of France.

The Earl and Countess of Beverley were among the most notable of Napoleon's British *détenus*, the civilians who were caught in France when the short-lived Peace of Amiens ended in 1803 and who were interned as enemy aliens. No hardship, however, befell the noble couple, who were allowed to live pretty much as they liked on condition that they did not try to escape to England. Since the earl loved France and had no desire to escape, he settled down happily with the countess in the Auvergne town of Moulins, free to make occasional excursions in his carriage to Paris and elsewhere. It was to this passive and idle *ménage* that, seven years later, the French authorities sent the captive Henry, and there he remained until after Napoleon's defeat and banishment to Elba in 1814. Even at that point the earl was in no hurry to return to England (in fact, he was still living in Moulins in 1821), but for the ambitious Henry things were very different: despite his personal merits and family connections, after ten years in the army he was still just a captain. His career as a staff officer had been cut short at Corunna, and his fighting career in the cavalry had lasted barely three months. Now there was peace, with all that implied for the prospects of army officers. He had not long returned to the family home in London that summer, however, when a golden opportunity came along. The Duke of Wellington, appointed British ambassador to Paris, recruited Percy to his personal staff with a promotion from captain to major. No doubt family influence again played its part (Wellington valued breeding), but Percy could also point to his experience at Moore's side and to his no doubt fluent French. And however briefly they had known each other in the Peninsula, he had impressed the duke in that time sufficiently to cause him to write to the French that his fate 'concerns me greatly'.

The young man was soon enjoying the diplomatic whirl of Paris, learning the duke's ways and no doubt turning a few heads. Upon Bonaparte's escape from Elba, however, he once again became primarily a soldier and travelled to Brussels as part of that 'family' of aides to the allied commander. In that capacity he was at the duke's side at Quatre Bras and again at Waterloo, and we have glimpses of him carrying orders through the thick of the fighting, liaising with the advancing Prussians and, in common with the unfortunate Gordon, failing to persuade the duke to be more careful of his own safety. At one point Percy's horse was shot dead under him. After the fighting ended he remained with his chief, riding out in pursuit of the retreating French and then turning back to the famous rendezvous with Blücher. And he was a member of the small party that trudged from there through the gloom and the horrors to the inn at Waterloo. How Percy came to be chosen next day for the honour of carrying the dispatch to London is not difficult to explain. First, this was a job for a member of the commander's staff, and with three members of the 'family' dead or wounded few candidates remained.

Second, by tradition the bearer of a dispatch announcing victory was rewarded with promotion. Since everyone knew this, it follows that such assignments were normally allocated by turns. After Waterloo it seems that Percy's turn had come.

A number of his belongings are preserved at Alnwick Castle in Northumberland, the ancestral Percy home, and among them is a woman's fashion accessory: a purple velvet pouch, or sachet, in which a handkerchief would have been kept. Tradition has it that this was a token given to him by a lady as he left the Duchess of Richmond's ball in Brussels on the night before Quatre Bras, and that four days later, as he set out for London, he drew the sachet from his pocket and slipped the dispatches into it for safe keeping on the journey. Since we do not know who the lady was, this story has lent a whiff of mystery and romance to Percy's mission ever since. And it also helps to put him in the cast of another poem that has a place in British history, *Childe Harold's Pilgrimage*, with its sumptuous description of the duchess's ball:

> There was a sound of revelry by night,
> And Belgium's capital had gathered then
> Her Beauty and her Chivalry, and bright
> The lamps shone o'er fair women and brave men;
> A thousand hearts beat happily; and when
> Music arose with its voluptuous swell,
> Soft eyes looked love to eyes which spake again,
> And all went merry as a marriage bell;
> But hush! hark! a deep sound strikes like a rising
>   knell!
> Did ye not hear it? No; 'twas but the wind,

Or the car rattling o'er the stony street;
On with the dance! let joy be unconfined;
No sleep till morn, when Youth and Pleasure meet
To chase the glowing Hours with flying feet.[4]

Soon, however, the true meaning of that 'deep sound' is understood: the French are on the march. Byron continues:

Ah! then and there was hurrying to and fro,
And gathering tears, and tremblings of distress,
And cheeks all pale, which but an hour ago
Blushed at the praise of their own loveliness;
And there were sudden partings, such as press
The life from out young hearts, and choking sighs
Which ne'er might be repeated: who would guess
If ever more should meet those mutual eyes,
Since upon night so sweet such awful morn could
    rise!

Percy was certainly at the ball and no doubt was as handsome, chivalrous and worthy of those choking sighs as any officer in the room. All of Wellington's well-bred aides-de-camp were in attendance, and as the news from the frontier sank in they would have been among the first to be drawn away from the dance-floor and sent off to copy and deliver orders. Nor is there any reason to doubt that, when the moment came to leave, some tearful admirer, fearing that Percy was going to his death, pressed the velvet sachet into his hand. Just how eligible for romance the major considered himself to be, however, is another matter.

Percy may have been blue-blooded, single and twenty-nine, but he was also a father twice over. It had happened in his years as a prisoner of war in rural France: while living with his parents in Moulins he met a Frenchwoman called Durand, whose first name was either Marion or Jeanne, and in 1812 they had a son who was christened Henry Marion Durand. Another son followed, probably called Percy Durand. Though Henry Percy did not marry their mother and did not formally acknowledge these illegitimate boys as his own, those names – Henry and Percy – imply a genuine bond. Indeed there are grounds to believe that he was proud of them and after he joined Wellington's staff made no secret of their existence among his colleagues.[5] He may also have been in touch with their mother in the spring of 1815 from Belgium: an entry in his diary for 1 April says cryptically: 'Wrote to M. D.'[6] No woman called Durand, however, figures on the lists of guests at the Duchess of Richmond's ball, so it seems unlikely that she was the giver of the velvet sachet.

On Monday 19 June Henry Percy was still wearing the bright red dress coat with short square tails and high, black embroidered collar that he had put on before going to that ball, though it was now stained with blood. He had almost certainly managed a little sleep every night – that, at least, is what Wellington would have expected – but he had also experienced five days of intense and on occasion harrowing activity. Now he had orders to rush to England. Besides the dispatch – probably two copies – and a bundle of other letters, he also had some important items of baggage.

Though Wellington had carefully avoided a tone of triumph in his official report, he was not above a flourish for the benefit of the Prince Regent. The final paragraph of the dispatch thus declared: 'I send with this dispatch two eagles, taken by the troops in this action, which Major Percy will have the honour of laying at the feet of His Royal Highness.'* These were war trophies of the most precious kind. Eagles were the standards of Napoleon's regiments, emblems he had copied from the legions of imperial Rome and which he did everything in his power to imbue with an almost religious significance for his soldiers. For eleven years they had accompanied Frenchmen in victory after victory across Europe, and such was their potency that after Napoleon's defeat and exile in 1814 the returning Bourbons rounded up every eagle they could trace and had them ceremonially destroyed. Once the emperor had returned from Elba, he therefore made a point of distributing new eagles to his soldiers in a spectacular public ceremony in Paris. 'I entrust to your hands the Imperial Eagle!' he cried out to his assembled army. 'You swear here to defend it at the cost of your life's blood against the enemies of the nation?' And the call came back loud and clear: 'We swear! We swear!'[7]

Both eagles captured at Waterloo were seized in a single famous charge. At about 2 p.m. a French advance against

* Two eagles or three? Many later accounts asserted that there were three, but there is no doubt that the number of eagles captured at Waterloo and carried by Percy to London was two. The confusion may have arisen because Wellington, in his own draft of the dispatch (preserved at the British Library), originally wrote 'three', and this was corrected to 'two' in the fair copy. While the fair copy, saying two, provided the basis for the official dispatch as subsequently published in the *London Gazette*, Wellington's own uncorrected draft, saying three, appears to be the version relied on for the collected *Dispatches* published by Gurwood in 1838 (vol. 12, p. 484).

the left of the allied line reached the crest of the ridge and threatened to break through, and the response was a mass attack by the Union and Household cavalry brigades. In the midst of this a tall Scottish sergeant, Charles Ewart, caught sight of an eagle being ushered out of danger towards the rear of the French line. Plunging forward and laying about him with his sabre, he took hold of it and killed its bearer. Next he parried a thrust from a lancer, killing him too, and then he fought off the desperate bayonet thrusts of a foot-soldier, dealing him a blow to the head. 'That finished the contest for the eagle', he wrote later.[8] Soon afterwards, and not far away, Captain Kennedy Clark led his squadron in an attack on another eagle party, killed the bearer and took up the standard. These trophies – displayed to this day in British museums – were as significant to their captors as they had been to the regiments that lost them. They had already been paraded through Brussels, and now Percy was to convey them to London and present them personally to the Prince Regent. They were magnificent, dramatic objects, as a description from this time shows:

The eagles taken belonged to the 45th and 104th [actually the 105th] regiments and were superbly gilt and ornamented with gold fringe. That of the 45th was inscribed with the names of Jena, Austerlitz, Wagram, Eylau, Friedland etc., being the battles in which this regiment, called the Invincibles, had signalised itself. The other was a present from [Empress Maria] Louisa to the 104th regiment. One was much defaced with blood and dirt, as if it had been struggled for, and the eagle was also broken off from the pole, as if from the cut of a sabre, but it was nevertheless preserved.[9]

As travelling companions, however, these objects were not convenient. The gilt copper birds weighed three and a half pounds each, while the flags were broad, with those heavy gold fringes, and the staffs were sturdy ten-foot oak poles.[10] So it was into a carriage from whose windows jutted two large, heavy enemy flags that Percy stepped that afternoon: whether he liked it or not, his passing on the road would attract attention. After bidding his chief and colleagues farewell his first objective was Ghent, to call upon the King of France, and from there he would travel to Ostend and take ship for England. Ghent was thirty miles off, and the road, like most of Belgium's main roads, was a good one by the standard of the time. Percy had travelled it on the duke's behalf more than once in the previous three months, so now he wove his way through the streets of Brussels to the north-western exit, left the city for the country and headed through low hills towards the town of Alost.

*

The Duke of Wellington was far from being the only British soldier to pick up his pen that day. Hundreds, if not thousands, seized whatever chance they could to send news home, and many of their letters survive. The chief and most urgent message they wanted to send, naturally, was that they were alive. 'My dearest father,' wrote one infantry captain, 'I am writing a few lines in haste on my knee, it is now sunrise and I take therefore the earliest opportunity of informing you that an all-kind providence has preserved me in two most sanguinary conflicts.'[11] An ensign wrote to his mother: 'I take the earliest opportunity to tell you that we have had some very hard fighting, but that we have gained a most complete victory, and also that I am quite well and safe and have escaped unhurt.'[12] A third soldier thanked God for his preservation and informed his father: 'I am in good health and capital spirits, our loss is horrid to think of, for we have lost the greatest part of the British army, but however it is the forerunner of Bonaparte's downfall and quiet of Europe.'[13] Pithiest of all, surely, was James Cocksedge of the 15th Hussars:

Dear Jones,

The fight is over, I am safe. Napoleon beaten with loss of 40,000, all his baggage and artillery; 3 days fighting, half the cavalry on our side destroyed, and the infantry and artillery suffered immense. Love to all, yours always,

J. C. C.[14]

Some writers had more difficult tasks. An officer wrote: 'by the request of your son I am pained to inform you that in an attack on the enemy yesterday he received a musket shot on his right breast'.[15] The Earl of Uxbridge beseeched his wife, Charlotte: 'Be bold, prepare for misfortune, I have lost my right leg.'[16] And then there is the case of Captain Philip Wodehouse, who on the day after the battle sat down and composed this anguished message to a Miss Parry, of Charlotte Street in London:

Though I cannot persuade myself that the wish that you once so kindly expressed is still as lively as then, yet not to use you as you appear to use me, I write to say that I suffered no harm from the affair of yesterday, even though the charm has not arrived. How brilliant and decisive it was, the Gazette will inform you. I only send these few lines written according to your desire in hurry and confusion to assure you that in spite of your forgetfulness, my affection for you is as strong as ever and that if a cannon ball hits me tomorrow I believe I shall die thinking of you. Good bye, believe me ever yours, Wodehouse.[17]

Some soldiers expressed joy and pride: 'When you learn the details,' wrote one to a friend, 'they will excite your astonishment and admiration of the invincible spirit of the British lion.'[18] From a bivouac on the Charleroi road Captain James Nixon informed his father: 'England has to thank the talents of her consummate general and the bravery of the troops of different nations under his command. Their steadiness and great endurance of privations for yesterday's total victory, are equalled by none of modern days, excepting Leipzig.'[19] As for himself, Nixon wrote, 'I never was better in my life.'

What became of these letters, which in their diverse ways convey the news of Waterloo just as effectively as the official dispatch? We must assume that most of them travelled to England by the army's postal service, but it is clear from what they wrote that the senders did not expect them to reach their destinations before the recipients had seen Wellington's account in the press, for again and again they refer their friends or relatives to the official dispatch for fuller details than they can provide. They assume, in other words, that Wellington's post would be faster than theirs. And there is one suggestion, in a letter from Captain Courtenay Ilbert, an artillery officer who throughout this period maintained a busy correspondence with his wife, Anne, in Sevenoaks, that army mail was deliberately delayed to ensure that the commander's dispatch reached London first. In a letter from Brussels dated 20 June he wrote: 'I found this morning when I sent my packet of letters to the post that like a great many others I had been taken in; for in order to prevent private accounts reaching England as soon as the dispatches, the dragoon had been sent off three hours before the usual time.'[20] Ilbert persuaded a colleague to send his letters by courier through Antwerp instead.

Many letters written after Waterloo thus began their journeys to Britain at around the time that Percy set out, but the duke's messenger had priority just as only the duke had authority to provide the official account. At least one person, however, found a way to ensure that his correspondence would arrive no later than the dispatch. Thomas Creevey, having spoken to Wellington in the course of the morning, went home and dashed off a quick letter to his friend and fellow MP, Henry Bennet. He then rushed back to Wellington's residence and gave it to Percy to deliver.

Unknown to Creevey, however, and to Wellington and to Percy and to the rest of the army in Belgium, someone else was aiming to be the first to get the news of victory to London, and he was already hours ahead of the official messenger.

*

On the night of the battle, as we saw, Wellington gave permission for a single letter to be sent reporting the outcome of the battle. This, it was agreed, was to be written by Count Carlo Andrea Pozzo di Borgo, the representative in Belgium of the Tsar of Russia, and it would inform Louis XVIII of France of his enemy's defeat. Pozzo, as he was known, was Corsican, and therefore French, but he had a longstanding personal feud with that more famous Corsican, Napoleon Bonaparte. Exiled from his own country, he had become an itinerant plotter, touring those courts of Europe where Bonaparte did not hold sway, including London, until Tsar Alexander I took advantage of his talents and connections. By 1815 Pozzo had been serving Russia as a diplomat for a decade, but everyone knew that his personal mission was to see Bonaparte toppled for good and Louis XVIII secure on the French throne. When, on Sunday night, the need to write to Louis was discussed and Wellington declared himself too tired for the task, Pozzo was thus the obvious person for the job, and all the more so because he intended to ride that night to Brussels.

On reaching the city, Pozzo took up his pen:

Brussels, 5 a.m.

Sire,

The Duke of Wellington, from whom I parted at midnight, has charged me with informing your majesty of the events of yesterday. His grace has won the most complete, the most glorious and perhaps the most momentous victory in history. The rival and the enemies of France have been defeated after nine hours of combat. The Duke has surpassed himself in heroism, and military science has never been put to a greater test. The enemy is in full flight. He has lost his artillery and today has lost the rest of his scattered army.

I will have the honour of giving your majesty the details of this memorable day, and until then I beg you to accept my congratulations and my profound respect.[21]

Such news was most anxiously awaited at Ghent. Louis was fifty-nine years old and since losing his brother to the guillotine had spent two decades enduring the relentless indignities of exile before, in 1814, finding himself at last upon the throne of France. Then came the ultimate ignominy: when Bonaparte reappeared, France chose the Corsican and Louis ran. At first he headed for England, but with the allied powers rallying he was persuaded to linger in Ghent to await the outcome of the new war. There was no guarantee of restoration for him – other candidates were available – but at least in Ghent he would be on hand. From there he had watched in alarm as Bonaparte concentrated his forces just over the border, and his little court was thrown into consternation by the French attack on Thursday morning and the fighting that followed, some of which could be heard from the walls of the city. Many urged the king to retreat at once to Antwerp, but Louis knew well that the slightest intimation of cowardice at this moment would end his hopes.

Through Sunday scraps of information came in from Brussels, where, as we know, people were in no position to give an accurate account of the fighting. Every report that the French had entered the Belgian capital thus had its echo a few hours later in Ghent, and the terror grew among those aristocrats and officials who had thrown in their lot with Louis that Bonaparte, by some bold deployment of cavalry, was about to capture them all. Wellington himself, however, in a letter written early on Sunday morning and delivered that evening, strongly advised Louis to ignore all rumours and to leave for Antwerp only 'on certain news that the enemy has entered Brussels'.[22] The king knew that what he was hearing from Brussels did not qualify as 'certain news' and so, displaying a kind of desperate dignity bordering on courage, he refused to run. His bags were packed and his carriage stood ready in the courtyard, but that night he remained in his little palace, went to bed and waited.

In Brussels, after 5 a.m., Pozzo di Borgo entrusted the delivery of his letter to the Comte de Semallé, a French royalist exile whom he knew well. In his youth de Semallé had been a page-boy at the court of Versailles, but now he was in charge of keeping the exiled royalists informed. He had spent several hours that day close to the battlefield at Waterloo, observing by telescope, and had returned to Brussels in confident mood to await confirmation of victory and ensure its transmission to the king.[23] Pozzo's letter gave him what he needed, and he decided to dispense with couriers and take it to Ghent in person. He rode first to Alost, the town at the half-way stage which was the headquarters of the meagre French forces that had remained loyal to Louis (and of which Wellington had such a low opinion that he would not trust them in battle). Having passed on his news there, de Semallé switched to a carriage for the remaining seventeen miles to Ghent. Given the distance and the heavy traffic on these roads, it must have been approaching 9 a.m. on Monday when he arrived, but he found the gates still locked and the city braced for a French attack. Negotiating his entry, he made first for the main square, where his carriage was quickly surrounded by people desperate for news. In that crowd was a friend of his, the Marquis de la Maisonfort, who takes up the story:

> His face [de Semallé's] was pale and his manner troubled. I approached and told him quietly: 'In the name of Heaven, say nothing!' This was what he wished. To judge by his expression the odds were a thousand to one that all was lost. I have never seen a messenger look more despondent. We followed him to the king's residence. The Comte de Blacas, as alarmed as we were, showed him in. Only the Duc de Duras and the Duc de Gramont followed, and we remained with ears pricked up, almost glued to the door.[24]

Behind that door, we are told, the king guessed the truth before his visitor could speak. 'It is de Semallé in person?' he asked. 'That can only mean favourable news.'[25] And, sure enough, the messenger handed over his letter and spilled out all he knew besides, including that the Prince of Orange was wounded and that Wellington had lost many of his own staff. After a brief interval the door was thrown open, and the Duc de Gramont, holding aloft Pozzo di Borgo's letter, announced the victory to a crowd that must by then have numbered in the hundreds. 'What a contrast when the fear of bad news makes good news spring up!' remarked de la Maisonfort. 'Semallé had played his part in admirable style, reserving for the king the prize of victory that he had brought.'[26]

In his three months in Ghent, Louis had maintained something like an open house. Though he had no common touch, he was evidently persuaded that he must befriend the city folk and also the allied officers who passed through from Ostend or were billeted in the area. His borrowed residence, the Hotel d'Hane de Steenhuyse, was among the grandest private houses in the city, and its location on a busy street and its broad ground-floor windows made it suitable for ostentation. Passers-by had become accustomed to watching the king and his courtiers dine, and some had even found themselves invited inside to join the company. Now, with this sensational news, all of Ghent was allowed to share in the celebration, and it did so with gusto. De la Maisonfort recalled 'universal delirium'. No doubt for the locals the joy lay at least as much in the knowledge that they would not be overrun by an invading army as that the Bourbon monarchy had been saved, but certainly there was joy. A local paper would record: 'When the victory was known, the delight of the population erupted with a vivacity rarely seen.'[27] Bells rang; strangers embraced in the street; the king, yielding to the demands of a boisterous crowd, appeared at his window and was enthusiastically serenaded with patriotic songs. The toasting and revelry continued all day and much of the night.

To this excitement there was an important witness who was struck by an idea. Here is a newspaper report about him that appeared a few days later:

he was on Monday at Ghent opposite the
hotel of Louis XVIII when at 1 p.m. an officer
arrived covered with dust, and as the king
receives every dispatch openly, he instantly
entered the hotel with the officer, who forth-
with congratulated his majesty on the great
victory just gained. 'We have taken all the
heavy artillery,' he exclaimed, 'and a great and
decisive victory is ours.' There was immediately the greatest joy among the personages
assembled. The king embraced the officer with
transport. The officer then said that the battle
of Sunday had been general along the whole
line and had continued for nine hours, that a
great number of prisoners had been taken, the
French retreating with the greatest confusion,
leaving all their heavy artillery behind them.[28]

We do not know this observer's name or what he was doing
in Ghent, but according to the same report he 'instantly' left
for London with the aim of becoming 'the first bearer of the
great news'. Although this report suggests that de Semallé
reached the king at 1 p.m., that is probably a mistake: around
9 a.m. is a more likely time for that. Another newspaper
report gave 1 p.m. as the time when the unnamed observer
set off for London, which is plausible.[29] If that is correct,
then he had a head start of at least three or four hours on
Major Percy, who at that time was more than thirty miles
behind.

5

Monday–Tuesday: Extraordinary Agitation

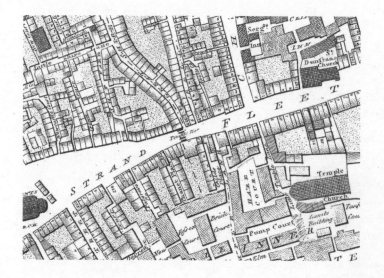

Most of the London newspaper industry in 1815 was to be found along the bustling, mile-long thoroughfare that ran from the foot of the hill below St Paul's Cathedral to the junction known as Charing Cross. The first half of this was Fleet Street, which ended at an elegant but narrow gateway called Temple Bar, and beyond that it became the Strand, so called because the River Thames was close by. Among the hundreds of shops that lined Fleet Street and the Strand, or in some cases tucked into courtyards and alleyways behind, were the offices of most of the fifty-six newspapers then in production. Printing had arrived in this district fully three hundred years earlier, when William Caxton's protégé Wynkyn de Worde set up his press, and the location had proved an excellent one in which to pick up news. To the east lay the City, that square mile of tangled streets ruled by its own Lord Mayor and aldermen where stood the Bank of England, the Stock Exchange and the offices of bankers, brokers and trading companies. Farther east, and also to the south, were the docks of the world's busiest and richest port. And to the west, where the Strand ended, stood what was known, by way of contrast with the City, as the Town. Turn right at Charing Cross and you were soon among the grand residential squares of the new Georgian London – St James's, Grosvenor, Berkeley, Hanover. Turn left and you were in Whitehall, at the far end of which, beyond Downing Street and government offices including the headquarters of the army and navy, stood the Houses of Parliament. To and fro along Fleet Street and the Strand, therefore, flowed the traffic between the world of finance and trade at one end and the world of politics and high society at the other, a traffic fruitfully observed by those working in newspaper offices.

Of the dozen or so morning papers produced along these streets every weekday, three led the market: the *Morning Chronicle*, the *Times* and the *Morning Post*. Of these the *Chronicle*, located at 143 The Strand, enjoyed the highest reputation – so high, in fact, that although it almost always supported the Whig opposition, it was considered essential reading by many on the Tory or 'ministerial' side of politics. This distinction it owed to its editor and proprietor of twenty-five years, James Perry, a Scottish carpenter's son who as a young man in the 1780s had taken the London newspaper world by storm. A shrewd businessman as well as a fine journalist, Perry built the *Chronicle*'s reputation both as a political and as a literary journal. Its parliamentary reports were always at least as good as any other paper's, even if their focus tended to be on what Whigs had to say. The leading articles were well informed, forcefully argued and often brave, while the other writers whom Perry persuaded to contribute on literary, social and political matters included the finest of the age, among them Hazlitt, Sheridan and Coleridge (though they were rarely identified in the pages by name). It is a measure of Perry's stature that, although he had been clearly wrong on some of the great issues of recent years – for example, on the significance of Napoleon's Russian campaign of

1812 and on the chances of his defeat in 1814 – the political credit of the *Chronicle* remained very high.

By this date, however, the great editor had probably passed the peak of his powers, worn down both by long service and by personal tragedy. In 1812 his oldest daughter had died aged only thirteen, and then his wife, Anne, became gravely ill, probably with tuberculosis. A spell in the warmer climate of Portugal produced some improvement in her condition, but on the return voyage her ship was seized by pirates and she was taken as a captive to Algiers. There her health collapsed again, and although she was eventually freed, she never made it home to rejoin her husband, dying in Bordeaux in February 1815. Perry's friends recorded that he was deeply distressed and that his own health began a long decline.

The *Chronicle*'s coverage of the events following Bonaparte's return from Elba none the less displayed considerable editorial vigour. When it came to a choice between the *ancien régime*, as represented by Louis XVIII, and the modern order personified by the emperor, Perry's paper unflinchingly opted for the latter, pointing out that the people of France seemed to have done the same. The *Chronicle* knew Bonaparte's faults and crimes and did not conceal them, but nor could it conceal its distaste at Britain's alliance with the leading autocrats of the age for the purpose of reinstating a Bourbon on the French throne. As the weeks passed and conflict became inevitable, however, the *Chronicle* suffered the stresses that all newspapers experience when their calls for peace have been in vain: it is hard to be an enemy to one's own country, so scepticism gives way to patriotism, or at least to a certain loyalty to those marching behind the national flag.

No such anxieties afflicted the *Times*, which operated from relatively grand premises shared with the *Evening Mail* in Printing House Square, near the eastern end of Fleet Street. The *Times* was unequivocally pro-war, in fact too much so for its own good. Younger than the *Chronicle* by sixteen years, it had been founded by John Walter in 1785 in a vain attempt to promote a new type-setting method he favoured, but control of the paper had since passed to his abler and more far-sighted son, John Walter II. Although the *Times* was not yet the titan among newspapers that it would be a generation later, one important foundation stone for success had been laid: it was the only paper in the world being printed by a steam-powered press. The younger Walter had also taken steps towards getting the *Times* a reputation for being quick with the news, but capable though he was, he was not a journalist or writer, and in 1815, like Perry, he was also suffering personal difficulties. That spring, after lengthy haggling with his bride's family over her settlement, Walter had finally married, only for his new wife almost immediately to fall dangerously ill – like Anne Perry, with tuberculosis. She would die before the year was out. Unsurprisingly Walter abandoned the affairs of his paper to his editor, but unfortunately this was not an editor who brought credit to the *Times*.

Dr John Stoddart, a former lawyer who had been hired on a generous contract a year before, suffered from what a colleague called an 'outrageous Bourbon zeal'. In younger days he had welcomed the fall of Louis XVI, but now no French aristocrat who had lost close relatives to the guillotine could hate the Revolution more than Stoddart did. And even more than that, he hated Napoleon, whose name he could barely bring himself to write. This animosity extended far beyond Bonaparte and his family, whom he mocked and insulted in every way possible, and even beyond those French people who supported the emperor, for whom his contempt was remorseless. Anyone in British politics or the press who detected the slightest merit in any action of Bonaparte's was in his view no better than a bloodstained revolutionary. It follows, of course, that Stoddart had a particular loathing for the *Morning Chronicle*, and the two sparred almost every day. Stoddart, as editor, employed a ranting, abusive style that was lampooned that summer in a pamphlet spoofing the *Times* entitled *Bonaparte-phobia, or Cursing Made Easy*. This offered a long glossary of terms of abuse for the emperor of the Stoddart kind – 'vile Corsican', 'execrable villain', 'disgrace of the human species', 'blustering charlatan', 'hypocritical impostor', 'atrocious brigand' and many more.[1] Stoddart himself acquired the nickname of 'Dr Slop', after a blustering physician in Laurence Sterne's *Tristram Shandy*. The official historian of the *Times* records that 'with few exceptions the political and literary writers of London during 1815, whether Tory or not, disliked the intemperate zeal of John Walter's principal writer'.[2] The proprietor, however, was not in a position to intervene, and so it was Stoddart who provided the voice of the *Times* through these dramatic days.

The editor and proprietor of the *Morning Post*, located at 335 The Strand, was an Irishman who on the face of it was no less zealous in his politics than Stoddart. So staunch a Tory was Nicholas Byrne that he named his son William Pitt Byrne after the greatest Tory of the era, and when Byrne bought the *Post* in 1803 it was for the express purpose of transforming it from a Whig organ to a Tory one. Yet, as the years passed, Byrne found a niche for his paper that was not chiefly political, so that by 1815, although its leading articles never wavered in their support for the ministry, the *Post* was best known for its society coverage. War or no war, the *beau monde* of Regency London insisted upon living life to the fullest, and the *Post*, in columns under the heading 'The Fashionable World', did its best to follow this. The balls and masques, the 'routs' and conversaziones, the opera evenings and formal dinners – all would be announced in advance in the columns of the *Morning Post* and then lovingly described after the event, with lists of guests beneath in challengingly small type. Though the paper liked gossip, it was not primarily interested in mischief or scandal; on the contrary, many of the entries were so breathlessly enthusiastic they could have been written by the hosts and hostesses, as no doubt some were. This editorial approach was both popular and profitable, and Byrne made the most of it, while taking care also to deliver a fair share of coverage of parliament, politics, courts and stock prices. Like his chief morning rivals, in the summer of 1815 he had personal distractions to contend with, though his were of a different character. A married man, he had for ten years been openly attached to Charlotte Dacre, a well-known author of Gothic novels, and the couple had three children out of wedlock. Now, following the death of his first wife, Byrne and Charlotte were about to marry, with the ceremony set for 1 July.

The *Chronicle*, the *Times* and the *Post* were the leading morning titles of the time, at least by reputation, with the *Morning Herald* a close fourth. No reliable information survives about newspaper circulations, but it is likely that the *Chronicle* and the *Times* normally sold in the region of five thousand copies per day and the *Post* and *Herald* somewhat fewer. Such figures may appear small in the context of a London population already in excess of one million, and this was, as we saw, no accident, the stamp duty doing its job of keeping papers out of the hands of the masses. In practice, however, many more people read these papers than could afford to buy them, for copies were frequently borrowed, rented, exchanged or handed on. Some were read aloud in pubs, some circulated in reading rooms and coffee houses and many were posted after reading to country cousins who would study them and pass them on again. A single copy could thus be read by a dozen or more people, and might still be in circulation a week after publication. It helped that the rag-based paper on which they were printed was far more robust than the wood-pulp newsprint of later years.

With modest sales and high taxes to pay, newspapers were inevitably small organisations. The *Chronicle*'s home on the Strand, for example, was a narrow building on four floors next to the Turk's Head tavern, with just two windows on each floor facing the street. Here were accommodated the presses, the printers and compositors, the shorthand report-ers (when they were not in Parliament), the advertising clerks, the cashiers for sales at the door and, of course, the editor and any other writers he employed. The editor set the tone of his paper by deciding what to include and what to leave out, what should have prominence and what could be dealt with in a line or two. But above all it was his task to write the leading article. Stoddart was formally contracted to this;

Perry, his own boss, did it so routinely that he was accused of denying others the opportunity; less is known about Byrne's practice, but since he lived a short step from his business we can take it that he was usually on hand to be consulted, at the very least. Leading articles then, as now, were unsigned, so we cannot be certain that these three men were person-ally present in their newsrooms on the evening of Monday, 19 June 1815, but given what we know of them and, above all, given the importance of the events that were unfolding – events which were undoubtedly pushing up demand for newspapers generally – we can assume that they were.

During the night one of these men would suddenly find himself in possession of a sensational scoop, but that was still several hours off. For the moment all of them must have felt a good deal of frustration as they reviewed the material available for publication in the next day's edition. It was not that there was no news; indeed in other times they might well have considered the fare to be good. Parliament was sitting and, though the business had been brief and dreary, there was enough in it for a column or two. The domestic development of the day was a robbery from a Birmingham stagecoach, supposedly with the loss of the fantastic sum of £14,000. The money, in notes issued by the Chipping Norton Bank, had been left in the coach by a bank partner while he dined in an inn at High Wycombe. Exciting though this was, and even though it had occurred more than two weeks earlier, none of the papers was able to make more than a few paragraphs out of it. From abroad, meanwhile, there was word that Franz Mesmer, the physician who had won inter-national fame for describing and practising hypnotism, had died in Germany – this too was hardly fresh, since Mesmer had breathed his last in March. But such *faits divers* were mere distractions, fit to fill odd corners of the news pages. As the evening papers had announced, the country was at war; indeed a decisive battle might already have been fought. For the readers, the London public, nothing mattered more, and when those readers bought their papers in the morning they would expect to find news of the conflict. As it was, however, there was nothing of substance to add to that item that had already appeared in all the evening papers, declaring that 'hostilities began yesterday, the 15th of June'. No official messages had arrived from Belgium, nor any newspapers or private letters. To their relief, the editors were spared from having to dwell upon this sorry state of affairs in their pages, for to their surprise late in the evening they received from the Post Office a summary of French newspapers fresh up to Saturday. Remarkably, these papers had been acquired with the unintended assistance of Napoleon's niece.

It happened this way. The emperor had a famously troublesome brother, Lucien, with whom he had fallen out long before – because, in essence, Lucien was more of a revolutionary and more of a democrat than he. In 1810 things got so bad between them that Lucien, then living in Italy, attempted to emigrate with his family to the United States, only for his ship to be captured in the Mediterranean by a British frigate. The whole exotic party was brought to England as prisoners of war. Rather like the Earl of Beverley in France, Lucien and his considerable household were allowed to endure this status in comfort, and they lived for the best part of four years in Thorngrove House, a fine country residence near

Worcester. There they dined with local families, who became accustomed to the sight of Lucien passing them on the road in his carriage emblazoned with the letter B. The government never quite dropped its guard, and all Thorngrove House mail was secretly opened and read by trusted agents, but it seems that Lucien was engaged in nothing more sinister than composing an epic poem about Charlemagne.[3] With the peace of 1814 the family soon swapped Worcestershire for the continent, but they left behind one teenage daughter, Christine-Égypte. Named because she was born in 1798, when her uncle was conquering Egypt, she was by all accounts an accomplished young lady, but because she showed signs of developing a curvature of the spine her parents had placed her in the care of a pioneering orthopaedic physician, Robert Chessher, of Hinckley in Leicestershire. After her uncle's escape from Elba, however, and with Britain once again at war with France, Christine's presence in England became an embarrassment for all parties, and so on the very day of Waterloo a ship called the *Wensleydale* made a special crossing from Dover to Calais with this teenage girl as its sole official cargo. The Calais authorities permitted the *Wensleydale* one hour in harbour under armed guard, and officers and crew were forbidden to disembark, but somebody managed to hand over a bundle of French newspapers. The following evening extensive transcripts from those papers, produced with unusual swiftness by the Post Office bureaucracy, landed on the desks of grateful London editors.

In the newspaper style of the time, the information was passed on to readers in generous helpings – in the case of the *Times* filling no less than half the space available for news that day. There were speeches at Napoleon's court, debates from the French chamber of representatives and upbeat dispatches from Bonapartist forces contending with royalist rebels in the western French provinces. All had self-evidently been crafted as propaganda to be consumed by the French public, and all were now reproduced deadpan for a London readership. A bulletin from the French war ministry, for example, began:

> Honest hearts, true Frenchmen, those who cannot without a feeling of profound grief cast their eyes on the internal convulsions of the country at the moment when the dangers from without so imperiously require that it should concentrate all its means and display all its strength, will learn with joy that the news from the departments of Morbihan and Finisterre are satisfactory, and allow us to hope that, far from making any progress, the troubles which threatened to desolate these countries will be stifled in their birth.

Readers of the *Post*, the *Times* and the *Chronicle* were accustomed to such fare and no doubt read the extracts with interest. Here and there they may have gained insights into the thinking and the posture of the enemy, but they will have searched in vain for any revelation about the progress of the war. Paris on Saturday, it seemed, had been no better informed about the fighting in Flanders than London was on Monday night.

Perry's *Morning Chronicle*, true to its Whig tradition, found a way to make this the government's fault, repeating in its leading article what was already known – that the French had attacked and that Wellington was on his way to meet them – and then declaring sulkily: 'The above is all which it has been thought prudent to give to the public.' Over at the *Times* the leading article struck a desperate note. 'The present is assuredly a moment of great interest', it said, revealing in those bland words that the paper had no idea what was actually happening. Stoddart speculated that Bonaparte could have no more than 130,000 men in his northern army (a fair estimate, as it turned out) and then, referring to the parliamentary debates in France reported on the opposite page, he yielded to a familiar fury:

> They seem intended for no other purpose than to amuse and occupy the childish Parisians while their country is bleeding at every pore and while the mad leader of a fierce banditti [Bonaparte] is preparing for that country, ruin if he should be beaten, and slavery if he should prove victorious.

Over at the *Morning Post* Byrne may well have been grateful that he did not depend as heavily as others on political content for his paper's sales and reputation. He was instead able to devote space to news of an event no doubt of the greatest interest to his readers: a 'Grand Baronial Fête' given jointly at their respective Sussex seats by the Duke of Norfolk and the Earl of Egremont to mark the six-hundredth anniversary of Magna Carta. This elaborate mock-feudal gathering, which had been running for five days, involved dancing, pageants, hunting, theatre, cards and phenomenal feats of eating and drinking. The *Post*'s latest bulletin reported that on Saturday 'the morning had been taken up in rusticating through the park', and then at 4 p.m. there was a 'most sumptuous dinner' at Petworth Castle for forty guests, lasting until 9 p.m., after which the participants, perhaps unsurprisingly, proved 'too much fatigued' to make a night of it. The report continued:

> The retinue attached to the numerous families
> now in the castle is prodigiously large, there
> not being less than two hundred servants in
> constant attendance. The consumption of each
> day is on an average of one of, three sheep,
> three calves, besides venison and sweetmeats
> in great profusion.

An update from Sunday announced that forty more visitors were expected that afternoon, and in preparation 'four turtles have been cut up this morning'. Elsewhere in the *Post* appeared reports of lesser parties and dinners in London, as well as this little paragraph:

> Madame de Staël, it is said, intends to set out
> soon for Greece and the Levant. Her motive
> for making such a journey is conjectured to
> be to collect materials for a poem on a second
> crusade.

But the *Post* did not ignore the momentous events on the continent; indeed Byrne devoted four entire columns to transcripts from those French papers, and his leading article provided a brief if dull summary of the news, accompanied by the optimistic assertion:

> Bonaparte's force was estimated at 130,000 men; that of the Duke of Wellington and Prince Blücher, which doubtless came immediately in cooperation, would greatly outnumber the enemy; and under two such distinguished and glorious chiefs everything is to be hoped for and nothing to be dreaded in the result.

The *Post*'s pages would later be transformed by the arrival of its scoop, but for the moment these were the best newspapers their editors could manage on the night. The approved texts were given to the compositors, who assembled the words letter by letter into lines of lead type, and then line by line into columns, to fit in a frame and make up a 'forme' for each page. There were few headlines worthy of the name, merely plain headings of one-column width: for example, 'French Papers', 'Flanders Mail' and 'United Parliament'. And there were no illustrations. Composition was a laborious business even in the most professional hands, and once that was complete there was the equally laborious matter of printing. All but one of these papers used presses so little different from the earliest ever made that Gutenberg himself would have been comfortable operating them. Where his machine had turned out one hundred and fifty pages an hour, these models – the fruit of three and a half centuries of improvement – could print no more than two hundred and fifty per hour.

This is another reason why circulations were small. Even to achieve sales in the thousands, papers had to operate two or more production lines, with duplicate page forms and all the additional labour and expense that implied. The one title free of such constraints was the *Times*, which seven months earlier had introduced the world's first steam-driven press. When this was inaugurated, a leading article declared:

> Our journal of this day presents to the public the practical result of the greatest improvement connected with printing, since the discovery of the art itself. The reader of this paragraph now holds in his hands one of the many thousand impressions of the *Times* newspaper, which was taken off last night by a mechanical apparatus.[4]

The bravado was justified. The new steam press, designed by two German émigrés, Frederick Koenig and Frederick Bauer, was capable of printing 1,100 pages in an hour. This meant that the *Times* could be produced more quickly and later in the night than any of its rivals. In time this would become a tremendous business advantage, but in June 1815 its impact had still to be felt.

*

During the hours of darkness along Fleet Street and the Strand those disappointing Tuesday editions were piled up for distribution, and soon the first carts set out around town to make the first deliveries. Across the Channel, meanwhile, the 'gentleman who came from Ghent', as he would be described, having picked up his important news outside the residence of Louis XVIII and made all haste to Ostend, had discreetly boarded a ship, the *Nymph*, and was under sail for Dover. Behind him, somewhere in northern Belgium, Major Percy was still labouring through the darkness along the road to the coast, the captured tricolours fluttering from his carriage windows. Neither of these messengers, however, would be responsible for the communication that would set London abuzz on Tuesday morning, for they were about to be forestalled by the arrival in the capital, and at the door of the *Morning Post* on the Strand, of one Daniel Sutton of Colchester. Why he chose to bring his story to this particular paper is no great mystery: in his home town he had for years been secretary of the True Blue Club, firm supporters of the government of Lord Liverpool and devoted to the memory of William Pitt the Younger. Those were also the *Post*'s politics and those of Nicholas Byrne, so Sutton was probably a reader of the paper and, if not, may have been directed to its office by some political contact of Byrne's. At what hour he turned up is not certain, though a report in another newspaper put it as late as 5 a.m.[5] This is the story that he told.

He was a ship-owner, operating a ferry service between the port of Colchester and Ostend. He was licensed by the Post Office to carry mail, so his vessel, the *Maria*, was, in the jargon of the time, a packet ship. Recent weeks had been busy for him – the *Maria* helped ferry the Scots Greys to Belgium, horses and all – and on Sunday evening he had found himself once again in Ostend, hoping to pick up passengers for the homeward voyage. As he waited at the dockside, sensational news reached the town from the battlefront. Sutton knew how eagerly such news was awaited in London, and he saw instantly what he must do. 'With great zeal and alacrity,' as a subsequent account put it, he 'ordered one of his vessels to sea without waiting for passengers, and made the best of his way to town to relieve the anxiety of government and the public by the earliest information'.[6] On reaching Colchester he made all haste to London, about fifty miles away, arriving at the Strand in the early daylight hours of Tuesday. Fortunately for the *Post*, he had delayed long enough in Ostend to gather some details of the allied triumph.

The French, he could confirm, had crossed the frontier at dawn on the previous Thursday between the towns of Charleroi and Givet, but this was taken at first to be no more than a foraging expedition – plundering supplies to feed the main French army camped on the other side of the border. Before long, however, it was realised that the whole French force was on the move, that this movement was rapid, that Bonaparte himself was in charge and that the aim was to drive a wedge between Blücher's Prussian army to the east and Wellington's allied force to the west – and by this means to expose and capture Brussels. On learning of this, Wellington threw his army into action, leaving Brussels on Friday morning and advancing to meet the threat. Thus far, Sutton was telling the *Post* more or less what London already knew, although his account added colour to the narrative. But he had more to report. Wellington, said Sutton, slept that Friday night in the village of Genappe, which lies seventeen miles to the south of Brussels, and on

Saturday morning at 7 a.m. he attacked the French. After long and bitter fighting the French army broke off and fell back, with the allies in hot pursuit. Bonaparte's men attempted to make a stand at Charleroi but soon burned and abandoned the town, and on Saturday night they were seeking safety across the border.

It was the best possible news. Not only did it answer the question all London was asking, but it provided exactly the answer that London most wanted to hear: Wellington had beaten Bonaparte and sent him scuttling back to France. At the *Post*, the order was given to stop the presses and get the story into print as quickly as possible. At such an hour this was no small commitment, not least because the first edition, produced at some effort and expense, was largely unsold and would soon be unsellable. But Sutton's tale was surely worth the price. Rapidly it was written up as a new leading article, and just as rapidly the compositors set it in type. Meanwhile the printers broke out a column of the existing page 3 to make space for the new material. As soon this was fitted into the forme the printers swung into their rhythm again, inking the type, slipping pages into the machine, tightening the press and releasing it, and quickly lifting out the printed pages. As soon as the ink was dry, the bundles went out of the door. By the time London society surfaced for its breakfast, therefore – something it did not tend to do before 9 a.m. – the newsboys of the *Morning Post* had a cry to trump all others: 'Glorious Intelligence! Bonaparte Defeated!' Before long, we may be sure, there was a queue of excited customers at the window of 335 The Strand.

The effect of this, as one paper later put it, was like an electric shock. Twenty-four hours later the *Morning Chronicle* would look back and observe:

> The town was yesterday morning put into the highest state of exultation by an account published in a second edition of the *Morning Post* announcing the commencement of hostilities with the most glorious *éclat* to the allies, and particularly to the British.

An out-of-town paper struggled for words: 'On Tuesday, at a very early hour, the metropolis was thrown into a state of extraordinary agitation which it is vain to attempt to describe.'[7] The *Post* would later boast of thousands of extra copies sold that day, probably doubling or trebling its usual circulation, and it seems that the presses ran through the morning and into the afternoon to meet demand. The paper gave its readers the best account it could of the provenance of its information. Sutton was a packet-ship operator and a gentleman, it explained, who had learned of the victory in Ostend on Sunday night and rushed to London to pass on the news. His story tallied in its earlier elements with what was already known in London, and this gave it credibility. But despite the paper's brash confidence, and despite the welcome nature of what it reported, many readers must have asked themselves, could this man Sutton be trusted? Was his tale not too good to be true? And if people were sceptical, they had good grounds. Many that Tuesday morning will have cast their minds back just over a year to the notorious de Berenger hoax. That story too had been brought by an unknown, had told of a French defeat and had been greeted with joy, but it had taught an unforgettable lesson.

It had begun in Dover in the small hours of 21 February 1814, when a red-coated officer calling himself Colonel du Bourg presented himself at the Ship Inn declaring that he had just come ashore from a French boat bringing sensational and glorious news. He promptly wrote a letter to the naval commander at Deal, ten miles away, at the end of the telegraph line to London. In this letter du Bourg introduced himself as an aide-de-camp to the British ambassador to Moscow and announced that the French had been decisively defeated in battle and that the allies had captured and occupied Paris. More than that, Bonaparte himself had been hunted down by Cossacks and literally torn to pieces. In short, the emperor was dead and the war was over. Having dispatched his letter and stirred up a mood of jubilation in Dover, du Bourg made all haste to London and in the course of his journey proved unable to stop himself, as it seemed, from sharing his all-important message with almost everyone he met. On entering the capital, however, he suddenly became discreet, eventually changing carriages and disappearing into the West End. Word had none the less travelled before him, and by the time the City markets opened at 10 a.m. everyone knew that peace had come and Bonaparte had breathed his last. Stocks rose sharply and at lunchtime the excitement increased when a laurel-decked carriage of exiled French royalist soldiers, wearing their distinctive blue coats and white cockades, paraded through the City scattering leaflets and crying: *'Vive le Roi!'* and *'Vivent les Bourbons!'*

Crowds gathered at the Mansion House and in Downing Street as people sought confirmation of the great news, and it was only in mid-afternoon, in the absence of any official word, that doubt started to get the better of hope, whereupon a great scandal began to surface.

The deception had been carefully prepared. The part of du Bourg, it was clear before long, had been played by Charles Random de Berenger, a hard-up adventurer of German background who had travelled down to Dover for the express purpose of stirring up a bow-wave of rumour that would run before him into London. A pair called McRae and Lyte confessed to being the fake royalists in the carriage and described how they had been taught their lines. And a search of relevant stock exchange transactions pointed the finger of suspicion at a group of investors who had profited by all this and were likely accomplices. Among them, adding further spice to the scandal, was Lord Cochrane, a nationally known naval hero and popular radical politician. The outrage at this fraudulent conspiracy was great, and the chief suspects were in due course convicted and jailed, although Cochrane always insisted he was an innocent dupe in the affair. The story that du Bourg had told, of course, was false: Paris did not fall in 1814 until the end of March, and no Cossack had laid a finger upon Bonaparte.

Now, just over a year later, here was another unknown person arriving in London bearing similar news that was also very likely to affect stock prices. He could not simply be taken at his word, so who was he? Byrne must have asked exactly that question, and on the face of it Sutton's credentials were good. He was in his mid-forties, and he really did own a packet-ship business. In addition he was a solicitor of long standing and, no less, the town clerk of Colchester. He even held the title of vice-admiral of Essex, though that probably sounds more impressive today than it did then, since it conferred only minor powers. On top of all this, he was the son of a famous doctor, also called Daniel Sutton, who had been a leading promoter of inoculation against smallpox. Daniel senior was now retired and living very respectably in London. How much of all this Byrne could have been able to verify at short notice we can't tell, but he evidently saw enough to be satisfied that the man in his office was not another de Berenger.

We know now that further enquiries of the kind that Byrne's deadline did not permit might have given pause for thought. For one, holding public office in Colchester at that time was something less than a guarantee of probity: the town council was afflicted by feud and faction to such a degree that an incoming mayor had recently been forced to sue his predecessor for the return of the regalia of office. It was also the case, and must have been well known in Essex, that Sutton was a chronic spendthrift. The elder Daniel Sutton had made a fortune from his quick, simple inoculation technique, but his son and namesake inherited neither his medical skill nor his business acumen. As one historian has put it, forgivingly: 'Brought up to see the guineas flowing in with so little apparent effort, it is not surprising that young Daniel Sutton could never properly appreciate the value of money, and always made it go faster than it came.'[8]

Though he did indeed practise as a lawyer in Colchester, he far preferred messing about in boats. He had a grand house by the Colne estuary, where he built his own dock, and he acquired a number of boats and small ships to which he seems to have devoted most of his time. Some of that time, the relevant authorities were aware, he spent smuggling, and locally he was associated in particular with the plundering of a wrecked cargo of Dutch gin in 1813. But even these illicit profits never stuck to him, and his family had had to bail him out more than once. In 1815, despite the rush of traffic through Colchester prompted by the renewed war, the Sutton shipping business was in trouble. In short, therefore, the *Morning Post*'s source for its great scoop had more than a whiff of Toad of Toad Hall about him, for, besides being a solicitor, ship-owner and town clerk, he was also a reckless enthusiast, a smuggler and a near-bankrupt.

In hindsight it is obvious that that there was something seriously wrong with Sutton's story. The earliest that anyone at Waterloo itself could have known the outcome of the battle was after 8 p.m. on Sunday, which was the moment at which the French Imperial Guard began to fall back. Sutton, it would be reported, sailed from Ostend with his news at midnight. More than eighty miles separate Waterloo and Ostend, and even in ideal circumstances it would have been impossible to complete that journey in less than eight hours. Sutton, in short, could not possibly have known about Waterloo and the defeat of Bonaparte. In fact the victory he reported, the victory that threw all London into the highest state of exultation that Tuesday morning, was not a victory at all but the battle of Quatre Bras, which took place two days before Waterloo and a few miles farther south. Wellington and his army were proud of what they achieved there, but even they would not have called it a victory; indeed they had come perilously close to a defeat that would have handed Bonaparte the keys to Brussels. Hesitation by Ney, tenacity by the allies and some clever improvisation by Wellington had saved the day, so when the fighting ended – and this happened on the Friday, not the Saturday as Sutton reported – the allies still occupied the crossroads of Quatre Bras. The French, however, far from fleeing back across their own border that night in disarray, made camp in good order just a few miles off. Indeed, if anyone could be said to have retreated, it was the allies, who the next morning fell back to Waterloo in preparation for a further French onslaught.

How did this become a story of glorious victory and ignominious French retreat? Sutton may have been a scallywag, but he was not a hoaxer. There are strong grounds to believe that, although he may have added some embellishments, the tale he told was one he had genuinely heard that night at Ostend. In other words, the responsibility for making a victory out of Quatre Bras lay elsewhere. The events of Thursday and Friday, as we saw, caused panic in Brussels, and the authorities there felt the need to calm people. At 10 a.m. on Saturday, the morning after Quatre Bras, Baron van der Capellen published the following bulletin on behalf of the Dutch administration:

> The affair was bloody and glorious for all the troops of his majesty and his allies. Our army kept the field of battle and bivouacked there during the night. The enemy was repulsed far

beyond Quatre Bras. The Prince of Orange, who was in the heat of the battle, is perfectly well. The colonel left him this morning at half-past six o'clock. The affair was going to begin again this morning: all promises the happiest success.[9]

For the most part this was no more than a brave and optimistic interpretation of events. The battle had been bloody; the allies had shown courage; the crossroads had been held. One phrase, however, goes farther: van der Capellen asserts that the French were 'repulsed far beyond' the battlefield. This was doubtless welcome news to the people of Brussels, for whom the proximity of the French army was at that moment a pressing concern, but it was not correct. The baron said he based this account on the Prince of Orange's report from the battlefield, which was written at 2 a.m., but the record shows that the prince had not used the words 'repulsed far beyond' Quatre Bras. Instead he wrote that the enemy's advance had been halted and he had been 'repulsed to a certain distance'.[10] The baron thus improved on the facts at his disposal, and though the change may have seemed a small one, it was sufficient, by the time the message reached Ostend, to transform a draw into an outright victory. Less easy to explain is the dramatic claim made in the *Post* that the French had burned down Charleroi as they retreated to the border, a detail that appeared to elevate victory into decisive triumph. Charleroi, thirty miles south of Brussels, was the last substantial town containing the last bridge over the last river before

France. If Bonaparte had retreated beyond that point, he was more or less back where he had started on the 15th. But van der Capellen never made such a claim, and the truth is that the French captured Charleroi on 15th and retained full control of it until the night of the 18th, and that it was never burned.

To cap all this, absent from Sutton's narrative was any mention of the second battle that had been fought on that Friday: Ligny. There, in an afternoon, Bonaparte had overcome superior numbers of Prussians, forcing them to retreat northwards and narrowly failing to kill or capture Blücher. The outcome at Ligny could be said to have wiped away any advantage that might have been gained by Wellington's stand at Quatre Bras, since as soon as the duke learned of the fate of the Prussians he had to abandon that position.

Sutton's information, then, was fundamentally wrong, and in that light we might expect that subsequent reports reaching London from Belgium on Tuesday would correct the picture. As luck would have it, the opposite happened. Almost every scrap of information that could be added by the evening papers on Tuesday afternoon seemed to confirm the thrilling story in the *Morning Post*. The *Courier* published a letter from a 'private source', datelined Ostend at 10 p.m. on Sunday, stating that Wellington and Blücher had together faced Bonaparte and after two days' fighting had driven the French back across the border. The *Courier* also published 'further particulars from an officer arrived at Ostend', which identified the 42nd and 44th regiments as having borne the brunt of the fighting and suffered the most. Losses on both sides were considerable, and two French generals had been captured. And beside these was an item which purported to relay the contents of a message sent by Wellington to the King of France, declaring:

> Bonaparte has been completely repulsed at Genappe; the battle was very bloody and the Duke of Brunswick was killed; two English divisions suffered considerably . . . The Duke of Wellington wrote on the field of battle that he is in pursuit of Bonaparte with Marshal Blücher.

With Sutton's tale apparently confirmed, the evening papers did not hide their delight. The *Courier*, beneath the heading 'Auspicious opening of the campaign; Complete repulse of Bonaparte', declared:

> Although no official accounts have reached the government, we believe we may congratulate the country that the war has commenced under the most happy auspices, and that the Duke of Wellington has at last measured swords with Bonaparte, and been again the conqueror.

The *Sun* went further. 'The battle of the 17th has been "fought and won"', it told its readers, claiming that these words came 'from authority' and were 'worthy of perfect confidence'. Six paragraphs followed, all in quotation marks as if spoken by an official source, describing the battle and stating that the allies 'had most completely driven the enemy over the frontier'. The *Star*, meanwhile, reported:

The rout of the enemy was complete, and when
the accounts came away the allies were in full
pursuit . . . We are happy in being thus enabled to satisfy the public anxiety with a correct
statement of the result of this dreadful battle.

*

Strikingly, a mirror image of these events occurred in Paris.
In just the same way that van der Capellen put the best gloss
possible on the events of Friday, so did the French. On the
evening of Ligny and Quatre Bras Napoleon's chief of staff,
Marshal Soult, sent the following message to the government in Paris:

The Emperor has just obtained a complete victory over
the Prussian and British armies, united under the command of Lord Wellington and Marshal Blücher. The army
is advancing in pursuit of the enemy through the village
of Ligny beyond Fleurus.[11]

This reached its destination on Sunday morning, probably
with the assistance of the French telegraph system. The
cannon battery at Les Invalides soon fired off a *feu de joie*
to greet this 'complete victory', and people thronged the
streets to share the news, passing around a special one-page
edition of the official newspaper, the *Moniteur Universel*,
which was distributed free of charge. And as with Sutton's
story in London, fresh information confirming and embel-
lishing the victory soon appeared. Wellington, it was said,

had been taken captive (he almost was, at Quatre Bras) and Blücher was mortally wounded (also almost true, at Ligny), while 25,000 allied prisoners had been taken (untrue). A letter from a French officer near the scene of battle reported that the allies had lost 50,000 men (a huge exaggeration). Such was the general delight in Paris that the president of the Chamber of Representatives, Comte Lanjuinais, sent a formal letter of congratulation to the emperor assuring him of the unshakeable devotion of France's legislators. By telegraph, meanwhile, a message went out across France announcing this victory over Wellington and Blücher. Thus Paris and London were both celebrating the outcome of fighting in which they were on opposite sides. Both had been misled.[12]

6

Tuesday: An Awful Moment

Besides its morning, evening and Sunday papers, London
had a handful of newspapers that appeared twice a week,
usually on Tuesdays and Thursdays. One such was the *St
James's Chronicle*, which, perhaps because of its more lei-
surely schedule, had a wordier style than its daily rivals and a
more circumspect attitude. In a 2 p.m. edition that Tuesday
the *St James's* declined to join the mood of exultation and,
though it published reports of a French retreat, it was quick
to stress: 'We cannot vouch for this – the messenger has not
yet arrived.' Nor, it warned its readers, should Wellington's
messenger necessarily be expected imminently:

> As the battles of modern days are not as formerly of a
> few hours' duration, but comprise a series of disparate
> and persevering struggles on a most extended theatre of
> operations, the final result cannot be fully ascertained
> till the lapse of perhaps three or four days.

And it added:

> We understand that government has received some offi-
> cial accounts, but till they know the final result, will
> probably not publish an official communication.

This assumption that, so far as events abroad were concerned, the government must know more than the public, was a common one, and there were good grounds for it. Not only did the Post Office, on behalf of the government, control the flow of correspondence and newspapers into the country, but ministers could normally assure priority for their own communications, and they had professional messengers whose passports guaranteed them swift passage whenever and wherever required. In addition there was the magic spell cast by the mechanical telegraph: few people had followed the fate of the Admiralty telegraph lines and so it was generally taken for granted that the system was still operating fully. Even in newspaper offices it seems to have been widely accepted that intelligence was continually reaching the government from Belgium by this means. That very week, in fact, several papers published this paragraph:

> Government has employed the means for the most rapid conveyance of news which the ingenuity of modern discovery will allow. A succession of vessels are stationed between Ostend and Deal, provided with all the expedients of telegraphic communication both for the day and night; and from Deal the land telegraphs, it is well known, confer with the Admiralty. By the application of these contrivances to maritime intercourse the event of a battle will be transmitted from Ostend in a few minutes.[1]

This was fantasy. No such fast transmission line existed, and indeed the general faith that week that ministers must know more than the public was equally unfounded, as the experience of Robert Peel demonstrates. The future prime minister, at twenty-seven, was then in his first big government job as Chief Secretary for Ireland, a position just below Cabinet rank. Around noon on Tuesday he wrote from London to Lord Whitworth, the Lord Lieutenant of Ireland, who was in Dublin:

I send an extra express for the purpose of conveying to you with more expedition the important intelligence which has this day reached London. I have little doubt that the substance of the following account will appear in the evening papers – probably with some additions – I believe the account to be accurate, though the officer with the dispatches is not yet arrived.

On the 17th Bonaparte made a feint attack on Blücher and a real one on the Duke of Wellington. The Duke attempted to draw the French into a plain for the purpose of employing his cavalry. The French halted and the Duke attacked them. A desperate contest ensued which terminated in our favour. The French retreated, burning, it is said, Charleroi. On the 18th the Duke and Blücher were in pursuit and advanced into French territory.[2]

This is Sutton's tale with a few embellishments, and the reply from Dublin would make clear that Whitworth had received similar information in a separate letter sent the same day by the Home Secretary, Lord Sidmouth. Both

ministers, in other words, had fallen for the story published
in the *Morning Post*. And it may be that even the War Secretary, Lord Bathurst, had done so, for at 3 p.m. the *Star*,
an evening paper, announced: 'Ministers have this instant
issued a confirmation of the defeat of Bonaparte in the following bulletin.' Impressively headed 'War Department,
June 20 1815', the bulletin was given in full:

> A captain of one of the Ostend packets brings an account
> of much severe fighting between the British and Prus-
> sians, and the French commanded by Bonaparte in
> person. The Duke of Wellington, having reached Niv-
> elles on the 16th, attacked Bonaparte on the 17th and
> after a most obstinate struggle drove him back in the first
> instance to Fleurus, and subsequently across the Sam-
> bre to Charleroi, which was burnt by the French. It was
> supposed that the British and Prussians were following
> up their success, as cannonading was heard on the 18th.

On the face of it, this does no more than report to the
public what has been asserted by 'a captain of one of the
Ostend packets' and does not say that the War Department confirms the information. Yet for the ministry clos-
est to these great events to issue a formal bulletin in such
terms amounted almost to the same thing, which was why
the *Star* billed it as 'official confirmation' and why it also
appeared in some morning newspapers the next day. There
is a possibility, however, that the bulletin was a fake – the
rival *Sun* warned its readers that afternoon that other papers
were publishing 'pretended official documents', and another

paper, the *Statesman*, denounced the *Star* next day for having presented 'as if it were a kind of bulletin' news that came from a mere sea-captain.

Whatever the truth about the bulletin, this much is evident: on that Tuesday ministers were no better informed than the public about events in Belgium, and some were at least privately giving credence to what was, after all, nothing more than a piece of hearsay picked up on the docks at Ostend. This was poor judgement, but there is an explanation for it, because this government was desperate to hear good news from Flanders.

*

They were not a team of ministers that inspired enthusiasm, even among their own supporters. The Prime Minister, Robert Banks Jenkinson, second Earl of Liverpool, had taken office three years earlier in inauspicious circumstances. The vacancy arose upon the assassination of Spencer Percival by a madman, and when the Prince Regent picked Liverpool to fill it the House of Commons had to be bullied into accepting him. Although in the two centuries that have followed no one has become prime minister younger (he was forty-two) or held the post longer (fifteen years), and although his term of office included not one but two great victories over Napoleon Bonaparte, Lord Liverpool has left only a faint footprint in British history. Disraeli's nickname for this tall, untidy, bookish character – the Arch-Mediocrity – may be harsh, but there is at least some truth in it.[3] More impressive figures came before him, would follow him and served under him, and the best that is usually said of Liverpool is that he was competent. Napoleon's return from Elba, and all that followed it, had been a stern test of that competence.

At first, all was brisk decisiveness. From Vienna the allied powers, Britain included, issued a declaration stating:

> Napoleon Bonaparte, by again appearing in France with projects of confusion and disorder, has deprived himself of the protection of the law and has manifested to the universe that there can be neither peace nor truce with him. The powers consequently declare that Napoleon Bonaparte has placed himself without the pale of civil and social relations and that, as an enemy and disturber of the tranquillity of the world he has rendered himself subject to public condemnation.[4]

This fiery document, known from its two final words in French as the '*vindicte publique*' (sometimes translated as 'public vengeance'), was swiftly followed by a treaty that set out in detail what each of the great powers would contribute to the effort to remove this usurper from the throne of France. However, though abrupt action of this kind was a relatively simple matter for autocrats such as the Tsar and the Austrian emperor, it caused problems for Liverpool and his colleagues. Britain, with its rotten boroughs and its bought MPs, was hardly a democracy, but it was none the less accustomed to a measure of parliamentary scrutiny of government policy. Ministers and parliament also had to contend, at least to a degree, with public opinion – an amorphous and relatively new phenomenon that involved classes outside the aristocracy and its clients and friends. So whatever Lord Liverpool's diplomats might have agreed in Vienna, he did not have the power to embark on a war merely on their authority, and this was soon made plain to him. To general embarrassment, therefore, the government was obliged to issue a statement of clarification: although Britain had signed the treaty in Vienna, it explained, that was 'not to be understood as binding His Britannic Majesty to prosecute the war with a view to imposing on France any particular government'.[5]

Prime ministers can sometimes count upon a surge of patriotic enthusiasm to carry a country into war, but this was not one of those occasions. The fight was unwelcome. People had been looking forward to stability and the possibility of prosperity after long years of struggle, loss of life and high taxes. As Liverpool himself had observed shortly before Napoleon's escape: 'The truth is, the country at this moment is peace mad.'[6] The government would now need to explain why war could not be honourably avoided, and this raised ticklish problems. Napoleon had been under British guard at Elba; how had he been allowed to escape? And was there any truth in his claims that money he was promised for the government of Elba was never delivered? In short, did Britain or its allies, rather than Bonaparte, bear responsibility for what had happened? Most troubling of all was the matter of legitimacy. A year earlier Britain had played its full part in placing Louis XVIII on the French throne, but Bonaparte's triumphant return had brutally exposed the king's inability to command loyalty among his subjects, whether they were aristocrats, generals, functionaries, soldiers or members of the Paris mob. In consequence no one could seriously claim that this would be a war to liberate France or the French people from an unwanted oppressor. On the contrary, British soldiers might die on foreign fields for no better cause than to foist a monarch on a country that might well take the next opportunity to throw him out yet again. And it was not as if the Bourbons had ever been popular in Britain: on the contrary, for a century before the French Revolution it had been a patriotic duty to hate them. To cap it all, the *vindicte publique*, besides declaring Bonaparte an outlaw, read very like an invitation to assassinate him, which was hardly the posture of a law-abiding country. Taking all of this together, there was at least an argument that Britain should hesitate before embarking on what might prove a long conflict, and there were voices in Parliament ready to make that case. An opposition operated in both houses, and, though it was usually weak and unorganised, it included some genuine masters of debate for whom a subject such as this was a brilliant opportunity. Even among the ministry's supporters, moreover, there was dissent – Wellington's own brother, the Marquess of Wellesley, opposed war.

When the moment came, Liverpool's competence was enough. Skating over the difficulties of legitimacy in his speech in the House of Lords, he stressed instead arguments of expediency and national security. Bonaparte, he declared, was a man of the sword who could never be trusted to rule France in a peaceful, stable fashion, and Britain could not afford to wait until he committed an overtly aggressive act. Russia, Austria and Prussia were ready for war now, but there could be no guarantee that they would be so determined and united in, say, a year's time. By then Europe, and by extension

Britain, might be at Bonaparte's mercy. Strong action now, in other words, was the only safe course. On the day, this case was sufficient to carry Britain into war, but Liverpool and his ministers were in no doubt that it must be a quick war or they would soon be in trouble.

With that in mind they resolved to spare no effort. As the Foreign Secretary, Lord Castlereagh, put it: 'If we are to undertake the job we must leave nothing to chance. It must be done upon the largest scale.'[7] There was no doubt that Wellington, Britain's greatest general, must have the command, but ministers also insisted that he would be given every resource that could be mustered. Again and again in the past two decades governments had been guilty of half-hearted support for armed action and of short-changing the generals in the field; this time would be different. Inevitably, and to Wellington's frustration, this was easier to promise than to deliver, for while the Tsar's army had not even made it home to Russia, Britain had already cashed in its peace dividend. Tens of thousands of soldiers, including many Peninsular War veterans, had been abruptly returned to civilian life as an economy measure, and of those who had not been discharged a large number had been sent to America to fight in the 'War of 1812' against the United States, which had only recently ended.

To make matters worse, soldiers were also needed at home because civil unrest was simmering both in Britain and in Ireland. The new Corn Law, which had the effect of increasing the price of bread, was extremely unpopular and uniformed soldiers had been required on the streets to maintain order. Circumstances, in short, did not favour a large-scale military deployment abroad. Yet in March, April and May Liverpool's ministers worked wonders. Almost the whole army that had been fighting the Americans in Louisiana was rushed back from America, with many proceeding to Ostend with no fresh equipment and with their terms of service unilaterally extended. After a slow start, substantial resources of cavalry and artillery were rounded up in Britain and Ireland and transported across the North Sea. Guards regiments were extracted from their comfortable London barracks and dispatched to Ramsgate and Margate and onward to the continent. And, after an awkward delay caused by uncertainty over whether Britain was legally at war with France (as opposed to being in a rather less clear state of hostility against Napoleon personally), part-time militias were eventually called out in Britain and Ireland to relieve regular troops from police duties and free them for transfer to Belgium. Wellington could never have enough men, but by June, with substantial reinforcements still coming in and more due right up to September, he was no longer complaining. Things really were being done 'upon the largest scale'.

Everyone was well aware, however, that all of this activity was only a part of the British contribution to the alliance. The allied countries recognised that Britain, primarily a maritime power, could not field a large army by the standard of the times. The Russians and Austrians might each muster 200,000 men under arms, with as many more in reserve, but in Britain all the king's horses and all the king's men could never approach such a number. By June, even after intense ministerial effort, fewer than 50,000 British and Irish soldiers were in Belgium. On the other hand, as a nation of shopkeepers and sea-going traders that had never suffered occupation by Napoleon's armies, Britain far outstripped its allies in disposable wealth. With this in mind, the deal struck in the latter years of the earlier war against France had been that the British should make up in cash what they lacked in manpower. Large subsidies in gold coin thus flowed out from London in 1813 and 1814 to help pay the armies of the other great powers. The same would be done in 1815: the treaty underpinning the renewed alliance bound Britain to pay millions of pounds in subsidies for foreign armies. Where would this come from?

If Britain as a country was relatively rich, the British government was not, or so it seemed to ministers. Paying for the war since 1793 had entailed raising old taxes to unprecedented levels and also introducing new ones, including the especially unpopular income tax. And even these measures were not nearly sufficient to meet the bills, so successive governments had borrowed, again on a scale without precedent. Before the conflict Britain's gross national debt had stood at around £250 million and was already a cause for concern. By 1814 it was three times that figure, and concern had sharpened into acute anxiety. How could a debt of £750 million ever be paid off? By law a 'sinking fund' of cash was set aside from government revenue every year for the purpose, but it had long before been dwarfed by the debt itself. The peace of 1814, welcome as it was, had brought these matters to a head. Public expectations were very high – this was what Liverpool meant when he wrote that the country was 'peace mad'. In the same letter he lamented: 'Many of our best friends think of nothing but the reduction of taxes and low establishments.' Even loyal supporters in Parliament, in other words, were demanding to see some benefit from the peace, and they looked to the Chancellor of the Exchequer, Nicholas Vansittart, to deliver it. Vansittart was considered a financial wizard, but he struggled to see how the government could cut taxes while keeping up payments on the debt. And then, out of the blue, Napoleon escaped from Elba, Britain was at war again and millions had been promised to the allies. There was only one thing to do: borrow more, and Vansittart did not stint. Having prepared the ground as best he could, on the morning of 14 June, just four days before Waterloo was fought, he met a deputation from the Stock Exchange and agreed with them the terms of the largest single loan that had ever been raised by a British government, amounting to £36 million. As he explained to the House of Commons that evening, due to 'extraordinary and unprecedented circumstances' it was necessary to make provision 'for the prosecution of a war on the most extensive scale', and he regretted that this must happen 'while the country was yet labouring under the burdens thrown upon it by a former contest'.[8]

Vansittart spoke of 'the most extensive scale' and Castlereagh of 'the largest scale': this was the Liverpool government's great gamble. All possible resources and all possible force would be thrown into the conflict in the hope of a quick, decisive and crushing outcome. And Castlereagh, Liverpool and Vansittart all knew what they were risking, for if things did not work out as they hoped, the government would not survive. Only six years earlier, at a moment when it had seemed that a decisive British intervention in the Netherlands would tip the war on the continent against

Bonaparte, the Earl of Portland's ministry had dispatched the largest invasion force ever to have left British shores. This was the Walcheren expedition, to which the journalist Peter Finnerty had attached himself. It could hardly have failed more miserably: not only were no military gains made but the impotent army was also devastated by disease. As dying soldiers arrived home by the shipload, the ministry collapsed.

Days before Waterloo, Lord Liverpool revealed the depth of his anxiety in a letter to an old political friend. Apparently believing the allies to be rather more advanced in their military preparations than was the case, he informed George Canning: 'We may now be in daily expectation of hearing that the allied armies have entered France.'[9] The Russians and Austrians would attack across the Rhine, he expected, while Wellington and Blücher would launch their assault from Flanders. 'It is impossible ever to answer for the result of military operations; but the chances are certainly all in our favour.' None the less he remained a worried man. 'During the twenty years we have passed in political life,' he told Canning, 'we have never witnessed a more awful moment than the present.' In those twenty years there had been times when invasion had seemed imminent, when British forces had been defeated in battle and when Britain had stood alone against Napoleon. Yet for the Earl of Liverpool nothing matched the awfulness of June 1815, as he waited for news from the battlefront. He was leading an unsettled and unhappy country into a war it did not want and which it could scarcely afford, and if things went wrong not only would his government surely fall, but the whole Tory system of government might be at risk. How tantalising for ministers, then, was Daniel Sutton's story of almost instant victory, and the apparently confirmatory evidence trickling in from Ostend that Tuesday. No wonder some were persuaded that the French were on the run. It was what they needed to hear.

*

Scarcely less eager than the government to learn of a victory, but more cautious about whom it believed, was the financial community in the City of London. Today we associate the Stock Exchange mainly with shares in joint-stock companies, but in 1815 its principal business was the trade in government debt. These were 'the funds' – in the form of government securities such as three-per-cents and consols – into which many people with capital sank their wealth. Generally speaking, they lent the government cash in return for a guaranteed income, and they could sell their slice of the debt at any time for the going price, or buy more if they chose. The buying and selling was done in a fine new building at Capel Court, near the Bank of England in the heart of the City, though some informal trading in the funds also happened outside in what was known as 'Change Alley. For the Stock Exchange as for the government, Vansittart's new £36 million loan was a very big deal, and in these June days it stood at the centre of the City's concerns and hopes. One kind of stock, known as omnium, was what the market now cared about above all, and omnium and the war were intimately linked.

Although government debt was spread across a range of securities, a new loan was traded independently for the first ten months or a year under this label of omnium. This arrangement allowed the market as a whole to adjust to the change while the instalments were being paid. There had been no omnium on the market since the spring, when the previous loan had been fully paid and consolidated into the funds, but on Wednesday 14 June, after Vansittart's transaction with the Stock Exchange, a new omnium immediately came into being. Initially it traded at 4 per cent premium, meaning that a £100 investment in the loan could now fetch £104. Predictably, some investors promptly sold so they could have that profit without further risk, and as a result the price slipped to 2½ per cent premium by the end of that day. This was considered a solid beginning by past standards, but everyone involved knew that over time omnium prices could go down as well as up. In May 1810, for example, a new omnium had opened at a premium of 1 per cent but four months later slumped to a discount of 10 per cent – at which point one of the principal contracting brokers, Abraham Goldsmid, took his own life. By contrast a loan of November 1813, which opened at 3 per cent premium, rose in less than three months to a premium of 30 per cent in response to successive victories over the French. Many investors made fortunes as a result. Now in 1815 the City, the government and investors around the country were watching to see what direction this new omnium would take, and once again the key was the progress of the war. A quick war, it was assumed, would be good for the economy and the government's credit, and would send omnium up; a longer campaign was likely to drag it down. By Saturday – the market operated on Saturdays – it had risen to 3⅜ per cent premium. Sunday's *Observer* newspaper noted:

A number of large speculators on the Stock
Exchange have been within the last two days
very considerable buyers, and yesterday it was
said that they had purchased in the various
funds upwards of a million of stock.

This eagerness was attributed in part to rumours of a French
peace initiative, suggesting that there might not be a war
after all.

On Monday omnium opened down at 2½ per cent premium as the peace rumour proved unfounded, and it slipped
to 2¼ with news that war had broken out, but confidence
returned and it ended the day at about 3¼ per cent. One
investor in the new loan, the economist Thomas Malthus,
has left us a clear picture of his feelings on that day. Offered
the opportunity by his friend the stockbroker David Ricardo,
one of the leading contractors for the loan, Malthus had
invested £5,000 and had been one of those to sell on the
first day and take his profits. On Monday 19th he wrote to
Ricardo explaining why he had been cautious:

Should the allies be successful at the commencement of
the campaign, omnium will certainly rise very consid-
erably; but on the other hand if Bonaparte should begin
prosperously, I think there might be a panic which would
occasion a rapid fall; and though on the whole the prob-
abilities of a rise are perhaps the greatest, yet I am fully
and entirely satisfied with what you have done and beg to
thank you sincerely.[10]

Malthus, in other words, feared that if Bonaparte won an early victory the market would panic and the omnium price would slump, and he preferred a quick, modest profit to that kind of risk.

Then Tuesday brought the *Morning Post* and Daniel Sutton's tale of victory. The *Courier* reported that afternoon that there was 'much agitation' on the Stock Exchange in consequence, and the next day's *Morning Chronicle* suggested mockingly that the City was totally convinced:

> An impartial and unconcerned stranger who had gone yesterday into the Royal Exchange would have received accounts from the scene of action in Flanders, so positive and circumstantial, so full of particular details, and warranted from such high and responsible authority that he could not have questioned the truth of the statements – and he must have believed that the race of the French Emperor was run, that Napoleon and all the elite of his army were enclosed in the forest of Ardennes by 15,000 cavalry from which they must come out and be starved, and when they come out must be cut in pieces.

Omnium rose, but it did not soar. It opened roughly a point higher, at 4 or 4¼ per cent premium, and after wavering during the day and dipping back below 4 per cent at one stage, by the end of the afternoon it stood at 4½ per cent premium. While that is evidence of optimism among traders, it hardly confirms the kind of victory fever described by the *Chronicle*. By way of comparison, on the day of the de Berenger hoax in 1814, when the report spread that Bonaparte was dead and Paris occupied, omnium jumped 6 points in three hours before the truth dawned. Here in 1815 was a gain in the whole day of just 1¼ points. Robert Peel may have believed the Sutton story, but in the City it appears that wiser counsels prevailed. Investors were no doubt also aware of contrary reports that were surfacing, one of which was mentioned in the *Times* that morning:

> A brief and unintelligible report in France asserts that Bonaparte attacked his Grace [Wellington] and Blücher united and completely defeated them; but to this we give little credit . . . These statements of his pretended victory were forwarded by telegraphic messages to Boulogne, evidently with the very view and intention that they should be communicated to England.

Though the *Times* was dismissive, the same story soon surfaced again in copies of a paper from near by in Kent, the *Maidstone Gazette*, which took the information altogether more seriously. Both reports, in retrospect, can be traced back to Soult's telegraphic message to Paris claiming 'complete victory' after Ligny. London was thus hearing reports both of victory and defeat for Wellington, and neither was founded upon fact.

7

Tuesday Evening: The Green Knight

The Port of Ostend, *c.*1815

'The officer with the dispatches is not yet arrived,' wrote Robert Peel. 'The messenger has not arrived,' lamented the *St James's Chronicle*. The *Sun*, going to extreme lengths to keep an anxious public up to date, issued a special late edition to announce:

> When the public is looking with as much impatience for the arrival of further accounts from Belgium, we are sure we shall be thanked for stopping the press at this late hour to say that the expected dispatches have not yet reached government.

Rarely can a newspaper have published such a disappointing 'Stop Press' item, but there followed a breathless afterword:

> We have just heard that a telegraphic dispatch has reached the Admiralty saying that a messenger with official dispatches has arrived at Dover this day.

The *Star* had heard something similar, while the *Pilot* went one better, stating confidently that the messenger would arrive in town with Wellington's dispatch at 6 p.m. In reality that arrival was not imminent at all, for at five o'clock on Tuesday evening, far from being in sight of London, Major Henry Percy could probably still see Belgium.

When last sighted, Percy was just setting forth in a carriage with the duke's dispatch wrapped in that purple sachet and tucked into his uniform coat. His instructions were to pay a courtesy call upon Louis XVIII at Ghent and then proceed to Ostend and take the first available ship to England. Given the importance of his information and given also the delay since the duke had last reported to London, Percy can have been in no doubt that his mission was urgent, and yet it seems to have taken him nearly twenty-four hours to cover the seventy-eight miles to the coast, an average speed of a little over three miles per hour. Tantalisingly, a tiny red leather-bound notebook survives which Percy carried on this journey and in which, sometimes in ink and sometimes in pencil, he made occasional notes, but it sheds no useful light on why he was unable to travel any faster across Belgium than a man proceeding briskly on foot.[1]

It is unlikely that he stopped for a night's sleep. He was tired, for sure, after his exertions of recent days, but he was only a passenger in the carriage and, though the ride was doubtless bumpy and sleep difficult, all he had to do, in principle, was sit. That he made the journey overnight is of little consequence since night travel was fairly common, and in any case the night in question was a short one, with only four or five hours of darkness, and the moon was almost full. The route, moreover, was straightforward. It led first through the small towns of Assche and Alost, twisting across rich, rolling, well-populated countryside before straightening out in the approach to Ghent. Between Ghent and Bruges a choice had to be made between the slightly shorter but narrower road along the side of the canal that linked the two cities and a more northerly route through Eeklo and Maldegem. If Percy followed what seems to have been the preference of most British officers, he took the Eeklo option, through well-farmed, prosperous country admired by many foreign travellers and ending again in a long, almost straight approach to Bruges. The final leg crossed low-lying, almost empty fenland in the shelter of the coastal dunes and ended with a ferry crossing over the estuary to Ostend. Delays were always possible, indeed travellers expected them, but on this occasion Percy probably had particular problems to contend with. One was the shortage of horses. Almost the entire British army had travelled this route in the opposite direction over the previous three months, and armies required horses in great numbers. We can assume that every Belgian stable-owner had received offers for his stock and that many sold all they could spare. There followed the exodus from Brussels from Thursday onward, which must have caused a further surge in demand for post-horses along the way. Of course the Duke of Wellington's personal messenger carried special authority, but in a journey of this length Percy would need to change horses four or five times to maintain a decent speed, and at some of his halts fresh teams of decent quality may have been hard or even impossible to find.

As for the road itself, it was probably not easy going. In normal times these Belgian high roads, with their three carriageways, of which the central one was paved in stone, were admirable, but these times were far from normal. British forces, heavy equipment and supplies had been pounding along this route every day for months, and though the paved central carriageway was probably equal to the challenge, the softer outer ways were not. At the beginning of June a major in the Coldstream Guards had written that in wet weather the sides of the high roads were impassable,[2] and things must have been worse two weeks later, not least because there had been an apocalyptic rainstorm on the night of the 17th. Add to this the traffic on Monday as refugees fleeing Brussels in one direction met British reinforcements still coming in from the coast in the other. With the outer lanes boggy, the paved central lane probably had to serve wheeled traffic in both directions, so movement would have been slow at best and halts frequent.

Percy was probably also held up by a more pleasant require-ment to announce the good news where it was not known and to share in the celebrations where it was. He was, after all, highly conspicuous, if not suspicious, with great French flags waving from his carriage, and he was passing through towns and villages where British and French royalist forces were billeted and where the locals, too, had a keen interest in the outcome of the battle. Percy could tell them a great deal, for he was not merely a messenger but a witness and partici-pant in the battles and was carrying the first returns of killed and wounded. It is easy to imagine him being detained an hour, for example, among the exiled French troops in Alost. At Ghent, in the midst of the city's raucous revelries, he was no doubt given the grandest possible reception by Louis XVIII and his courtiers. Bruges, which had probably heard the news not long before he got there, was surely keen to toast the duke's man on his arrival, while British garrisons in every town and village along the way would have wanted to hear his story and ask about friends and comrades who were in the fighting.

Though no record survives of that journey from Brussels, we do catch sight of Percy arriving at Ostend, where he was the first to announce the news. The witness was a young artillery officer, Benson Earle Hill, who had just reached Ostend after service at New Orleans in the War of 1812. Hill had been intrigued that Tuesday morning by the curious mood of the locals and upon questioning some of them he discovered that they had copies of a printed proclamation announcing a French victory over the allies. It purported to have been issued by Bonaparte at Laecken, a Belgian royal palace that lies north of Brussels – that is to say, on the opposite side of the city from Waterloo. If Bonaparte was at Laecken, it followed that the French must have captured the capital. Hill was dismayed to find the Ostenders quite happy with this and remonstrated with them for believing propaganda. Indignantly, he headed off to report the incident to Admiral Sir Pulteney Malcolm, the officer in command of naval support for Wellington's forces, who had made his headquarters in Ostend. Hill's account, written some years later, continues:

We hardly had time to talk over the subject when a loud huzza was heard at some distance, which increased, as though approaching his house. Scarcely had we gained the window, ere a cabriolet drove up to the door, in which Major Percy was seated, displaying to the hundreds who had followed him the eagles of the 45th and 105th regiments, taken from the foe on the glorious plains of Waterloo. Admiral Malcolm's first inquiry was for the Duke. 'He is safe and well, and in full march on Paris,' shouted the gallant major. His countrymen, on learning that their noblest captain had escaped unhurt, rent the air with shouts, whilst the brave *Belges*, hearing that he was about to visit Paris instead of taking to his ships, sneaked off, uttering abundant *sacrés* and other emphatic epithets, with which they are wont to express their feelings. Major Percy alighted, and, in a few words, related to the admiral the leading features of that fight, on which the destinies of Europe depended. Having thus fortunately obtained such valuable information, I took leave, and hastened to apprize my brother officers of news so cheering.[3]

This was around midday on Tuesday, and Admiral Malcolm had good news for Percy. Anchored just off Ostend at that moment was HMS *Peruvian*, under Captain James Kearney White. It had arrived that morning to deliver reinforcements for the army, and Malcolm authorised it to depart as soon as possible to convey Percy and the dispatch to England. The *Peruvian* was relatively small – a two-masted brig-sloop with eighteen guns (HMS *Victory*, by way of comparison, had 104 guns) – but it was fast: the Cruiser class to which it belonged was said to 'sail like the devil'.[4] No time was lost, and Percy was quickly aboard. The *Peruvian*'s log for that day records that at 2 p.m. it weighed anchor 'with the Hon. Major Percy with dispatches for the War Office from the Duke of Wellington and a King's Messenger'.[5] (A King's Messenger is a

Foreign Office courier; this one had probably travelled with Percy from Ghent with messages from the British ambassador there.) At long last Henry Percy, the dispatch and the eagles were at sea. Forty-one hours had passed since he had seen Wellington and Blücher acknowledge victory to each other. Before him still lay a seventy-mile sea crossing to Kent and a seventy-five-mile journey from the coast to London.

*

By now the news of defeat had reached Paris.[6] There had been nothing from the war front since Sunday morning's victory message from Soult, and a general mood of satisfaction had since become tinged with anxiety. So far as we know, the first to hear of the outcome of Waterloo was the emperor's brother Joseph, who was in charge in the city.

On the night of the battle Napoleon had struggled through the chaos of his shattered army to put some distance between himself and the pursuing Prussians. He paused first at Genappe and then at Charleroi, where he was held up by terrible congestion at the bridge over the Sambre. After leaving Charleroi around 5.30 a.m. he broke away from the direct route to Paris and sought the relative security of the fortress town of Philippeville. On arriving there around 9 a.m. he paused, slept for an hour or so and then, having been joined by his secretary, dictated two important letters. The first was a formal report to his ministers in Paris – equivalent to the dispatch that Wellington was writing at exactly the same time. This, Bonaparte knew, would in due course be published in his official newspaper, the *Moniteur*

Universel. He began his account of Waterloo by pointing out correctly that, if Wellington's and Blücher's forces were taken together, the French army had been outnumbered.[7] As for the fighting itself, he too described a day of pounding but asserted that as late as 8.30 p.m. he was still confident that he would be able to seal a French victory. As he told it, disaster came out of the blue. In the midst of the fighting some French Imperial Guardsmen were surprised by British fire on their flank and there was a moment of disorder. Neighbouring French regiments caught sight of a few runaways and mistakenly believed the Guard was in full retreat. The cry went up, '*Sauve qui peut!*' and in the darkness and confusion it proved impossible to show the troops their mistake and make them regroup. The enemy seized the moment and in this way all was lost. In other words, Bonaparte blamed his defeat on an unfortunate lapse by his soldiers just when victory was in sight. He was more frank about the scale of the defeat, explaining that even his Old Guard, his 'immortals', had been swept away in the stampede, and that most of his army's hardware and baggage had been lost. He must have known how shocking this would be to his ministers and to the people of Paris, but Napoleon, as usual, had a plan, and this he spelled out in a separate, private letter to Joseph that began: 'All is not lost.'[8] The allies, he argued, could advance only slowly into France, and this would allow him time to muster French forces. Giving a rapid inventory of all the troops he believed could be raised – regular soldiers, militiamen, garrison forces and others – he declared: 'I will thus have 300,000 soldiers to immediately oppose the enemy.' In just three days, he insisted, he would have enough to start harrying the invaders, and before long he could add to that total with new levies from the provinces.

From Philippeville Bonaparte sent these two letters to Joseph while he paused to consider whether to follow them or to stay in the north to rally his forces. The messenger probably set out before 2 p.m. on Monday, around the same time that Henry Percy was beginning his mission. From Philippeville to Paris was about 160 miles of relatively good road, passing through Laon and Soissons. An ordinary citizen travelling by public coach would have taken two full days to complete the journey: for an imperial messenger in a hurry, twenty-four hours was probably possible. Sure enough, it was some time on Tuesday afternoon that Joseph Bonaparte convened the Council of Ministers to read his brother's shocking dispatch from the field. More than likely, word was by then trickling into Paris from other sources too.

*

In London at 5 p.m. British government ministers also held an urgent meeting, for at long last they were about to hear fresh news from Belgium that they knew they could trust. Half an hour earlier a post-chaise carriage from out of town had drawn up at the colonnaded entrance of Admiralty headquarters on Whitehall. Enquiries were made for the First Lord of the Admiralty, and the answer came that Lord Melville was at the House of Lords, where a shipping bill was under consideration. Thither the carriage had rushed. His Lordship was summoned, and very quickly he gathered together most of his Cabinet colleagues in the parliamentary office of Lord Eldon, who as Lord Chancellor was the speaker of the House of Lords. Among those present was the Prime Minister, Lord Liverpool, who also had business in the Lords that afternoon.

The bearer of the news was the Rt Hon. Maurice FitzGerald, then aged thirty-nine, a member of Ireland's grandest aristocratic family who bore the exotic title of Knight of Kerry. This was one of three hereditary knighthoods associated with the FitzGeralds, each identified by a colour: white, black and green. As the eighteenth Knight of Kerry in a line stretching back to the thirteenth century, FitzGerald was the Green Knight. He was also MP for the county of Kerry. With him in the Chancellor's room that afternoon was his travelling companion, James Butler, another MP and, as the younger brother of the Marquess of Ormonde, another Irish aristocrat of ancient family. These two men, meeting Cabinet ministers, were among friends. The knight, in particular, was well known and well connected in London political circles, and he knew at least two members of the Cabinet of old: Lord Castlereagh, the Foreign Secretary, and William Wellesley-Pole, the Master of the Mint (who was another brother of the Duke of Wellington). Both ministers, like the knight, had been involved in politics in Dublin before the Irish parliament was abolished in 1801.

The knight and Butler had rushed to London from Belgium at the personal request of Admiral Malcolm, charged by him with delivering news of the military position there. It was an unexpected mission for them since they had been travelling as tourists and had expected to continue doing so for some time longer. They had gone to Brussels at the begin-

ning of the month and, Wellington being another old friend
from Dublin days, were entertained there at the highest level.
When Napoleon attacked on 15 June they were touring the
south of the country, but they were safely back in Brussels in
time to attend the Duchess of Richmond's ball, where the
knight chatted with Malcolm. Although he did not witness
the fighting at Quatre Bras the next day, he visited the scene
of the battle on Saturday morning and spoke with the duke
as the army began withdrawing towards Waterloo. After this,
he and Butler intended to visit an infantry division farther
to the west and they paused at Ghent on their way, dining
with a friend who commanded a regiment stationed there. It
was now Sunday, the day of Waterloo, though of course they
knew nothing of the progress of that battle, and by the time
their dinner was over it was between 6 p.m. and 7 p.m. Their
plan was to leave Ghent at midnight to travel to the town of
Halle, and the knight, having made the necessary arrangements, was just entering his hotel when a carriage drew up.
This was Admiral Malcolm, who had come from meeting
Wellington at Waterloo that morning and was in a hurry
to deliver an urgent message for the King of France.[9] Malcolm begged the knight to wait at the hotel because he had
something very important to ask him. Here is the knight's
account of what followed:

> I waited accordingly; on his return he pressed me in the
> most earnest manner to proceed to London and commu-
> nicate to the government what had occurred. He argued
> the necessity of such a course, from the Duke of Welling-
> ton having declared to him that morning that he would

not write a line until he had fought a battle, and from the false and mischievous rumours which had gone to England, and the total ignorance of the English government as to what had taken place. He said that he was desirous of writing to the First Lord of the Admiralty, but that etiquette precluded his entering into any details on military subjects when the general [Wellington] had not written: that if I consented I would greatly relieve the government and do essential public service as, independent of the Prussian case, of which I knew more than any other individual could communicate to the government, there were subjects of a most confidential nature which he would entrust to me to be told to Lord Castlereagh, our Foreign Minister; that he would put me in a sloop of war at Ostend and send me across at once.[10]

Although the knight had been hoping to follow the campaign against Bonaparte all the way to Paris if that proved possible, he dutifully agreed to break off his holiday as Malcolm asked.

A striking element of the knight's account is Malcolm's concern to counter 'false and mischievous rumours which had gone to England'. This cannot have been a reference to the tale of victory that Sutton brought to the *Morning Post*, since Malcolm could have known nothing about that in Ghent on Sunday. Much more likely is that Malcolm feared the opposite: that London would believe that the allies had suffered a heavy defeat at Quatre Bras. That, after all, had been the interpretation placed on events by many in Brussels, and not without reason since it was Wellington's army that retreated the next day. And the duke himself was worried about how this withdrawal would appear, remarking to one of his officers on Saturday morning after Quatre Bras: 'I suppose in England they will say we have been licked.'[11] Wellington knew the power of the croakers in London, who would exploit any set-back for political advantage, and equally he might have been concerned about the possibility of panic if people believed he had been 'licked'. The Knight of Kerry's narrative supports this idea that the chief purpose of his mission was to reassure London that all was not lost. And no sooner had he agreed to go than Malcolm explained the military picture on the ground at Waterloo in as favourable a light as possible:

> He then told me that he had left the Duke at half-past ten that morning [Sunday] with the army in position on ground which he had already examined, determined to give battle and confident of success, and that he was in military communication with Marshal Blücher.

The knight, his friend Butler and the admiral proceeded 'at once' from Ghent to Ostend, travelling through Sunday night. On arrival at his headquarters the admiral wrote a note to the First Lord of the Admiralty and, true to his word, laid on a naval vessel, HMS *Leveret*, for the crossing. He himself remained in Ostend. According to the knight, just as the *Leveret* weighed anchor a 'gendarme' came up beside them in a small boat to hand over some mail bags and pass on word that 'the Duke of Wellington was driving the French at all points' – another overblown report of

Quatre Bras like the one Sutton had picked up the previous evening. The *Leveret* sailed, carrying the knight and Butler, at 2.45 p.m. on Monday. (Sutton had sailed from the same port about fifteen hours earlier, and Henry Percy would leave nearly twenty-four hours later.) The knight wrote that they had 'rather a slow passage', and this is confirmed by the log of the *Leveret*, which records only light breezes in what proved to be an eighteen-hour crossing. They dropped anchor off Deal at 9 a.m. and their coach reached the Admiralty at 4.30 p.m., twelve hours or more after Sutton had turned up at the office of the *Morning Post*.[12]

Standing before the Cabinet in the Lord Chancellor's room, the knight began, not unreasonably, by asking his audience what they knew, and was told that they knew nothing, that there had been 'reports by smugglers' but that 'nothing was certain'.

> I then gave a detail of all the circumstances that had come to my knowledge, and endeavoured to impress on them the utmost confidence in the success of the Duke of Wellington in any battle that should take place.

The knight's information was enough to strip all credibility from Daniel Sutton's tale. He knew precisely what had happened at Quatre Bras, having heard it from Wellington's own lips the morning after, and he could testify that it was no decisive victory. He could also report, because he had been there when Wellington had learned of it, the grim news of the defeat of the Prussians at Ligny the same day – the first word of it to reach London. He knew nothing of the battle of Waterloo itself beyond its imminence on Sunday morning, but he was able to pass on Malcolm's assessment, which was that Wellington was in a good position, confident and still in communication with the Prussians.

According to the knight's account, written thirty years later, his information was greeted by ministers with 'great relief and gratification'. They told him that London 'had been inundated with the most alarming and dangerous rumours, and that from the length of time since they had received any positive communication from the Duke of Wellington, considerable anxiety undoubtedly existed, but that I had effectually removed it'. To be sure, ministers must have been relieved no longer to be at the mercy of unknowns such as Sutton, but it is impossible to believe they were as gratified as the knight described. Perhaps his perception was coloured by that mistaken expectation that, before his arrival, they would have understood Quatre Bras as a heavy defeat. In reality the knight's news sank the hopes raised by Sutton and thrust ministers back into the 'awful moment' of uncertainty that Lord Liverpool had written of a week earlier. That Wellington was in confident form was a consolation, but ministers knew it was Napoleon Bonaparte that he was about to fight and, shockingly, Bonaparte had already beaten the Prussians.

What to do with the knight's information? It was not a formal dispatch, indeed it was close to a breach of the dispatch protocol, but it was most definitely news and important news at that. Most of London, it was suddenly clear, was labouring under an illusion, and it was surely the responsibility of ministers to give people the facts, however incomplete and disappointing those facts were. At this hour, however

– it was after 6 p.m. – how to give people the facts was a problem, since it was too late for any report of Kerry's news to appear in an evening paper. In the circumstances a formal bulletin for the morning papers might have been justified, but that option was not chosen. Perhaps ministers felt the awkwardness of an announcement which said that there had been no victory when it was still possible there might be one, or perhaps they simply expected Wellington's messenger to arrive during the night and settle matters either way. Bathurst made special arrangements for this, a newspaper reporting that 'the attendants at the War Office were directed to be in waiting the whole of the night, to be ready to receive any arrival from Flanders'.[13] In the event, nothing formal seems to have been done that evening to spread the news that the knight had brought. Instead Lord Castlereagh took upon himself the task that would today be called briefing. Speaking to 'anxious inquirers' in the lobby of the House of Commons that evening, he related that

> according to the advices he had received no decisive affair had taken place – that there had, indeed, been fighting, that the armies were, at the date of his accounts, in sight of one another, and that the allies were acting purely on the defensive and had not entered France.[14]

Charleroi had not been burned, he added, and people should treat with caution all reports of individual casualties that had so far reached London.

*

From the Commons Castlereagh headed for the opera, which he attended frequently with his wife, Emily. Theirs was a happy marriage, despite what many considered a sharp contrast in character: he the cerebral, calculating politician and she the chatterbox and socialite. Opera was one of their shared loves; their home in St James's Square was a stroll from the opera house in Haymarket, and Emily often threw after-show parties for select members of the audience. As he set out from the Commons that evening, however, the Foreign Secretary is likely to have been preoccupied not only by the knight's news and how to communicate it but also by the matter of his own safety, for only a few nights earlier he had turned a corner in Westminster and found himself in the midst of a hostile and threatening crowd. Nor was that the first time, for Castlereagh was roundly hated by the London radicals, partly because a reputation for bloodlessness and cruelty had followed him from his young days in Irish politics. It was not unknown for troops to be called out to ensure he got home safely. Once again this Tuesday evening the streets were full of people, but, as the *Morning Herald* would report next day, the mood was very different:

> The evening of yesterday having been fine, and the placards of the many-edition papers having been very profuse of various, if not contradictory, intelligence, groups of people remained to a late hour in the Strand, some arguing for one, some arguing for another construction of the news from Flanders. About the Horse Guards the crowd was greater, and

> the Park was thronged, all the evening, with people waiting for the dispatches. The feeling was evidently and strongly British, notwithstanding the laborious arts of the Bonapartian journals to produce a contrary spirit.

It is a vivid picture of a population in a ferment of anticipation. These people were desperate for news, and since they knew they would not get it at home they whiled away the long June evening in those places – the Strand was the home of the press, and Horse Guards and St James's Park abutted Whitehall – where the news would first be known. And the *Herald* makes clear that there was no consensus on what news they expected. Despite the report in the *Post* and its eager endorsement by the Tory evening papers, opinion was divided – 'some arguing for one, some arguing for another construction of the news'. And if, as the report says, the majority was optimistic of an allied victory, many would surely have changed their view if they had known what the Knight of Kerry had just reported. Castlereagh, however, was not the man to enlighten them. It would have been neither practical nor, given his unpopularity, wise for him to begin addressing the milling multitude in the park. Nor, for that matter, was he a man who cared much about the opinions of crowds. Once he reached the safety of the theatre he was again among people of his own class, and there he did his best to spread the word. The *Chronicle* would report:

> Lord Castlereagh, who was in the pit of the Opera last night, considered the position which

they [Wellington and Blücher] have taken as
secure, and that the result of the sanguinary
conflict is glorious to the British army.

In other words, while the first encounters may have passed
off satisfactorily, it was not all over.

The performance seen by the Foreign Secretary began
with what the advertisements called a 'grand serious opera',
Barseni Regina di Lida, by Portogallo, with Madame Sessi in
the lead female role. Also on the bill, as a '*divertissement*', was
a new short ballet entitled *Endymion*, and then came a second
full-length production, 'by popular desire', entitled *Le Prince
Troubadour*. Long bills such as this were the custom in the
great London playhouses. On that same night the Theatre
Royal in Drury Lane was offering two plays: *Rule a Wife and
Have a Wife*, a comedy featuring the celebrated Charles Kean
('he failed not to convulse the house with laughter', wrote the
Post), followed by a new work, *Charles the Bold*. But it was the
audience at the Theatre Royal in Covent Garden who would
experience the most memorable evening, and for reasons that
had nothing to do with the theatrical fare on offer. They were
to see a performance of *Love in a Village*, a light opera by
Thomas Arne, followed by *Bombastes Furioso*, a boisterous,
tragi-comic affair, and then *The Sleep Walker* – 'in which', the
bills declared, 'Mr Mathews will introduce the comic song of
Manager Strut Was Four Feet High and a variety of his celebrated imitations'. This was Charles Mathews, a great com-
edian of the time and no doubt the ideal act with which to
bring down the curtain. As patrons at Covent Garden took
their seats, the chatter was no doubt more animated than

usual, for they must have been infected by the giddy mood of the throng in the streets outside. The dispatch, they believed – because the evening papers insisted on it – might arrive at any moment. And sure enough, in the course of the evening there came a sensational interruption, though it was not the dispatch. The music stopped, actors and audience fell silent and the following announcement was read from the stage:

> Lord Cranborne, son of the Marquess of Salisbury, is just arrived from the headquarters of the Duke of Wellington with an account of the defeat of Bonaparte, with a loss on the part of the French of 20,000 men and fifty pieces of cannon.[15]

At this, we are told, 'the theatre rang with shouts of joy'. Alas, management and audience alike had been duped. The story of Lord Cranborne was at best another symptom of collective hysteria progressively gripping London, and at worst a hoax. As several newspapers would point out the next day, Cranborne had been nowhere near Belgium in the preceding weeks and had no knowledge whatever of events there.[16] In fact, on that same night he was across town attending the opera in the same audience as the Castlereaghs, and afterwards, presumably unaware that the patrons of Covent Garden considered him a hero, he mingled at a party in St James's with dukes and duchesses, marquesses and marchionesses, earls and countesses, all lovingly listed in Byrne's *Morning Post*.[17] Perhaps Cranborne even chatted with Lady Castlereagh, who was also in the company, though it appears that her husband had gone to bed.

8

Tuesday: The Rothschild Legend

If there is one well-known fact about the news from Waterloo, it is that the first man in London to know of the victory was Nathan Mayer Rothschild, the founder of the British bank N. M. Rothschild and Sons. You can find this in histories both academic and popular, in novels both literary and romantic, in children's books, reference books and business manuals, in films and television documentaries and on websites by the dozen. It has featured as a fact or a probable fact in *Encyclopaedia Britannica* and the *Dictionary of National Biography* as well as in histories of the City of London, of Jews and Judaism and, of course, of the Rothschild family and of Waterloo. Wellington's most prominent biographer, Elizabeth Longford, repeated it in the 1970s, as did Niall Ferguson in recent works of financial history. The one-time CIA director Allen Dulles told the story in his 1963 book *The Craft of Intelligence*, and it also appears in a 2009 novel by Sebastian Faulks. In these many, many tellings the story has taken a great variety of forms, but most of them have in common two points: first, that Rothschild acquired exclusive word of the victory; and second, that he exploited it to make a fortune on the Stock Exchange. Since most versions also assert that he knew on Tuesday 20 June or even on Monday 19th, and since this narrative has reached Tuesday evening without mentioning him, the time has come to consider this.

Nathan Rothschild was thirty-seven years old in 1815 and doing extremely well for the third son of a Frankfurt merchant who had come to Britain sixteen years earlier with no contacts, no English, an abrupt manner and very little idea of how to run a business. He began in Manchester, dealing in textiles, and despite ruffling many feathers he prospered, but it was his move to London in 1808 that set him on the path to fortune. Now he became a banker, exploiting a talent for bold deal-making and a remarkable memory for figures. He had already married Hannah Cohen, the daughter of a prominent member of the London Jewish community, and he was also able to draw on a wide network of family connections, notably four of his own brothers scattered across the great capitals of Europe. So when in 1813 the British government turned to him for help in paying Wellington's army in Spain, he was well placed to oblige. The duke refused to let his soldiers live by plunder and required them to pay their way as they went, which meant that they had to receive their wages regularly from the government. Acquiring enough gold and silver coin for this purpose and getting it to Spain, or later southern France, was beyond the capability of British officials and of most banks, but not beyond those of Rothschild and his family. They gathered great quantities of coin across Europe and thanks to the efforts of James Rothschild in Paris were even able to smuggle them across France itself. This discreet but important business was very profitable and also earned Nathan trust from the government and respect in the City. It did not, however, make him famous, and by 1815 most readers of London newspapers would still not have recognised his name.

Jump forward thirty-one years now to 1846, by which date few literate people in all of Europe were unaware of the great Rothschild banking family. That summer in Paris a pamphlet was published titled *Histoire édifiante et curieuse de Rothschild 1er, Roi des Juifs.** Its author signed himself simply and strikingly 'Satan', but he was soon revealed to be Georges Marie Mathieu-Dairnvaell, a prolific left-wing writer and controversialist. A small but important part of Dairnvaell's pamphlet concerned Waterloo, and for this he set the scene by explaining that in June 1815 the destiny of Europe was in the balance. As he put it, the vulture (Nathan Rothschild) had tracked the eagle (Bonaparte) to the field of battle:

> Nathan Rothschild was in Belgium with his eyes fixed on Waterloo. He had arranged a relay of horses to Ostend; when he saw the Imperial Guard fall, overwhelmed, dying but not surrendering, he set off at full gallop. At Ostend he found a sea-storm brewing and sailors declared the crossing impossible; but does greed admit anything is impossible? By force of gold Rothschild persuaded a few men to leave with him in a fishing-boat; like Caesar, Meinherr Nathan was risking his fortune. Success crowned his bravery; he reached London twenty-four hours before the news; he gained twenty million in a single coup, and his other brothers backed him up so that the total made in this fatal year reached 135 million![1]

* 'The edifying and curious history of Rothschild I, King of the Jews.'

Dairnvaell's purpose in writing this was political. The 'King of the Jews' in the title of his pamphlet, and the real target of his hostility, was not Nathan but Baron James de Rothschild, the head of the family in France and, since Nathan's death in 1836, the senior figure in the Rothschild family internationally. James was by 1846 fabulously wealthy and enjoyed great political influence. He was also happy for people to know it, with the consequence that he achieved a public prominence probably greater than any other Rothschild before or since. Besides his business dealings he bought chateaux and vineyards, collected art, moved in high society and was married to a glamorous younger woman (his own niece) whose tastes helped define the styles of the age. The phrase 'as rich as a Rothschild' probably acquired its currency in association with James, and in the year 1840 his public image gained an important additional dimension when he locked horns with the French government over the 'Damascus affair'. This was an allegation that a Catholic priest in Damascus had been ritually murdered by Jews, reports of which stoked anti-Semitism across much of Europe in a way few other events have done. The priest was French, and the French government joined in a popular mood of vengefulness towards Jews, but James was quick to denounce the allegation as fraudulent and to criticise the government's response. This he did in a most public manner, taking out advertisements in the daily press. When the Damascus story proved false he was vindicated, and from that time he was seen not only as a mighty banker and leading society figure but also as a defiant leader of Jewish opinion.

Soon James was making headlines again, and it was this

that drew him to the attention of 'Satan'. France experienced a railway mania in the 1840s, and James stood out as the force and the money behind the great new Compagnie des Chemins de Fer du Nord. Dairnvaell saw the new railway companies as a cruel scam at the expense of ordinary people. He had already published one pamphlet denouncing this when in 1846 two events redoubled his anger: first came the extravagant public inauguration of the Chemins de Fer du Nord service and then, just three weeks later, a company train derailed near Arras with the loss of fourteen lives. Dairnvaell now identified James de Rothschild as the personification of all that was wrong in the railways and most of what was wrong in France, and his attack was strongly informed by the mood of bigotry that followed the Damascus affair. Nathan Rothschild's apparently ruthless financial coup after Waterloo – a fortune gained over the dead bodies of thousands of gallant French soldiers – was to Dairnvaell the natural precursor to James's deadly railway profiteering. 'It is to the gold of this Jew [Nathan] that France owes its disaster,' he wrote, 'just as it is to his brother's gold that it owes the shameful swindles of 1845 and the deaths of passengers on the Chemin de Fer du Nord in 1846.' Now, as in 1815, the French people were victims of the Rothschilds: 'This family is our evil genius.'

The Satan pamphlet reached a remarkably wide readership, as is testified by no less a witness than Friedrich Engels, writing that September in the radical English newspaper the *Northern Star*. Here was proof, declared Engels, that people were turning against the 'money lords' of international capitalism. 'The success of this pamphlet (it has now gone through some twenty editions) shows how much this was an attack in the right direction', he wrote. 'The public have taken up the controversy with the greatest interest. Some thirty pamphlets have been published pro and con.'[2] Dairn-vaell himself claimed that 60,000 copies in French were sold in a few months and that it had been translated 'into all the languages'.[3]

In this way, almost incidentally, the story of Nathan Rothschild and Waterloo first reached an international pub-lic. There had been occasional whispers here and there before – Dairnvaell did not quite conjure it from nothing – but from now on it became a widely accepted fact, and all the more so because it lent support to anti-Semitic prejudice. Like the best of legends, the tale has never stood still but instead has grown, changed and adapted to new circumstances. Through the rest of the nineteenth century, as the Rothschild wealth grew ever more fabulous, the story of Nathan's opportunism and greed in 1815 flourished in parallel. In English, French, German and even Hebrew it was retold in ever more elab-orate forms. Nathan, it would be asserted, spent the whole day of Waterloo on the battlefield itself, riding a fine Indian charger; he was present at the meeting of Wellington and Blücher; he paid no less a sum than 2,000 francs for his perilous crossing from Ostend; once in London, he cruelly observed the despair of financial markets convinced of defeat while he discreetly bought up cheap stock. Then, when news of victory sent prices soaring, he cashed in at a mountain-ous profit.[4] One writer even hinted that Rothschild was no mere spectator at Waterloo but that he directly influenced the outcome by underhand dealings with one of Napoleon's marshals, de Grouchy.[5]

The story probably had its most exotic flowering in English in 1887, in the hands of a writer called John Reeves, who placed Rothschild in Wellington's personal entourage at Waterloo, where he was able to question Pozzo di Borgo, among others, on the progress of the fighting. Once he was certain of victory, Rothschild made for Brussels – 'his solitary ride in the darkness must have been intensely exciting to his already highly taxed brain'. From there a carriage swept him to Ostend, where the hapless fisherman who was induced to ferry him through the storm to England held out so little hope of his own survival that he insisted on leaving his lavish payment behind in the safe keeping of his wife. According to Reeves, Rothschild reached the Royal Exchange in London on the morning of Tuesday 20 June to find the market mood extremely anxious. Taking up position beside his favoured pillar, he then deliberately stoked this worry into a panic by reporting the (correct) news of the defeat of Britain's Prussian allies at Ligny while carefully withholding his first-hand knowledge of the subsequent triumph at Waterloo. Tuesday's trading ended 'with not a ray of hope to brighten the all-pervading gloom', but the following afternoon word of victory brought a dramatic rebound in prices. 'Many pitied Rothschild for the enormous losses he had, as they thought, suffered', wrote Reeves. 'They little suspected that, while his known agents had been selling openly, his unknown agents had bought up secretly every piece of scrip they could secure. Far from losing, he had by his manipulations pocketed nearly a million sterling.'[6]

This story was obviously damaging to the reputation of the Rothschilds, and eventually the family and their associates took steps, as they perceived it, to set the record straight. In 1903 Leopold de Rothschild, Nathan's grandson, was guest of honour at a newspaper industry dinner in London, and he used the opportunity to address a tale which, as he noted, even then was told in many forms:

> The authentic story will appeal to you as pressmen, for the news really came through the medium of a small Dutch newspaper. It was published in three big-letter lines, 'Great Victory of the English' at Amsterdam. My grandfather, who owned some ships, had told his captains whenever they went to the Dutch coast, or to any place where there were newspapers procurable, always to bring him the latest publications of the kind. When my grandfather – who believed, as we all do, in the accuracy of whatever was printed in a newspaper (laughter) – saw this announcement, he immediately took it to the Treasury and gave the information to Lord Liverpool without saying how he got it. Strange to say, the news was scouted [disbelieved], because at the very same time intelligence had arrived that the English troops had been defeated on the previous day.[7]

These remarks by a leading member of the family, duly reported in the press, provoked a minor historical controversy. The idea that the news might have travelled to London through Amsterdam, a long northerly detour that would have cost many hours, was at best surprising. As for the suggestion that a Dutch newspaper had given the English credit for a victory in which the Dutch army was so heavily involved, that too seemed hardly credible. Leopold had tried to reframe the Waterloo story in a way that made his family appear less sinister, but he was no historian and he found himself on shaky ground. To his rescue came an English journalist called Lucien Wolf, who asserted with an air of great authority that Leopold's version, though faulty in detail, was correct in outline. Wolf soon published an entirely new narrative, which in summary goes like this. Nathan Rothschild was acutely aware of the commercial value of having information first, so shortly before Waterloo he sent a relative to the French Channel port of Dunkirk to organise an express courier service between there and Brussels. At midnight on the night of the victory at Waterloo a special *Gazette* was published in the Belgian capital, and this was immediately rushed by Rothschild's special private relay to Dunkirk, reaching there at about 10 a.m. on Monday morning. A Captain Cullen, waiting offshore, ferried it across the Channel to Deal, where another express rider was ready to dash with it to London. By this means, Wolf wrote, 'the news was placed in Rothschild's hands some time during the night of Monday'.[8] According to Wolf, in other words, Rothschild in London knew the outcome of Waterloo even before Daniel Sutton began telling the *Morning Post* his overblown tale of Quatre Bras.

Dairnvaell and his successors had never adduced any evidence for their tale, but Wolf was more serious. His narrative, he admitted, rested partly on conjecture, but he had consulted Nathan Rothschild's correspondence at the headquarters of the family bank in London, and this had revealed to him what he called the 'mechanism' involved in transmitting the news. Once this mechanism was under-stood – the couriers to Dunkirk, the fast boat in the Chan-nel, another relay of horses to London – he insisted that it was easy to detect it at work in this particular case. Backed by historical research as it seemed to be, Wolf's narrative had the immediate effect of killing off the notion that Nathan had been present in person at Waterloo. The idea simply disappears from the histories, and even a Nazi propaganda film of 1940, *The Rothschilds: Shares in Waterloo*, which does all it can to blacken the Rothschild name, does not show Nathan riding from the battlefield and inducing a sailor to take him through a Channel storm. Instead, in the film the banker receives the news in London from a sailor who has brought a newspaper from Ostend – and who is casually cheated by Rothschild of his due reward.

Wolf's revision of the story was less effective, however, in clearing Nathan Rothschild of the charges of profiteer-ing and insider trading. Responding to the suggestion that Nathan had exploited or even engineered a slump in stock prices to buy cheaply before the news of victory arrived, Wolf asserted instead that he 'bought largely and openly, in face of an incredulous and falling market'. As proof of this Wolf pointed to a report in the *Courier* newspaper of the afternoon of Tuesday 20 June saying: 'Rothschild has made great pur-chases of stock.' Wolf also endorsed Leopold de Rothschild's claim that before Nathan began buying, indeed as soon as he knew of Waterloo, he loyally reported his information to the government, only to find that ministers, for their own reasons, chose not to believe him. By Wolf's account, there-fore, Rothschild is acquitted of anything dishonourable or underhand. Though this version of events was embraced by some historians, it never acquired a wide currency. Instead, the idea persists that was put forward earlier by writers such as Reeves, that Rothschild covertly manipulated the market to generate the greatest possible profit. This is the form in which the story appears in Sebastian Faulks's *A Week in December*, where reference is made to the need for someone to 'do a Rothschild'. This is explained as follows:

> Everyone in Lombard Street was aware that Nathan Rothschild would be the first to know how the Battle of Waterloo had ended, and this made it impossible for him to trade on his knowledge; his competitors would copy him and no one would want to be on the other side. So, with exaggerated furtiveness designed to draw attention to itself, he began to sell small amounts of government bonds. The herd followed, and the bond market crashed. Unknown to his rivals, Rothschild had, by using intermediaries, accumulated huge long positions in government bonds. When victory at Waterloo was announced, the patriotic rally in bond prices delivered him the largest fortune the City had ever seen.[9]

A different story again is told by Niall Ferguson, official historian of the house of Rothschild. By his account the victory was inconvenient for the family because, as in 1813–14, they had been buying up in large quantities the gold that allied governments would need to pay their armies. The sudden end to hostilities threatened to leave the family over-committed, and so, in Ferguson's words, 'a frantic

Nathan sought to make good the damage' by buying stocks as fast as he could – from the Tuesday onward. His gains cannot have been very great, Ferguson cautions, as the volume of trading at that time was simply not high enough to yield in a few days fortunes of the kind needed to impress a Rothschild.

It is a remarkable array of conflicting tales, some undoubtedly rooted in anti-Semitism and some in a fascination for intrigue and mystery. Where does the truth lie? Or rather, what does the evidence point to? One certainty is that, just as Lucien Wolf asserted, Nathan Rothschild was not at Waterloo. Not only are the *dramatis personae* of the battle well known, with the banker conspicuously absent, but his own correspondence files show him writing letters in London dated 16 and 20 June, which is sufficient to make a journey to and from Waterloo in the interval highly unlikely.[10] Nor is there any hint in the content of the letters of these days, even in confidential exchanges with his brothers elsewhere in Europe, that he left England. As for Wolf's claim that Nathan had prepared an express news service through Dunkirk, that does not survive the evidence test either. Contrary to his claims, nothing in Nathan's correspondence with agents in Dunkirk, or with those in other ports along the coast such as Calais, Ostend and Antwerp, supports the idea. On the contrary, the agent in Dunkirk wrote to Rothschild on 5 June to complain that he had been 'for some time deprived of your favours', and to 'lament this inactivity of your correspondence'.[11] Far from being busy carrying out Rothschild's plan for a fast news service, in other words, the agent was struggling to revive a business connection that had lapsed.

One piece of evidence that has been cited, not by Wolf but by others making the same case, is the published diary of James Gallatin, a junior member of a diplomatic mission from the United States that was visiting Britain in 1815. The entry for 18 June, the day of Waterloo, records Gallatin's impressions of the mood in London, and mentions Rothschild:

> Great anxiety. Consols have fallen terribly. I have never seen greater depression; everybody one sees seems frightened. A rumour today that a battle had been fought and that the Duke of Wellington was crushed; tonight that is contradicted. One cannot believe anything. They say Monsieur Rothschild has mounted couriers from Brussels to Ostend and a fast clipper ready to sail the moment something is decisive one way or the other.[12]

From this it appears that, even as the battle was being fought, informed people in London were talking of Rothschild having couriers and a fast ship ready to convey news – just what Wolf later described. But the Gallatin diary is not what it seems. In 1957 it was exposed as a fraud, probably confected after 1879 and relying on works published long after Waterloo and also long after Dairnvaell had done his work.[13] The story of a Rothschild 'mechanism' for acquiring the news from Brussels first does not stand the test of evidence any better than the tale of the banker himself riding post-haste from the battlefield.

Indeed no convincing evidence has come to light to show that Rothschild knew about Waterloo on Tuesday at all, by whatever means he might have employed. Both Wolf and

Ferguson relied on that quotation from the *Courier* of Tuesday afternoon saying: 'Rothschild has made great purchases of stock.' By implication, it is suggested, he was acting on exclusive information. The problem is, and this was pointed out as long ago as 1858, that no such sentence appears in the surviving copies of the *Courier* of 20 June. The quotation has come down to Wolf, Ferguson and others, it appears, from a nineteenth-century historian called Sir Archibald Alison, author of *A History of Europe from the Commencement of the French Revolution in 1789 to the Restoration of the Bourbons in 1815*. Alison may be little remembered today but was tremendously popular and successful in his own time. He brought out the first volume of the first edition of his vast survey in 1833 and the final and tenth volume in 1842 and then immediately set about revising and enlarging the entire work. Further revisions followed, while at the same he embarked on a no less substantial sequel describing European history after Napoleon. In 1848, in the midst of this great torrent of words, he added an eccentric footnote to page 9 of volume twenty of the seventh edition of the first series. It concerned the 'almost supernatural' ability of news of great events to travel long distances at speed, and it referred to a London newspaper which reported on the Tuesday after Waterloo a rumour that Napoleon had suffered a great defeat on the Sunday night. It continued: 'The same paper (*Courier*, June 20, 1815) mentions that "Rothschild had made great purchase of stock, which raised the Three per cents from 56 to 58."' To all appearances it is a standard reference in an ordinary footnote in a very widely read history book, but like Gallatin's diary entry, it is not what it seems. To repeat, no such reference to Rothschild can be found in the surviving copies of the *Courier*, or in any other surviving evening paper of that day. Where Alison got the idea we will probably never know, though a writer so prolific is likely to make more mistakes than most. As for Nathan Rothschild, he will surface in this narrative in due course, but on Tuesday evening that moment is still some way off.

9

Wednesday Morning: A Gentleman from Ghent

The *Observer* newspaper, published the following Sunday, would look back over this historic week and observe that Wednesday in particular had been 'an interval of painful suspense'. This was an understatement. Certainly there was suspense, and it was painful to endure, but this long day also brought teasing possibilities and aching fears, so that for Londoners it was a period of sharp and disorienting mood-swings. The hunger for news that had been seen on the streets and in the theatres the previous evening turned into a kind of fever. People were desperate to know – because they had relatives or friends fighting in Wellington's army, because they were fired up by patriotism or party loyalty, because their savings were at risk in the funds or because they simply longed for peace and dreaded the consequences of a French victory. And another force was at work: the thrill of living in a moment of history, which brings with it an urgent and not always discriminating desire to be part of what is happening, to know more than the next person or to have something to remember in later years. Thus every titbit of fresh information reaching London became significant, and every theory or rumour became a matter of joy or alarm.

Ministers had gone to bed on Tuesday night knowing, thanks to the Knight of Kerry, that Sutton's story of a beaten Bonaparte fleeing into France on Saturday was untrue, and that instead Wellington had probably fought a battle of consequence against the French south of Brussels on Sunday. Nothing was yet known of that battle but, since two whole days had now passed, Lord Liverpool and his colleagues must have expected that they would wake on Wednesday morning to find the duke's messenger in town. In this they were disappointed. And when they opened their newspapers their dismay must have deepened, for it was clear that the knight's information had not had the calming effect it should have. Indeed the excitement and the expectation of victory provoked by Sutton's false information had intensified, most notably in those that supported the government.

At the *Morning Post*, where Byrne and his staff had spent every hour since Sutton's arrival promoting their scoop as hard as they could, there was no let-up: the story was now told again, and with renewed vigour. 'Glorious Intelligence', announced the leading article, 'Defeat of Bonaparte by the Duke of Wellington'. The *Post* proudly continued:

> We yesterday had the supreme happiness of announcing, not only in a second edition, but in some thousands of our regular publication, the important and glorious intelligence of the defeat of Bonaparte, in his first desperate efforts, by the great and illustrious Wellington, his country's first pride . . . and the destined saviour of Europe and the whole civilised world. The facts we have stated may be relied upon as accurate and undoubted. Govern-

ment are in possession of them from sources
perfectly authentic, but the dispatches from
our glorious heroic chief, owing to his wonted
indefatigability in the improvement of his
splendid successes, had not reached town at
a late hour last night. They are momentarily
expected.

Over the next three columns the paper published what it
called 'a variety of interesting details derived from the pur-
est authority' – no fewer than eleven letters, dispatches and
bulletins received from Belgium. Most had already appeared
in the evening papers of Tuesday, none was dated later than
Saturday and they all had this in common: they made no
claim that the French had fled over the border. Yet the *Post*'s
confidence was unshaken:

> The gratifying summary of all these accounts,
> as we had the happiness of stating yesterday, is
> that on the 15th Bonaparte, with an immense
> force, marched towards Nivelles. On the 16th
> he was met by the Duke of Wellington, who,
> after very severe fighting, defeated and drove
> him back. The French fled to Charleroi, which
> they burnt to prevent pursuit. The pursuit was
> continued by our illustrious chief.

Nowhere did the *Post* mention the Knight of Kerry or his
revelations about the true nature of events at Quatre Bras
and the Prussian defeat at Ligny, although as a staunchly

pro-government paper it would have been informed of all
this. Indeed a paragraph tucked away at the foot of the second column of dispatches betrays some knowledge of what
the knight reported, even if it brazenly dismisses it:

> Another second battle was expected to take
> place on the 18th, but of this no account has
> yet been received. The actual loss sustained
> in the first glorious encounter must be of
> serious magnitude to the rebel leader [Napo-
> leon] who has strained all his energies for the
> first blow and cannot supply the deficiencies
> which the sword has thus occasioned. . . .
> Thus auspiciously has the campaign opened.
> The next blow will be struck in the territories
> of France.

The *Post* thus admitted that there might have been a second battle on the Sunday but insisted it could be of little
consequence because the French had suffered so heavily in
the more important contest reported exclusively in Tuesday's
paper. Meanwhile the paper did not forget its debt to Daniel
Sutton, publishing prominently in its news columns what
amounted to an advertisement for his business:

> The *Maria* packet . . . in which Mr Sutton of
> Colchester arrived from Ostend early yester-
> day morning with the important information
> relative to the success of the allied forces
> under the Duke of Wellington and Marshal

Blücher, which we had the happiness of exclusively announcing yesterday, we understand
will sail from Colchester late this evening for
Ostend, with dispatches. We were not aware
of the facility with which communication
from the port of Ostend can be communicated
by the way of Colchester till we were lately
informed of the short passages which the
packets, lately established at Colchester, usually make to and from Ostend. Government
will probably feel it advisable to take more
notice of this port.

Over at the *Times*, Stoddart was if anything more gung-ho
than Byrne:

The first blow has been struck by Bonaparte,
and has failed. Yesterday morning the town
was filled with animation by intelligence that
the campaign had been opened in a manner
most glorious to the British and allied arms.
The first and fullest account was brought by
Mr Sutton, a gentleman of Colchester.

There followed an overwhelmingly positive account of the
battle of Friday. It had been Bonaparte's 'manifest object' to
drive a wedge between the British and the Prussian armies
and to seize Brussels, 'where he had actually promised to
dine the next day', but he had been 'completely deceived'
by Wellington. Despite affecting a total inattention to the

movements of the enemy, the duke had swiftly mustered his forces and, in a 'most sanguinary' combat, the British and their Belgian allies 'did their duty'. Wellington's army suffered heavy losses, but they 'annihilated' the French heavy cavalry and Napoleon was obliged to retreat. Stoddart could not resist adding the gleeful line: 'Bonaparte slept or, most probably from vexation and rage, passed a sleepless night, at Charleroi.' This was a long way from the truth. Far from duping his enemy at Quatre Bras, Wellington had struggled to get enough men in the field to put up a fight; the French heavy cavalry was not annihilated there, and Bonaparte did not command the French forces, and he spent the following night not at Charleroi but in a position some sixteen miles closer to Brussels. And Stoddart was not done. Looking beyond Friday's events, he wrote:

On the 17th there appears to have been only skirmishing, but fresh reinforcements were momentarily coming up to the Allies so that on the 18th Bonaparte was constrained altogether to abandon his attempt, and before Mr Sutton came away the cannonading in the line of retreat sufficiently proved that the French had sought refuge within their own frontier.

The *Times* thus continued to tell its readers that Bonaparte had been driven back into France, and it gave no hint at all of the news that the Knight of Kerry had brought; instead, Stoddart gave space to the dubious war department bulletin of the previous afternoon, reporting that the defeated French had fled beyond Charleroi. And so grateful was the *Times* to Daniel Sutton that it outdid the *Post* in promoting his business. It was surprised, it declared, that the government had neglected to arrange for the regular transmission of dispatches by the route that Sutton had taken.

> Colchester being but fifty miles from town, and packets sailing twice a week between that place and Ostend, it is reasonable to believe that the earliest intelligence of events from the important scene of military action would thus reach the metropolis.[1]

Londoners who bought James Perry's *Morning Chronicle* were presented with a very different picture. Unlike the *Times* and the *Post*, the *Chronicle* reported the news brought by the knight conspicuously, in large type, beneath the heading 'The Latest Accounts':

> M. FitzGerald Esq, Knight of Kerry, and the Hon. James Butler arrived last night from Brussels, which they left on Sunday . . . From the accounts brought by these gentlemen we learn that the reports first given to the public yesterday morning were greatly exaggerated, and that the encounter between the two armies, though dreadful in carnage, terminated without signal advantage to either side. It is most satisfactory, indeed, to find that this first attack of Bonaparte on the allies failed in its object. He did not separate the English and

the Prussians, as was obviously his design.
But the battle was most sanguinary, and the
French retained possession of Charleroi, which
of course is not burnt. . . . Our readers will see
that the Duke of Wellington and Blücher are
exerting themselves to concentrate their force,
and that they have retreated and taken up a
defensive position at Waterloo.

This was an accurate summary, suggesting that Perry or one
of his staff had spoken to the knight or had been briefed by
Castlereagh. The information evidently arrived at the *Chronicle*'s office late in the production process – that much is clear
not only from the heading of the report but also from the
content of the leading article itself. It had clearly been written in ignorance of the knight's news, and there had been no
time to change it.

Beginning in a reflective vein, it reminded readers that
the *Chronicle* had not wanted this war and had made the
case that British lives should not be sacrificed merely
because the French chose to be ruled by one man rather
than another. This argument had been rejected and now
there was war, and in these changed circumstances the
Chronicle loyally hoped for an allied victory. In reporting the war, however, the paper had a duty to distinguish
between genuine news worthy of publication and 'the
fabrications intended for the omnium mart'. Naming the
Morning Post and Mr Sutton of Colchester, Perry then
painted the picture of the 'state of exultation' that had
gripped the town and in particular the City on Tuesday,

lamenting the impression that must have been made on anyone unfamiliar with such alarums.

> Those, however, who were acquainted with the habits of the Stock Exchange and who knew that on a loan of thirty- six millions there must be many thousand ready believers of every favourable story, enquired what account ministers had put forth. What bulletin had been sent to the Lord Mayor, or circulated in the public offices? What messenger had arrived with glorious tidings?

There was, of course, no ministerial account, no bulletin and no messenger. Perry was not quite accusing Sutton and the *Post* of participating in a stock market hoax in the style of de Berenger, but he was not far off it. Certainly he was accusing the traders behind the new government loan of ramping up, for motives of profit, the significance of a single report from a dubious source. When it came to military analysis, however, Perry proved little shrewder than his rivals, for his summary of the available reports ended with a bland acceptance that 'the French lost all the ground they gained before and were driven to Charleroi'. In other words, before the Knight of Kerry's news reached his office on the Strand, even Perry accepted Sutton's story.

He was on surer ground when he broached the problem of reporting casualties. All of the papers on Tuesday had used the same word about the battle: sanguinary. Allied casualties were said to have been between 2,000 and 3,000 killed, wounded or missing, and the *Courier* declared that regiments worst affected were the 42nd, the 44th, the 79th, the 92nd and the Guards. When it came to naming individuals, however, papers claimed to have scruples. The *Courier* explained:

> We have omitted the names of some of the officers who are reported to have been killed or wounded because the returns are not official and because we would not upon any less than official authority do anything that must shock the feelings of relatives and friends connected with them.

The *Sun* made a similar declaration, but in practice neither paper held back. Notably, the *Sun* had announced that the Duke of Brunswick was 'reported to be killed', while the *Courier* gave his death as a firm fact. Also reported dead in Tuesday's rush of news were Major-General Sir Denis Pack, Major-General Sir James Kempt and Lord Hay, while Sir Thomas Picton and Prince Frederick of Orange (younger son of the King of the Netherlands) were said to have been wounded. The *Morning Chronicle* was indignant:

> the names of distinguished persons have been too lightly mentioned as having fallen. We should not quote them if our silence could prevent the spreading of disastrous intelligence. But to show how vaguely the names of officers are stated, we shall particularise those of Lord James Hay, brother of the Marquess

of Tweeddale, and James Lord Hay, son of the Earl of Errol. Both of these gallant young men were with the army and one of them is said to have fallen, yet both are mentioned indiscriminately. In the Brussels paper the Duke of Brunswick is mentioned among the slain, and General Sir Thomas Picton is, we fear too truly, said to be wounded . . . In some of the accounts General Pack was said to be wounded. This is not true.

More was at stake here than an ethical principle. London society was small and closely interwoven, and many readers of these newspapers knew the officers being discussed personally. Where people were not relatives, they were often friends or acquaintances; the officer class in the army, after all, was in many ways an extension of that society. Pack and Kempt – both reported killed, though neither was even wounded – were well-connected men of high reputation. As for Picton, a great infantry commander in the Peninsula who was wrongly reported as wounded at Quatre Bras but was in fact killed at Waterloo, he was little short of a national hero. The families, friends and comrades of these men, as the *Chronicle* implied, were now reading reports of their death and injury that had been subjected to no verification of any kind – and, as events would show, were for the most part incorrect. And this effect extended beyond high society, for papers were no more careful or accurate when naming whole regiments. Several reports, for example, asserted that the 42nd Regiment was 'literally cut to pieces, with most of its officers wounded and only eighty private soldiers surviving the battle', but this was a considerable exaggeration.[2] A Highland infantry regiment later famous as the Black Watch, the 42nd had indeed experienced appalling losses, but final returns would show that of its six hundred officers and men more than three hundred survived.[3]

On one point, however, the reports were both unanimous and correct, and that was that the Duke of Brunswick had been killed. This alone was shocking news. Frederick William, Duke of Brunswick-Lüneburg and Oels, was not only an important ally to Britain and a close relative of the king and the Prince Regent, but he was also a war hero who had lived for some years in London and was well known in society. The duchy of Brunswick (or Braunschweig) bordered the Hanover lands in Germany, and the bonds between the ruling families could hardly have been closer. The duke's father had married a sister of George III and his sister, Princess Caroline, was the estranged, not to say loathed, wife of the Prince Regent and the mother of his only child, Princess Charlotte. The duke's military record combined valour with tragedy and personal dedication to a degree which, had his character been less stolid, would have made him a figure of romance. The previous Duke of Brunswick, his father, had died in 1806 as a result of wounds sustained at the battle of Jena, where he commanded the Prussian army in a vain effort to halt Bonaparte's conquest of Germany. The new duke subsequently accused Napoleon of denying his father a suitable burial, and this grievance developed into hatred. Driven from his duchy, Frederick William rallied German exiles to fight with the Austrians against France and then, after a remarkable march across Germany, to throw in their lot with the British, who gratefully redeployed them to the Peninsula. Their uniforms were black – it was said that the duke put his men into mourning until Napoleon's slight to his father was avenged – making them an unmistakable and dramatic presence on the parade ground and the battle-field. Returned to his lands in 1813, the duke had been one of the swiftest to rally to the allied cause in the spring of 1815, marching to Brussels at the head of his six thousand 'Black Brunswickers'. Now the Knight of Kerry had con-firmed that this dashing figure had died on the battlefield of Quatre Bras without gaining the revenge he longed for, and those left to grieve in London included the very highest in the land. Indeed the death of so close a relative of the monarch raised delicate matters of protocol. Ministers were obliged to inform the Prince Regent, who had known his brother-in-law well, and it appears that either Liverpool or Castlereagh made the necessary visit to Carlton House. It follows that the first family in Britain to know for certain that they had lost a close relative in the 1815 campaign was the royal family. There would inevitably be a period of court mourning, but the knight's word was not sufficient to trigger this; it must wait, like so much else, for formal confirmation in Wellington's dispatch.

*

Londoners on Wednesday morning thus found their papers telling contrasting stories. Whom did they believe? Close comparison of the reports could leave little doubt that the *Chronicle* was on firmer ground with its account of the Knight of Kerry's information, but few readers had the luxury of making such a comparison. In all likelihood most of them believed the story they wanted to believe, just as the editors did. The *Post* and *Times* wanted victory and promoted Sutton's story while ignoring the knight's, and to their readers, no doubt, the *Chronicle*'s reports must have looked like classic Whig croaking. That people generally preferred good news was demonstrated by the experience of Lord Sunderland. Unlike Lord Cranborne, Sunderland really did spend time in Belgium that June, and he travelled back on HMS *Leveret* in company with the Knight of Kerry and Butler. Reaching London on Tuesday evening and discovering the city in a state of enthusiasm unjustified by the facts as he knew them, he naturally attempted to put his friends on the right track. His reward was to be assailed 'for spreading unfavourable anticipations'.[4] No one likes a spoilsport.

This mood of denial could not last, and as midday approached doubt crept in. Once again it was the turn of the evening papers to compose their leading articles and, try as they might, they could not keep the balloon of optimism aloft. For one thing, the Knight of Kerry's information, strongly endorsed by ministers, was increasingly hard to ignore. For another, there was the absence of the dispatch. Like everyone else, the editors were longing for the duke's messenger to arrive and they were increasingly baffled that, hour after hour, he stubbornly failed to do so. If, as now seemed to be accepted, another battle had occurred on Sunday, then some sixty hours had elapsed since nightfall on that day. This was ample time for a messenger to make the journey. Why the delay? Had something gone wrong? The possibilities were dreadful: Wellington might have been prevented from sending a dispatch because his army was in headlong retreat, or because he had been captured, or even because he was dead. (This last was a haunting fear since no one could forget that ten years earlier Britain had lost its other great hero, Admiral Nelson, in battle.) Every hour that passed without the arrival of the dispatch seemed to make calamity more likely, just as every hour made Daniel Sutton's story less credible – after all, if Bonaparte had been roundly beaten as long ago as the previous Friday or Saturday, as Sutton said, London would surely have proof of it by now.

The *Courier* yielded to the new mood. Having rejoiced the previous day in the 'complete repulse of Bonaparte', it now conceded in its leading article that 'no general battle has taken place'. Its new narrative of the campaign abandoned Sutton and accepted the far more cautious account given by the Knight of Kerry:

> The Duke of Wellington, attacking Bonaparte, drove him back three leagues and was thus enabled to take up a strong defensive position in front of the forest of Soignes. He manoeuvred there with his cavalry on the plain in the front of his army. His headquarters were on the night of the 17th at Waterloo, Marshal Blücher was at Wavre, and thus they were in communication with each other.

The rival *Sun*, which on Tuesday had also crowed over Bonaparte's humiliating flight towards Paris, beat a retreat of its own. Wellington and Blücher, it now reported, had held a conference on the 17th and taken up a strong position, and 'nothing is yet known to government of the 18th'. Gingerly these papers were climbing back on to the fence in case the news of Sunday's action did not match expectations. Meanwhile the Whig *Statesman*, detecting no grounds 'for huzzaing like the *Morning Post* and the *Courier*', declared soberly:

> We regret that we cannot yet tranquillise the public mind as to the result of the dreadful struggles which now interest all feelings and engage general anxiety. No dispatches had arrived from the Duke of Wellington and no communication from office [government] on which we can rely had been made when we sat down to give the best account we could of the sanguinary engagements in which our countrymen have had such a large share in Belgium.

Just as caution was taking hold, however, a new element appeared. The first editions were not yet on sale when word reached the *Courier* that there was a man in town who claimed to know the outcome of Sunday's contest. This was someone we have met: he had arrived from the Channel coast during the night after a journey that had begun, not on the battlefield or in Brussels, but in Ghent, outside the residence of the king of France.

*

The *Courier* broke the news as an appendix to its leading article, timed at noon. It began: 'The following is said to have been brought by a gentleman who was at Ghent on Monday at one o'clock.' Then came the gentleman's story of entering the residence of Louis XVIII on Monday with an officer dusty from the road who congratulated the king on a 'great and decisive victory' the previous day, in which, after nine hours' fighting, all of Bonaparte's heavy artillery was captured and his army was left retreating 'with the greatest confusion'. Here, with the publication of this report, is an important moment: beyond doubt it is the earliest known evidence of authentic information reaching London about the outcome of the battle of Waterloo. This anonymous gentleman, in other words, has his place in history as the first person known to have brought news of Wellington's victory. And with hindsight the authenticity of his story is beyond doubt: the provenance can be tracked all the way to the battlefield through the chain of communication made up of Louis XVIII, the Comte de Semallé, Pozzo di Borgo and Wellington. As for the gentleman's journey from Ghent, he was reported to have crossed the Channel in the packet ship *Nymph*, and separate evidence confirms that the *Nymph* did indeed sail on Monday, reaching Deal some time on Tuesday. The Knight of Kerry had left Ghent after midnight on Sunday and reached London late on Tuesday afternoon; if, as reported, the gentleman left Ghent some twelve hours later, it is reasonable that he should also have arrived in London about twelve hours later than the knight, in the early hours of Wednesday. He might have made better time – one report said he sailed from Ostend less than six hours behind him –

and if so it is possible he reached London before midnight on Tuesday.

How was his story greeted? That it appeared in the *Courier* ensured it a substantial readership, for this was the biggest-selling paper in the country, outstripping not only all of its evening rivals but the morning titles too. In this Waterloo week, it has been said, its sales rose to 10,000 copies per day, which implies an extraordinary feat of printing. A lively and well-produced paper loyal to the government and accustomed to receiving official leaks, it was also the most popular London paper in the provinces. But on Wednesday at noon, importantly, the *Courier* did not know what we know about the source and accuracy of the new information from Ghent. Nor had the paper spoken directly to the gentleman who delivered it, for its report began: 'The following *is said to have been brought* by a gentleman . . .'. The tale was a vivid one, with the dusty officer and the royal embrace, but it came with very little to vouch for it. How should such material be handled? Could it be trusted? It was increasingly clear, after all, that one unofficial informant had led London badly astray, and now here was another unknown who, while he also spoke of victory, described a battle that was fought on a different day in a different place. Once bitten and twice shy, the *Courier* concluded its report with the warning:

> Such is the account in the City. We give it as we heard it, repeating, however, that down to the hour when our paper was put to press the official dispatches had not reached government.

'We give it as we heard it' is not far removed from 'Don't blame us if this is wrong.' At about the same time that the *Courier* appeared, its rival the *Star* also published a report about the gentleman from Ghent, and soon afterwards the *Sun* had the story too. Like the *Courier*, the *Sun* struck a note of caution:

> Of course we can answer for this intelligence no further than it is communicated to us, but we *know* that the gentleman got off from Ostend at eight o'clock on Monday night – that he positively asserts all that we have stated – and that we believe him to be worthy of credit.

There is irony in this. Sutton had been wrong but was widely believed; now another traveller had turned up with accurate news and his word was doubted. It cannot have helped that the new messenger remained anonymous, but the real problem was that Sutton had queered the pitch that week for all other unofficial informants.

The gentleman's actions are curious. The *Courier* declared that his aim was 'to be the first bearer of the news', and apparently for this he had dropped whatever he was doing in Ghent and put himself to the trouble and cost of a rushed journey of thirty-six hours or more, including a sea crossing. Yet once in London he did not seek public credit and withheld his name. Nor, it seems, did he exploit his knowledge for profit by hiding what he knew and buying shares – a kind of insider dealing that was then legal. It is clear that he took his news to the City in the morning and shared it readily and widely – so much so that within a couple of hours it was published for all to read in more than one newspaper. A little more light is shed on the gentleman and his actions by a report written later that day for the *Caledonian Mercury* of Edinburgh. After summarising what he had to say, the *Mercury*'s correspondent explained:

> This pleasing account was brought to government by a Mr C of Dover. He stated to the ministers that he was on Monday at Ghent.

This is the only report to give any form of identity to the gentleman from Ghent – as Mr C of Dover – and it also asserts that Mr C brought his news to the government and that he spoke to ministers.

It happens that there is other evidence suggesting that Mr C met ministers, though it is not of the most reliable kind. According to a biographer of John Wilson Croker, Secretary to the Admiralty, the gentleman from Ghent had an audience with Lord Liverpool himself and after that was questioned by Croker. The description of these encounters is not attributed but had presumably come to the writer directly or indirectly from Croker:

> Lord Liverpool could make nothing of the man and after examining him and cross-examining him for some time he felt increasingly sceptical as to the authenticity of the news that he brought. He then sent for Mr Croker and told him that the messenger had come from Waterloo with the tidings of victory, but that his story was confused, and it

was therefore difficult to accept it as genuine. Thereupon Mr Croker began to question the man, with all his legal acumen, but he succeeded no better than Lord Liverpool in making the narrative intelligible. When about to give it up in despair, as a last resort and led by a sudden impulse, Mr Croker questioned the messenger as to his interview with the French king, and asked him how the king was dressed. The messenger replied: 'In his dressing-gown.' Mr Croker asked him what the king did and said to him, to which the messenger said: 'His Majesty embraced me, and kissed me.' Mr Croker asked: 'How did the King kiss you?' 'On both cheeks,' replied the messenger; upon which Mr Croker emphatically exclaimed, 'My Lord, it is true; the news is genuine', and so, in truth, it proved.[5]

This was written nearly seventy years after the events described and nearly thirty years after Croker's death. It is one of several accounts of meetings between ministers and messengers in these few days that have come down the generations, all of them no doubt having some root in real events.[6] Some probably relate to Sutton – ministers may well have interviewed him – and some to the Knight of Kerry. In the case of this reported meeting between Liverpool, Croker and Mr C, as with others, there are problems. The messenger did not 'come from Waterloo', and far from being unintelligible and confused, his story, as recounted in the *Courier*, was coherent and plausible. None the less, it would have been natural for Liverpool and Croker, if they met Mr C, to test his information and to try and catch him in a mistake. And since Croker knew Louis XVIII he could well have exploited this knowledge in the attempt – though it is hard to believe that he would have placed such reliance on the king's manner of kissing.

Fortunately, against this background of uncertainty, there is one group in London whose response to Mr C's news can be measured with accuracy, and that is the City stock traders. What did they make of this first report of Sunday's battle? Omnium opened on Wednesday, presumably before Mr C's information had spread, at about 4¾ per cent premium, little changed from the previous day's close. From there, according to the *Courier* at noon, it 'gradually kept advancing', and at 1 p.m., by which time Mr C's tale was in general circulation, it stood at around 5½ per cent. At this point the *Sun* commented:

> The state of the money market affords strong presumption that similar intelligence [to Mr C's] has been received through other channels. Though nothing official was known upon 'Change, yet no doubt seems to be entertained of the success of the allies. The Jews, who seem to be in the secret, are buying largely.

This did not last, however, and omnium ceased its advance in early afternoon around the 6 per cent mark and then began to slip back. It seems that traders were encouraged by Mr C's victory story but not really convinced. What the Stock Exchange needed was what all London was aching for: the official dispatch. Nothing less would have the power, in the words of the *Statesman*, to 'tranquillise the public mind'. It is time once again to check on Percy's progress.

*

Wellington's messenger had set sail from Ostend the previous afternoon aboard HMS *Peruvian*, bound for Deal. The *Peruvian* was fast, known for chasing down and capturing an American privateer two years earlier, and its sole mission now was to deliver Percy with all speed. In favourable conditions it might have reached Deal or Dover not long after midnight, and the dispatch could have been in London before midday on Wednesday. Such, no doubt, had been the hope in Percy's mind when they sailed. On the other hand, he and everybody else knew that, sleek or not, sailing ships need wind, and weak winds could keep them at sea on this passage for a whole day, or even two. The log of the *Peruvian* records that Tuesday had begun with 'fresh breezes' off Ostend, but before noon these had become 'moderate' and by the time the ship weighed anchor for England they were 'light'. The progression was discouraging. 'Out studding sails' is the next entry, meaning that on departure Captain White had deployed every inch of sail he could. Even so, the canvas remained limp. Progress was very slow, and it seemed an age before the Belgian coast slipped over the horizon. There was nothing that could be done, however, besides pacing the deck and praying for wind, and later going below to dine and then trying to sleep. On a still sea, and with the ship doing little more than drifting on the currents, it must have been a quiet night if not a restful one.

This was an experience as ancient as seafaring. Seasoned sailors accepted the powerlessness and the waiting as part of the job, or else, like the Ancient Mariner, endured it as the work of fate. Percy had spent time at sea, in the Mediterranean and sailing to and from the fighting in the Peninsula, and no doubt he had known calms before, but he can be forgiven frustration on this occasion. It had taken him much longer than he could have expected to reach Ostend, and now, when a bit of luck with the wind might have allowed him to make up time, he was all but becalmed –

> . . . stuck, nor breath nor motion;
> As idle as a painted ship
> Upon a painted ocean.[7]

Wednesday morning brought no improvement, the log recording: 'Light airs and clear.' Captain White was able to assure Percy that the ship's progress, slow as it was, at least tended in the right direction – their destination was gradually getting nearer. But the hours passed – 7 a.m., 8 a.m., 9 a.m. – and still the wind did not pick up. Ten o'clock came and went, and they had been at sea twenty hours; as a newspaper would later report, 'the anxiety of Major Percy to get to England was extreme'. Before 11 a.m. something changed at last: land was in sight. The first glimpse would have been from the rigging, the white tower of a lighthouse just above the horizon to the west. Very slowly, chalk cliffs appeared below it, aglow in the morning sunshine. This was North Foreland in Kent, a sight well known to sailors, and a telescope would have brought it tantalisingly near. The tension now was too great to be endured, and even White was feeling it. He knew that his superiors at the Admiralty would expect him to do everything possible to hasten Wellington's dispatch towards its destination, and he did not wish to fail. So he proposed to Percy a drastic measure. The same newspaper report explains:

> Capt. White, the commander of the vessel, offered to convey him to Broadstairs in five hours, if he would entrust himself and his dispatches to his care. Major Percy immediately accepted the offer. Captain White ordered his boat to be lowered overboard, and, together with the Major, took his seat in her, with four picked men.[8]

The ship's log put it pithily: 'Out gig, Captain and the Hon. Major Percy left the ship with the dispatches.' It was 11 a.m. and they were rowing for it. Their objective was the fishing village of Broadstairs, between fifteen and twenty miles off and the nearest landing place to North Foreland.[9] It was not a port for warships, but there was a beach, an inn with horses and a road out that led towards London. The gig was small and better suited to harbour business, but in such calm conditions it was equal to the job. Whether White and Percy took turns at the oars is not recorded, but Percy may have been more useful than the average landlubber since he is said to have rowed as a schoolboy at Eton. Either way, the relief of being in motion and under power, albeit merely human muscle power, must have been tremendous. Two whole days after he parted company with Wellington, Percy could at last see England getting nearer.

Wednesday Afternoon: Rumours and Letters

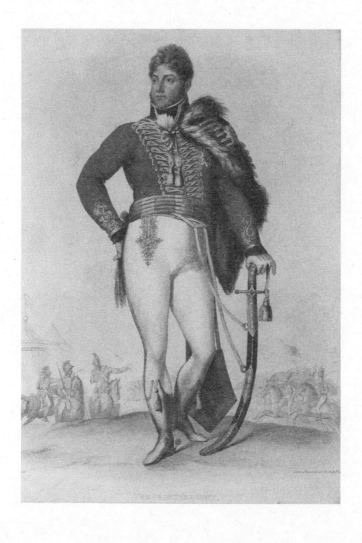

In London that afternoon all twelve ministers in the Cabinet found themselves 'unexpectedly summoned', as the court bulletin would put it, to the residence of the Prince Regent at Carlton House. Besides the Prime Minister, the Foreign Secretary and the War Secretary, the presence was also required of such ministerial officers as the Master of the Mint, the Lord Privy Seal and the Chancellor of the Duchy of Lancaster. And when they reached the cavernous gilt-and-plush halls that had been so lavishly and reluctantly funded by the taxpayer in recent years, they found themselves in company with others of rank. The Archbishop of Canterbury was there, as was the Commander-in-Chief of the Army, who was the prince's brother Frederick, Duke of York and Albany. So too were senior courtiers, including the Royal Steward, the Master of the Horse and the Groom of the Stole (a post originally created for the person who assisted the monarch in the lavatory). They were assembled for a purpose: His Royal Highness had decided that this was a moment for him to show that the 'First Gentleman of Europe', as he styled himself, was more than a gaudy adornment upon the constitution of his country.

Regent since his father had succumbed to mental illness in 1811, the future George IV was fifty-two years old in 1815 and combined wanton habits of self-indulgence with a deep sense that he was unfulfilled. Historians, especially those of the Victorian age, have not been kind to him. This was the verdict of the *Dictionary of National Biography* in 1890:

> That he was a dissolute and drunken fop, a spendthrift and a gamester, 'a bad son, a bad husband, a bad father, a bad subject, a bad monarch and a bad friend', that his word was worthless and his courage doubtful, are facts which cannot be denied, and though there may be exaggerations in the scandals which are current about him, and palliation for his vices in an ill-judged education and overpowering temptations, there was not in his character any of that staple of worth which tempts historians to revise and correct a somewhat too emphatic contemporary condemnation.[1]

Today we acknowledge his style and wit, and we give him credit for endowing his capital city with a grandeur that it had lacked, but if we were asked the question that William Makepeace Thackeray once posed – 'Would we bear him now?' – the answer would still be a resounding 'No'.[2] The Prince Regent's political clumsiness and his prodigal way with public money, to say nothing of his other vices, make even the most feckless of his successors seem virtuous in comparison. The ministers of his own time, however, did not have the consolation that better was to come; they simply had to endure and manage him, and it is one of the achievements of Lord Liverpool and his colleagues that, most of the time, they coped. They knew that the prince resented his constitutional exclusion from the high table of European diplomacy alongside the Tsar, the

Emperor of Austria and the King of Prussia – Britain's business was done by its government and not its monarch – and
they did their best to find compensations and distractions for
him. They were also familiar with the mood that was probably
preying on him on this occasion: an old yearning for some
kind of military accomplishment to justify the sumptuous
field marshal's uniforms he loved to wear.

It was one of the prince's grievances against his father,
George III, that he had never been allowed to experience
active service. His great-grandfather, George II, had commanded an army in battle, at Dettingen in 1743, but since
then only the monarch's younger sons had been permitted real military careers. In 1783, when he was twenty-one,
George was made colonel of the 10th Light Dragoons, a
dashing cavalry regiment which he proceeded to render more
dashing with uniforms of his own design and the very best
equipment. When war with France came in 1793, he begged
his father to allow him to lead his regiment overseas, only to
be told that 'military command was incompatible with the
situation of Prince of Wales'.[3] As the old king knew, not only
was it unwise to risk your heir in battle but young George
also had none of the qualities needed for making war. The
prince, however, still longed for command and, when his
dragoons sailed off to fight, he wept at the dockside. In 1803
he begged again: 'I am aware I do not possess the experience
of actual warfare; at the same time I cannot regard myself
as totally unqualified or deficient in military science, since I
have long made the service my particular study.'[4]

This was ignored. By June 1815 all hope was gone, but the
prince's lingering regret can only have been sharpened by the

martial mood of the moment and by the discovery that his brother-in-law, Brunswick, had died a hero's death in battle. Nor was it a consolation that his country's forces were led in Belgium by a truly great commander, for Wellington was not the prince's cup of tea. For one thing, the duke didn't wear any kind of uniform, let alone an ornate and interesting one, and for another he rarely drank alcohol to excess in the way that the prince and the Duke of York believed men of substance should. One historian described Wellington's relationship with the prince and duke tartly: 'Men who are in complete control of themselves are seldom popular with those who are not.'[5]

On this Wednesday afternoon the Prince Regent had gathered together Britain's highest and mightiest so that they could endorse an exercise of his limited powers that was intended to contribute to the war effort. This was announced in due course in the *London Gazette* as follows:

> Whereas His Majesty is engaged, in concert with His Allies, in a just and necessary war against France, His Royal Highness the Prince Regent, acting in the name and on behalf of His Majesty, and by and with the advice of His Majesty's Privy Council, is therefore pleased to order, and it is hereby ordered, that general reprisals be granted against the ships, goods and subjects of France.[6]

In other words, he was declaring that all French shipping was fair game, and that his government was free to issue letters of marque – the licence of the privateer – to any suitable sea-captain of any country who wanted to help himself to the booty. It was not an initiative likely to change the course of the war, but it was action of a kind and it even had a whiff of daring about it. No doubt those present were grateful to be able to please the prince by signing. Once the formalities were concluded, the regent had private audiences with four of his ministers, including Liverpool and Bathurst. Liverpool had seen him only the night before, but no doubt they lamented together the further delay in the arrival of Wellington's dispatch, and if Liverpool's interview with Mr C had occurred by this hour, the prime minister was in a position to discuss that.

By now George was probably the only one of the chief royal figures in the alliance against Napoleon still in ignorance of the victory. King William of the Netherlands, whose son, the Prince of Orange, had been wounded in the battle, received the news in The Hague late on Monday.[7] Tsar Alexander of Russia, the Emperor Francis of Austria and King Frederick William of Prussia were all in or near Heidelberg, which had become the military headquarters of the alliance since the Congress of Vienna had broken up. Word reached there in the course of Wednesday, stimulating some allies to quicken the march of their armies so that they might be in time to share any remaining glory with Blücher and Wellington. As for Paris, it had been digesting news of the defeat for nearly twenty-four hours.

Bonaparte himself reached the city at 5.30 a.m. on Wednesday, having decided that political manoeuvres in his capital must take priority over military manoeuvres in the field. According to a senior courtier, he was 'overcome by grief and exhausted by fatigue'[8] on arrival, and his first action was to take a bath. There he lay while his brothers and other trusted advisers briefed him and sought his decisions, but in contrast to the mood he had conveyed in his letter to Joseph the previous day, when he had briskly discussed a vigorous defence of France, Bonaparte now struck those around him as dazed and despondent. The momentum generated by his triumphant return from Elba was gone, and for once he did not know what to do. Nagging at him was the suspicion that his best hope of salvaging anything for himself or his personal posterity was to abdicate in favour of his four-year-old son, whom many both in France and abroad would see as preferable to Louis XVIII. But such a step at such a moment would be a desperate gamble: once he yielded power he could not hope to reclaim it, and the child would be left at the mercy of competing interests. While the emperor pondered this quandary in his bath, elsewhere in the Tuileries Palace and beyond many of those interests were uniting around the idea that he must go. Soon the two chambers of his parliament, which he could normally treat as a rubber stamp, were in permanent session and debating his future. Napoleon's supporters there, who as recently as Sunday had sworn undying devotion, were all but silent. His brothers – including Lucien, with whom he was reconciled – urged him to seize dictatorial powers so that he could lead the fight against the invaders, but on this occasion the consummate opportunist could not make up his mind.

Meanwhile Britain did not know whether it could expect news of a victory or should be dreading something much worse. It was as though the English Channel and the North

Sea, having preserved the island from invasion and conquest by Bonaparte, were now conspiring to prevent it knowing of his ultimate defeat. 'Every hour', as the *Sun* put it, 'may bring intelligence.' Yet the morning papers had come and gone, and the evening papers too, and still there was no messenger. While Percy alone could bring certainty, however, nothing could prevent the arrival of further unofficial information. Hundreds of letters had been written in the time it took Wellington to complete his dispatch, and even if army mail was held up, there were civilians on the road able to carry some of these to their destinations. The sea traffic from Ostend was busy: at least five ships reached English ports from there in the course of Tuesday, and there must have been plenty more since then. Any of the coaches and carriages that were coming into London on the Dover road might carry passengers with fresh and important news.

Sure enough, information arrived that afternoon, though it was not necessarily what people were hoping for. One person to receive a letter was Sir Robert Wilson, a soldier and diplomat of maverick spirit who in the Peninsular War had raised a volunteer Portuguese corps to fight alongside Wellington. Now back in London, he was making a name as a political radical, an opponent of the new war and, as one clubland acquaintance later put it, a 'constant harbinger of bad news'.[9] The letter he received from Brussels fitted the gloomy pattern, informing him that on Sunday 'the English were defiling out of the town by the Antwerp gate' – fleeing northwards – and from this he drew the conclusion that the city must soon afterwards have fallen to the French.[10] He was quick to spread the word. Similar news, meanwhile, had reached at least one evening paper, which reported that Bonaparte had occupied Brussels.[11] And another newspaper had this:

> At about half-past two a rumour gained credit with some individuals, which deserved none, and before the close of the market omnium fell to 4½ per cent, but at the close it a little recovered. The story was, that Bonaparte in great force had entered Brussels.[12]

Given what happened in the Belgian capital on Sunday, it is no surprise that echoes of it had now found their way across the Channel. Fanny Burney and Thomas Creevey had described a day of gloom and panic, and anyone leaving the city while that unfolded, as many did, would have carried that mood with them and transmitted it to others. The step that Wilson made, from learning that people had fled in panic to concluding that the French marched in behind them, was a short one.

But other information was also trickling in, and for this there is what may appear an unlikely source: the following Saturday's edition of the Edinburgh paper, the *Caledonian Mercury*. Among the dozens of newspapers published outside London the *Mercury* stands out as unusually well informed and thoughtfully produced. It did not simply rely on the London press for its national and foreign news, as other out-of-town papers tended to, but augmented it with 'private correspondence'. Among the advantages of this, for the *Mercury* and for posterity, is that the writers had later deadlines: London evening papers carried news that was fresh up to around 4 p.m., but the *Mercury* writers were able to sweep up later developments before consigning their letters to the mail coach that left central London for Edinburgh at 8 p.m. It was one of these items of 'correspondence', timed at 7.30 p.m., that identified the gentleman from Ghent as Mr C, and the same writer had more:

> In corroboration of the above account, we have seen a gentleman who left Brussels on Sunday evening, at which time the people were animated with the most heartfelt joy for a decisive victory obtained by the Duke of Wellington on that day.

Here again was a report of a decisive victory, and though it was vague and the informant is not named, it offered independent corroboration of Mr C's story, coming as it did from Brussels rather than Ghent. A second correspondent for the *Mercury* had an interesting source:

> Good news – to be relied upon – Lord Wellington was joined on the 18th by 20,000 Prussians under Bülow and beat Bonaparte completely, taking nearly the whole of his artillery. Omnium is now up at 6. This I have from good authority – one who has seen a letter from Ghent, received by Rosschild, the great stockbroker whose information is invariably the best. He is now at the Foreign Office.[13]

'Rosschild' is obviously Rothschild, and this is the only known occasion on which anyone writing in London that week mentioned Nathan Rothschild in association with news of Waterloo. The report states that the banker (he was not a stockbroker) had received a letter confirming the victory and had gone to the Foreign Office to report this. And though the letter came from Ghent, it was no mere echo of Mr C's information, since the one detail from it that is reported – that General von Bülow's Prussians had participated in the victory – is a detail Mr C does not seem to have known. And it is accurate too: that is to say, von Bülow's was the first corps of the Prussian army to reach the battlefield and was subsequently the most heavily engaged in fighting the French.[14] Nowhere in the reports about Mr C is this mentioned, presumably because the source of his information, Pozzo di Borgo's letter to Louis XVIII, did not mention von Bülow or the Prussians.[15] So the name of Nathan Rothschild can be added to the list of those who received independent intelligence from Belgium by Wednesday evening, and there is at least one more, for the same *Mercury* writer added the line:

> I have this news confirmed by a gentleman
> arrived at the Commissary-General's office
> – the whole ended in Wellington's complete
> success.

After the arrival of Mr C, therefore, at least three further, separate reports reached London announcing a victory for Wellington, while at least three more suggested that Brussels

had fallen on Sunday or was about to fall. It is very unlikely
that anyone in London had a clear picture of all this, still
less that anyone was counting and weighing the reports, so
the likeliest consequence was that people felt confused, or
felt an even greater eagerness to know what the official dispatch had to say. Once again the price of omnium serves as
a barometer of feeling. Having opened that morning at 4¾
per cent premium and then climbed to 5¾ or 6 per cent
in response to Mr C's information, it slipped back to 4¾
per cent in mid-afternoon and remained at roughly that level
until the close of trading. The Stock Exchange, in other words,
spent Wednesday afternoon in a state of uncertainty, which
is hardly a surprise. But to put this in perspective, omnium
traded all day Wednesday at a higher level than on Tuesday
or on Monday, indeed higher than at any time since the new
loan was launched a week earlier. Fundamentally, therefore,
traders remained optimistic, but, just as they had refused to
lose their heads over the Daniel Sutton report, so they took
a measured view of Mr C's information from Ghent and of
all the contrary reports that tumbled into London that afternoon. By close of trading they had struck a balance: 6 per cent
premium had been too high, but nor would they go below
that day's opening price. At 4¾ per cent, it seems, they considered themselves braced for whatever news Wellington's
messenger might bring. So, once again, where was Percy?

*

He and Captain White made landfall at Broadstairs around
3 p.m. Local tradition has it that they beached the gig and

walked up through the village bearing the eagles and flags, attracting around them a small but excited crowd who ever afterwards would claim they were the first in Britain to know of Waterloo. In an inn at the top of the village Percy hired a post-chaise and four, and as soon as the horses were in harness and the flags were secured he and White set off, leaving the locals celebrating in a special glow of privilege. The post-chaise, one of the glories of the coaching age, was the taxi service of the well heeled. Any gentleman or lady without a coach of his or her own, and who sought privacy, could travel by post-chaise for journeys long or short. A snug little box, open at the front, the 'yellow bounder' accommodated little more than a bench seat broad enough for two, but it was light and well sprung and as quick as anything on the road. Two horses were enough to draw it, but for speed four were employed, and the vehicle's principal oddity, or so it may now seem, was that those in the chaise itself had no control over it. The driver rode one of the horses, usually the rear left one, and passengers communicated with him by shouting. In 1815 most inns, even in a small place such as Broadstairs, kept at least one post-chaise for hire, with suitable horses in the stables.

Percy and White would have been told by the villagers that it was just under seventy-five miles to London. Their first stage would be a long one, and taxing for the horses. It took them uphill to the village of St Peter's and then south to join the bigger road that led out of Ramsgate. From here they followed a relatively straight and flat route to Canterbury, bordering the Great Stour river and passing the hamlets of Sarre, Upstreet and Hersden. Ideally the horses would have been changed after fifteen miles at most, but instead they pressed on, downhill into Sturry and then onwards to Canterbury, a full twenty miles. Entering by the Northgate and passing the cathedral on their left, they headed for the big inns strung along the east–west axis through the town. Which of these they chose is not recorded, but it is likely to have been one that had a regular arrangement with the Broadstairs inn. The change of horses can hardly have occurred without fanfare, for a post-chaise clattering into an English town with its horses in a lather and gold-fringed French tricolours fluttering on long poles from its windows could hardly fail to draw a crowd, especially as this was market day. There was a tradition of carriages being the bearers of news from town to town, and in the case of military and naval victories they would often be decked in ribbons and laurels, with the coachmen shouting or blowing horns. Percy and White may not have had trumpets, but their flags and uniforms – Percy in scarlet and White in navy blue – must have served just as well. So however swiftly the stable hands and the landlord performed their business, we may be sure that by the time the officers with the duke's dispatches headed out through Westgate, Canterbury was buzzing with the news of victory just as Broadstairs had been before it.

They now joined the Dover-to-London road, the most important in the country and the most historic. It followed roughly the line of the Roman Watling Street but was even older than that, and for centuries past had been the cord that linked London with the Channel and the continent. Almost every king and queen of England had travelled this route, some of them many times, and usually they paused along the way to pass the night at inns that themselves became famous. A host of distinguished visitors had come this way too – churchmen, poets, merchants and men of learning – and they would continue to do so until the railways arrived. And even for the humblest travellers the journey offered moments of splendour. After halting at Harbledown turnpike to pay the toll, the chaise climbed and eventually crested Boughton Hill, and from there its passengers beheld a magnificent view of the Kent countryside stretching far to the west, the straight road bisecting it to the horizon. When Percy saw this the time was roughly 6 p.m. and he was fifty miles from London.

II

Wednesday Evening: 'Victory, sir! Victory!'

It had rained in London in the afternoon, but in the evening the sky cleared and once again crowds gathered in Whitehall, the Strand and St James's Park. There they shared the suspense and the rumours, debated the possibilities and passed around newspapers, while all the time hoping that they would see the messenger arrive. The theatres were as busy as ever. At Drury Lane the popular William Lovegrove returned after a long illness to play Sir Peter Teazle in Sheridan's *School for Scandal*. At Covent Garden Charles Mathews was back on stage, this time topping the bill with ('positively for the last time this season') a medley of song, impressions and ventriloquy entitled *Mail Coach Adventures*. This included his ditty 'London Newspapers', with the lines:

> Then they differ in name, none alike, all the same,
> *Morning Chronicle* and *Day Advertiser*,
> *British Press*, *Morning Post*, *Herald*, *Times*, what
>   a host,
> We read every day and grow wiser.
> The *Examiner*, *Whig*, all alive to the gig,
> While each one his favourite chooses,
> *Globe*, *Star* and *Sun*, to keep up the fun,
> And tell all the world what the news is.[1]

Up the river at Vauxhall Gardens – that 'metropolitan Elysium', as the *Morning Post* called it, where the rich mingled thrillingly with ordinary folk – there was a gala night of fireworks and music. And in the most fashionable parts of west London there were dinners and parties aplenty, many of them announced in advance in the press, and especially in Nicholas Byrne's paper.

In Portman Square, for example, the Dowager Countess of Clonmell threw open her fine home for what was called a 'rout', a kind of reception that was meant to be crowded and filled with talk. This attracted no fewer than six hundred 'distinguished fashionables', according to the reports next day, including the Marquess of Exeter, the Earl and Countess of Mansfield, the celebrated actress Sarah Siddons and the Prince Regent's discarded wife, Mrs Fitzherbert.[2] In New Burlington Street, meanwhile, the free-spending Sir George Talbot, brother of the Earl of Shrewsbury, was host to an 'assembly' which also was 'numerously and fashionably attended', and in Great Cumberland Street Sir George Buggins gave a dinner. The carriage traffic must have choked the streets that evening, for there were also two grand dinners in St James's Square, which was among the most desirable of all addresses. One was a 'turtle dinner' given by Lord and Lady Grantham and graced by the Duke of Devonshire, the Earl and Countess of Jersey, the Barringtons and the Morpeths, and the other was surely the most exclusive of all the evening's gatherings: at 16 St James's Square Mr and Mrs Boehm were entertaining not only the Prince Regent but also his brother the Duke of York and the Foreign Secretary, Lord Castlereagh.

Dorothy Boehm, fifty-five in 1815, was proof that you did not need blue blood to scale the peaks of society in Regency England. The daughter of a merchant in Hackney, north of London, she was by no means poor by background, but nor was she an aristocrat. In 1781 she made a very good match, marrying Edmund Boehm, a member of a noted City family. German by origin but long established in England, the Boehms had fingers in important City pies such as the East India Company, the Bank of England and the Russia Company. Edmund was nearly twenty years older than Dorothy, and around 1800 he decided that he had made his pile and could take things easy, so he became the sleeping partner in the firm of Boehm and Taylor of New Broad Street and devoted himself, with Dorothy's shrewd assistance, to spending his money in the finest possible style. They bought a grand country seat at Ottershaw Park in the eternally fashionable county of Surrey and employed the architect James Wyatt to help with 'improvements' both inside and out. Their London home had been in the City, but in 1804 they acquired a plot on the west side of St James's Square and proceeded to build a town house of some elegance, possibly again employing Wyatt. Once this was complete Mrs Boehm began giving parties that became features of the society calendar, and she herself was soon a favourite of the *Morning Post*. The mere arrival of the Boehms in town, from Ottershaw or their other home in Bath, was a matter of which the *Post*'s readers had to be informed. Twice and sometimes three times a year Dorothy threw newsworthy balls and masquerades, routs, conversaziones and dinners, and she did so with such flair, taste and charm that they attracted the very best of guests. Byron would write of the young woman who

> the usual preparations made,
> Which you do when your mind's made up to go
> To-night to Mrs Boehm's masquerade.[3]

The Prince of Wales danced at a ball given by the Boehms as early as 1808, before he became regent, and after that he was their guest perhaps once a year. The Duke of York, a neighbour in Surrey, also graced several parties. Already in 1815, in May, there had been one important Boehm event, a masked ball, and on 13 June the *Post* had informed its readers:

> Mr and Mrs Boehm will entertain the Prince
> Regent, the Duke of York and a large party of
> distinguished personages, with a grand din-
> ner, on Wednesday, the 21st instant, at their
> house in St James's Square.

By Dorothy Boehm's expansive standards, in fact, this was an intimate affair. Besides the regent, his brother and Castlereagh (who lived two doors up, at number 18), there were Lord Alvanley, a famous wit, dandy and rider to hounds who was an old friend of the prince, and Joseph Jekyll, another wit and party favourite who in his more serious moments was the prince's legal adviser. Also present were Lord Lynedoch, a veteran Scottish soldier and MP, and the Earl of Westmorland, the long-time Lord Privy Seal. Among the ladies were Emily Castlereagh and Dorothy's niece Eliza

Henchman. We don't know how many there were in all, but this was not one of those events with a cast of hundreds and an hour-long queue of carriages at the door.

As the guests gathered and chatted – the hurly-burly of reports from Flanders gave them plenty to discuss – a few streets away in Grosvenor Square a smaller dinner was beginning which was rather more businesslike. The host was Lord Harrowby, the Lord President of the Council, and his guests were the Prime Minister, Lord Liverpool, and those of their ministerial colleagues not otherwise engaged. Such Cabinet dinners took place roughly once a month and were no doubt arranged some time in advance, but this one fell fortuitously for these anxious men. Over the previous couple of days they had spent a good deal of time fretting over the news and waiting for the duke's messenger. Now, seated around Harrowby's table, they could at least do their waiting together. What did they know? They knew that Bonaparte was expected to attack on Sunday and that Wellington had chosen his ground. They knew that unofficial word from Ghent suggested the battle had gone well, but they must also have heard those reports of Brussels having fallen. They could look across at the City and be assured that the omnium price had not collapsed, but then neither had it risen very much. And they could wonder to each other what could have prevented the arrival of the dispatch. Was there a more likely cause than defeat and retreat? Perhaps the story from Ghent was no more accurate than Sutton's tale, and instead of the French falling back it was the allies. Wellington might even now be trying to rally his beaten forces and escape through Ostend or Antwerp, or he might have died, like Nelson at

Trafalgar. Days earlier Lord Liverpool had written that he was living through an awful moment, with so much at stake for his government and the country; by now the tension must have been barely tolerable.

If there was one professional group in town feeling under even greater strain than the ministers, it was the daily newspaper editors. After the sensation of the Sutton story on Tuesday it had been a challenge to struggle through a whole edition without anything significant to add. To face a second night in the same limbo was agony, especially with demand for news so high. This was a priceless opportunity to win readers, but only if you had something to report. Once again the cupboard was not quite bare. There was parliamentary business to be reported, including a debate about a proposal to restrict the use of flogging as a punishment in the army. This could fill three or even four columns of the ten, and advertisements might occupy a couple more. After that the pickings were slim: a woman found with her throat cut in Drury Lane; an Essex farmer and his horse both killed by a bolt of lightning; a court case about whether canvas for theatre sets was subject to tax. All of this left a gaping hole: at least two columns would remain for war news and the leading article. The compositors and the presses were ready, the hole had to be filled and the editors contemplated another round of leading articles closing with that useless sentiment: only time will tell. As they toiled that evening in their offices on the Strand and along Fleet Street, they must all have had one ear straining for the cry from outside that would save them, the cry that said: 'The messenger has arrived!'

*

Percy was now travelling fast. From Canterbury to Sitting-bourne was fifteen miles of straight and lonely road, swiftly covered. And if there was one place in the kingdom where a traveller could count on a fast change and good horses it was Sittingbourne, for the little town lived by the coaching trade. Its main street pointing towards London was lined with inns, some of them, such as the George, the Red Lion and the Rose, known far beyond Kent. All kept stables of horses ready to work, and all could change a team of four in less than five minutes. A brief pause, some banter with the ostlers and the innkeeper, an exchange of money and official paperwork (post-horses were subject to tax, so every transac-tion had to be ticketed), accompanied perhaps by a snatched bite to eat, and they were on their way again, leaving behind another wildfire of excitement. From there it was eleven miles to Rochester and another team of fresh horses at the Bull, the Crown or the King's Head. Crossing the ancient bridge over the Medway, they came up to the turnpike at Strood and then on after Gad's Hill to another at Chalk Street. Each turnpike required a pause to allow the driver to pay the toll and in some cases hand over the ticket for the post-horse tax. Then the keeper would open the gate, the revenue nominally going to maintain the road and any sig-nificant bridges. After Windmill Hill, near Gravesend, came the Stonebridge turnpike and then beyond Galley Hill a descent to the bridge over the Darent and on into Dartford. Here, after another fifteen miles, they made their fourth and final change of horses. Broadstairs lay sixty miles behind, and they had fifteen to go. Once again the road was straight, and soon they were past Crooked Log turnpike, through Welling and at the foot of Shooter's Hill, the steepest and longest climb of the journey. Here it was customary for drivers and passengers, or at least the men among them, to alight and walk, easing the burden for the horses. And here again we tread in Byron's footsteps:

> Don Juan had got out on Shooter's Hill;
>   Sunset the time, the place the same declivity
> Which looks along that vale of good and ill
>   Where London streets ferment in full activity,
> While everything around was calm and still,
>   Except the creak of wheels, which on their pivot he
> Heard, and that bee-like, bubbling, busy hum
> Of cities, that boil over with their scum –
>
> I say, Don Juan, wrapp'd in contemplation,
>   Walk'd on behind his carriage, o'er the summit,
> And lost in wonder of so great a nation,
>   Gave way to't, since he could not overcome it.[4]

Percy reached the top later in the evening than Don Juan, and so the sun had set. But this was one night short of the summer solstice, so something like an hour remained before the last light faded from the sky. Below and to the north-west, therefore, Percy could clearly see the greatest city in the world stretched out in the twilight glow. The end of his journey was eight miles off.

Down the hill they clattered, through Blackheath to the

Deptford turnpike and on to the Marquis of Granby inn, where they left the county of Kent and entered Surrey. After another turnpike at New Cross the Kent Road, as it now was, took them west and then north, over the Surrey Canal to the final turnpike at the Green Man. These, at last, were the outskirts of London, and from here the route was mostly lined with houses. It was around 11 p.m. and only a faint dusky light remained in the sky, but with their haste, their fluttering tricolours and no doubt the occasional halloo from the driver they must have turned many heads as they went. At the Bricklayers' Arms, a travellers' landmark, the road forked. In 1815 there were three road bridges over the Thames in London, and the right fork led to the two more easterly ones, the new Blackfriars Bridge and the ancient London Bridge (by now stripped of the tall houses that had risen above it for centuries). Both led into the City, but that was not Percy's destination. He wanted the seat of government, which meant the left fork towards Westminster Bridge. So the yellow chaise zigzagged along Greenwich Road, London Road, Westminster Road and Bridge Road until, at or a little after 11.15 p.m., with its horses steaming and exhausted by the hectic pull from Dartford, it climbed the gentle slope to the middle of the great bridge and, to a joyous roar of greeting, descended into Westminster. For despite the late hour the crowd was still waiting, and the message of those flags was instantly clear to them: here was the duke's man at last, and Boney had surely been beaten.

Percy had two if not three missions that night: the first was to deliver the dispatch addressed to Earl Bathurst, the Secretary of State for the War Department and the Colonies;

the second was to present the flags and eagles to the Prince Regent, and the third was to give the copy of the dispatch to the Duke of York. Percy knew he was unlikely to find any of these men at their desks so late in the evening and he also knew enough about London society to realise that, this being the height of the social 'season', they would be out at dinner. His first call, therefore, was at Bathurst's ministry, housed in the Colonial Office, in the hope that there might be someone on duty who could give him directions. He had the driver turn right into Parliament Street and then left into Downing Street, while in the wake of the post-chaise there flowed a swelling and joyful crowd. Their approach sent a shiver of alarm ahead. Downing Street was also home to the Treasury, and the Secretary to the Treasury, an MP by the name of Charles Arbuthnot, had just returned there from an evening in Parliament. Hearing the noise, he feared for a moment that this was another dangerous protest against the Corn Law.

> Going down into the street to see, he perceived a chaise and four with eagles out of the windows, at the door of the Colonial Office, while enquiry was making within for Lord Bathurst. Arbuthnot knew that Lord Bathurst was with the rest of the Cabinet dining at Lord Harrowby's in Grosvenor Square, upon which he stepped into the chaise and drove there with Percy.[5]

By the standards of London at the time, Grosvenor Square was not close by: it lay beyond St James's Park and Piccadilly, near the edge of Hyde Park. As Arbuthnot guided them through streets lit by oil lamps and a full moon, the crowd behind thickened into a procession. By one account they were chanting: 'Wellington is safe! We don't know what the news is, but Wellington is safe!'[6] When they passed Charing Cross at the top of Whitehall, the noise surely carried down eastwards to the newspaper offices, alerting editors and printers who were probably already inspecting early proofs of feeble first editions. All that would now change; their night was just beginning.

An account of Percy's arrival at Lord Harrowby's has come down to us indirectly from Vansittart, the Chancellor of the Exchequer, who years later told a friend how pleased his colleagues had been to be dining with Bathurst that night, since they knew the dispatch must be brought to him. The story goes:

> They dined, they sat. No dispatch came. At length, when the night was far advanced, they broke up. Yet, delayed by a lingering hope that the expected messenger might appear, they stood awhile in a knot conversing on the pavement when suddenly was heard a faint and distant shout. It was the shout of victory! Hurrah! Escorted by a running and vociferous multitude, the Major drove up. He was taken into the house and the dispatch was opened.[7]

This dramatic entry was witnessed by Harrowby's fourteen-year-old daughter, who would live to the age of one hundred and describe it many times. By her account, at least some of the Cabinet must still have been indoors. She recalled watching from the stairs in her nightgown as an officer wearing a scarlet-and-gold tunic but looking weary and dishevelled rushed into the house asking for Lord Bathurst and crying: 'Victory! Victory! Bonaparte has been beaten!' Into the dining room he went, and soon there came a burst of cheering.[8] At this point Percy handed over the dispatch, presumably unwrapping it from the protection of that purple velvet sachet. The Vansittart account describes the effect as the ministers worked their way through its sixteen handwritten pages:

> On a first and hasty perusal the impression received was somewhat indefinite; the great fact of the final triumph stood not forth in sufficient relief, and the Cabinet were at fault. It was now certain that an important victory had been gained on the 18th, but they could not exactly gather from a first reading of the dispatch on what scale the allied armies had been triumphant or how far the success was final and complete. They turned for information to Major Percy but the gallant officer was dead beat – much more inclined to go off in a doze than to answer questions. In fact he was still feeling the effects, as it afterwards transpired, of hard fighting as well as hard travelling.

They quizzed him, and he reported that thousands of prisoners were taken and all of the enemy's cannon captured. And then, the story goes, he fell asleep. (This is a third-hand report, written forty-three years later, so we should not take it too literally.) At length, the ministers must have grasped the meaning of Wellington's climactic passage on the tenth page:

The attack succeeded in every point. The enemy was forced from his positions on the heights and fled in the utmost confusion, leaving behind him, as far as I could judge, 150 pieces of cannon.

There could be no doubt that this was a resounding victory. Outside, the crowd could wait no longer: they demanded to know what the dispatch contained. Another later account records:

Arbuthnot was sent out to the head of the staircase to announce to them the happy tidings. He ended by saying: 'In short, the French army is completely destroyed.' Upon which, says Arbuthnot, Lord Harrowby interposed in his usual critical way and cried out, 'I beg your pardon, Mr Arbuthnot, but not exactly. I think you are going a little too far.'[9]

Whether Harrowby really made such an interjection, and whether anyone heard it, is of no consequence: the crowd was satisfied, and the *Morning Post* would write of 'the universal and ecstatic cheerings of the populace' gathered in Grosvenor Square.

By now an hour must have passed since Percy had crossed Westminster Bridge, and word was already travelling far across town. At Vauxhall Gardens it had been a splendid evening, according to the *Chronicle*: 'The company were extremely numerous . . . and of the most respectable description, and although we cannot say first-rate fashion was predominant, yet of beauty and dash there was a very strong muster.' These

beautiful, dashing folk had been treated to brilliant illumina-
tions, while the fireworks, prepared by Messrs Bologna and
Hengler, were executed 'with a degree of neatness and preci-
sion truly astonishing'. But the evening had an unscheduled
climax, which came when a gentleman fresh from Westminster 'announced the arrival of dispatches from our immor-
tal Wellington'. With this, the *Chronicle* reports, 'the bands
were instantly directed to perform the national airs of *See the
Conquering Hero Comes* and *God Save the King*, in which the
whole company participated with the most enthusiastic joy'.[10]

At the Harrowby residence in Grosvenor Square the time
had come to get Percy, tired as he was, to the Prince Regent.
Carriages were called and the Major, followed by the Prime
Minister, the War Secretary, the Home Secretary and much
of the rest of the Cabinet, set off for St James's with the jubi-
lant, chanting crowd still in tow. For the ministers – these
were the men behind the Corn Law and the income tax –
such a moment of popularity must have been as dizzying
as it was unusual. For others, however, the parade brought
embarrassment. Its route led down St James's Street and past
Brooks's, the gentlemen's club, where at that very moment
Sir Robert Wilson and his opposition friend Lord Grey
were demonstrating to the satisfaction of members that
Bonaparte must by that time be in full possession of Brussels. Wilson was just delivering the final proof of this argument by reading aloud his letter from Brussels announcing
the flight of the expatriates when, as one who was present
recorded, 'the shouts in the streets drew us to the window,
and we saw the chaise and the eagles'.[11]

Someone at Lord Harrowby's was misinformed about the

Prince Regent's movements that evening, for Percy had been directed to the Castlereaghs', and so, on entering St James's Square, he went to number 18 instead of number 16. Lady Castlereagh's niece Emma Edgcumbe was there.

> I was sitting quietly alone, when suddenly there came a sound of shouting and the rush of a crowd, and running to the window to discover the cause of all this noise I saw a post-chaise and four, with three [*sic*] of the French eagles projecting out of its windows, dashing across the square and to Lord Castlereagh's door. In a moment the horses' heads were turned, and away went the chaise to Mrs Boehm's, leaving me in a state of excited bewilderment, but feeling that this haste, and the three eagles, and the cheering of the people, announced a victory.[12]

Inside number 16 the elegant dinner was long over. Such was the hour that the ladies had not only withdrawn, but after the usual suitable interval they had returned to join the gentlemen. Now there was to be dancing on the first floor, and for this additional guests had been admitted. Dorothy Boehm herself takes up the story:

> The first quadrille was in the act of forming and the Prince was walking up to the dais on which his seat was placed, when I saw every one without the slightest sense of decorum rushing to the windows, which had been left wide open because of the excessive sultriness of the weather. The music ceased and the dance was stopped; for we heard nothing but the vociferous shouts of an enormous

mob, who had just entered the square and were running by the side of a post-chaise and four, out of whose windows were hanging three nasty French eagles. In a second the door of the carriage was flung open and, without waiting for the steps to be let down, out sprang Henry Percy – such a dusty figure! – with a flag in each hand, pushing aside everyone who happened to be in his way, darting up stairs, into the ballroom, stepping hastily up to the Regent, dropping on one knee, laying the flags at his feet, and pronouncing the words 'Victory, Sir! Victory!'[13]

A dusty figure he doubtless was, but this hardly does justice to the force and presence of Percy, entering such company. When the tall, well-built, dark and handsome soldier thrust himself into the midst of the excited dancers, he came fresh from a scene of carnage as well as of triumph. There was a blood stain on his jacket, blood and mud spattered the flags and the eagles in his hands, and around him hung the smoky smell of battle. Three days on the road may seem a long time to us, but this sudden irruption brought war nearer than genteel London had known it in many years. So while that word 'victory' must have rung wonderfully around the room, and while the scene – with its princes, its flags and its dainty ladies – was worthy of 'grand serious opera', the major was delivering not only thrilling news but also a shocking physical message of violence and death.

Lord Liverpool, Lord Bathurst and the other ministers were close behind him, bearing the dispatch, and Percy had that second copy to give to the Duke of York. The gentlemen withdrew to read, and to experience at second hand

Wellington's emotions. 'Such a desperate action could not be fought,' he had written, 'and such advantages could not be gained without great loss, and I am sorry to add that ours has been immense.' He only identified by name the soldiers of rank, but these were the men most likely to be known to, or related to, this company, and the list seemed to go on for ever. Here, finally, was confirmation of the death of the Duke of Brunswick, and after that of General Picton and General Ponsonby, both popular and well-known figures. Then there were colonels and lieutenant-colonels, majors and captains, some of them staff officers and many with the most elite of regiments. The list of wounded, headed by the Prince of Orange and the Earl of Uxbridge and usually carrying the suffix 'dangerously' or 'severely', was twice as long – and in 1815 such a wound was at least half-way to death.

As the Prime Minister read the dispatch aloud, the Prince Regent wept. Gossips later reproached him for this – one declared that he 'fell into a sort of womanish hysteric'.[14] It may well be that he was in his cups and maudlin, as he often was, but all the same the criticism seems unkind on this occasion. Dorothy Boehm was with the ladies, and so not a witness to the reading of the dispatch. More than twenty years later she recalled that after a while the prince emerged, 'said a few sad words to us, sent for his carriage, and left the house'. Lady Castlereagh, meanwhile, had sent urgent instructions to her niece to dress and join her, and Emma's recollection is more detailed:

Lord Alvanley was the first gentleman who appeared, and he horrified us with the list of names of killed and wounded; and such names! great and distinguished in the campaigns of the Peninsula, and become almost house-hold words. There were several for whom I felt a true regard. The Guards, he said, had suffered severely – my brother was in them, but the fate of a subaltern could not be known! I had wished to hear more, and what I heard stupefied me; I could scarcely think or speak. Presently the Prince came in, looking very sad, and he said, with much feeling, words to this effect: 'It is a glorious victory, and we must rejoice at it, but the loss of life has been fear-ful, and *I* have lost many friends.' And while he spoke the tears ran down his cheeks. His Royal Highness remained but a short time and soon after, the party broke up.[15]

Mrs Boehm remembered the room clearing in less than twenty minutes, leaving her and her husband alone with the servants:

Such a scene of excitement, anxiety, and confusion never was witnessed before or since, I do believe! Even the band had gone, not only without uttering a word of apology, but even without taking a mouthful to eat. The splendid supper which had been provided for our guests stood in the dining room untouched. Ladies of the highest rank, who had not ordered their carriages till four o'clock a.m., rushed away like maniacs in their muslins and satin shoes, across the square; some accompanied by gentle-men, others without escort of any kind; all impatient to learn the fate of those dear to them; many jumping into the first stray hackney coach they fell in with, and hurry-

ing on to the Foreign Office or Horse Guards, eager to get
a sight of the list of killed and wounded.

Among those in the rush was Lord Sidmouth, the Home
Secretary, who made for the home of his friend Lord Ellen-
borough just a few doors away. The veteran Lord Chief
Justice, he found, had gone to bed and had to be roused.
'Bring me my clothes!' demanded Ellenborough on hearing
the news. 'I will not rob myself of one moment's enjoyment
of this glorious night.'[16] Outside in the square, even as Mrs
Boehm's guests flitted away, the crowd was warming up. The
Courier would report:

> They sang *God Save the King* full chorus, and
> filled the place with shouts and huzzahs. A
> more animated scene cannot be conceived.
> The flags and the two eagles were displayed in
> front of Mr Boehm's house, and loudly cheered
> by the people, who pressed forward, anxious
> to touch them with their hands, and it was
> with great difficulty they could be restrained
> from pressing into the house to obtain a more
> satisfactory view of them. All was joy and fes-
> tivity to a late hour.

The biggest social event still under way at that hour was
Sir George Talbot's assembly in New Burlington Street, a
little to the north. One guest arrived late: 'I found the whole
house in confusion and dismay; ladies calling for their carriages and others fainting in the anteroom, particularly the

Ladies Paget, who seemed in the utmost distress.'[17] This was the work of Alvanley, who according to Emma Edgcumbe had dashed from the Boehms' to deliver the news and 'certainly had the credit of having sent half the ladies into fainting fits and hysterics'. The Pagets had learned that their brother, Lord Uxbridge, had lost a leg. In the words of the *Courier*, 'the intelligence spread with lightning rapidity', and at another party in Berkeley Square the bearer of the news faced swift interrogation:

Has the Duke escaped? *Without a scratch*. William and Frederick Ponsonby? *Both killed*. Frederick Howard? *Killed*. Gordon? *Killed*. FitzRoy Somerset? *Lost an arm*. Lord Uxbridge? *Lost a leg*. Have the Guards suffered? *Dreadfully*.

Within ten minutes, we are told, that room too was deserted.[18]

Lord Bathurst, meanwhile, had work to do – the work for which he had kept his office staffed through two nights running. On behalf of the government he was required to provide formal and official confirmation of the news received from Wellington. Accordingly, and in short order, his department sent this bulletin to the press:

Downing Street, June 22 1815

The Duke of Wellington's dispatch, dated Waterloo, the 19th of June, states, that on the preceding day Bonaparte attacked, with his whole force, the British line, supported by a corps of Prussians, which attack, after a long and san-

guinary conflict, terminated in the complete overthrow of
the enemy's army, with the loss of one hundred and fifty
pieces of cannon and two eagles. During the night, the
Prussians under Marshal Blücher, who joined in the pursuit of the enemy, captured sixty guns and a large part of
Bonaparte's baggage. The allied armies continued to pursue the enemy. Two French generals were taken.

And for the information of the City of London he wrote a
letter to the Lord Mayor, timed at 1 a.m.

My Lord,

I have the greatest satisfaction in informing your lordship that the Honourable Major H. Percy is just arrived
with dispatches from the Duke of Wellington, dated
Waterloo, 19th instant, containing the account of a most
decisive and glorious victory having been obtained over
the whole French army by the allied forces, on the 18th
instant, the result of which has been the overthrow of
the French army with the loss of more than two hundred
pieces of artillery, an immense quantity of ammunition
and a part of the baggage belonging to Bonaparte.

The loss of the British army on this occasion has unfortunately been most severe. It had been impossible to make
out a return of the killed and wounded when Major Percy
left headquarters. The names of the officers killed and
wounded, as far as they could be collected, are annexed.

I have the honour to be your lordship's most obedient
humble servant,

Bathurst

So much for the press and the City; the proper way for the government to present important news to the British public was through the pages of the *London Gazette*, published, as it boasted, 'by authority', exclusively to announce official business. Sometimes, as after the victories at Trafalgar in 1805 and Vittoria in 1813, a special edition, or *Gazette Extraordinary*, would be rushed out to carry a single announcement, and this was surely an occasion for that measure. Bathurst gave the relevant instructions, ensuring that the *Gazette* printers around the corner in Cannon Row would begin work as early as possible on what would be one of their most famous and most-read editions. Meanwhile, a little farther north, Henry Percy, his great task complete and with appointments made for the next morning, escaped the throng outside the Boehms' and made his way to 8 Portman Square, the family home. There he was dismayed to find another crowd awaiting him, this time of anxious people hoping to learn the fate of relatives in the army. He did what he could to help and then, at long last, retired to his bed.[19]

Thursday and Friday: The Summit of Glory

For the daily papers it had been a close-run thing. As late as 11.15 p.m. they were expecting to lay before their readers in the morning nothing better than a desperate rehash of the previous day's reports and rumours, accompanied no doubt by generous measures of partisan point-scoring and *braggadocio*. Had Percy left his arrival only an hour or so later, they would have begun printing this, using up their precious taxed paper on a product that, at such a time of public frenzy, was bound to disappoint. Even as it was, Percy left them only sufficient time to insert one or at most two hurried columns, space that had to be used to maximum advantage. The most exuberant presentation came from the *Morning Post*, which in its excitement stacked up headings in capital letters over one column:

GREAT AND GLORIOUS NEWS.
ANNIHILATION OF BONAPARTE'S WHOLE ARMY,
AND HIS OWN NARROW PERSONAL ESCAPE.
CAPTURE OF THE TRAITOR'S PERSONAL
STAFF AND CARRIAGE
AND TWO HUNDRED & TEN PIECES
OF CANNON.

The article beneath overflowed with patriotic pride:

> With hearts grateful elate and all due thanks
> to Heaven for the event, we have this day the
> supreme happiness of announcing one of the
> most splendid and comprehensive victories
> ever obtained even by British valour, or the
> illustrious Wellington himself.

And farther down, after a description of the arrival of the
bulletin and a summary of its chief features:

> What renders this great and splendid achieve-
> ment the more gratifying to us is the proud
> circumstance of its having been accomplished
> chiefly by British valour, though every praise
> is due to the Prussian chief for his vigorous
> and cordial cooperation . . . Britain, therefore,
> may indeed now be truly considered as at the
> summit of glory.

The *Times* too resorted to capitals, though not quite so many.
Under the heading 'OFFICIAL BULLETIN' it reproduced
in full Bathurst's short statement, picking out the words
'ONE HUNDRED and FIFTY PIECES of CANNON and
TWO EAGLES' and later 'SIXTY GUNS' to impress the
reader. Then it wrote:

> Such is the great and glorious result of those
> masterly movements by which the hero of Brit-
> ain met and frustrated the audacious attempt
> of the rebel chief. Glory to Wellington, to our

gallant soldiers and to our brave allies! Bonaparte's reputation has been wrecked, and his
last grand stake has been lost in this tremendous conflict.

In his vanity, the *Times* wrote, Napoleon had underesti-
mated adversaries who were better soldiers, commanded by
a better general. But no one in Britain should be surprised,
it continued, for the official bulletin simply confirmed what
the City had known the previous day and Daniel Sutton
had reported two days before. Indeed the bulletin, according
to the *Times*, was a vindication of the paper's support for
Sutton's story. 'We were very well satisfied that Mr Sutton's
account, so far as it went, was correct', it declared, skating
over the problem that the victory it was now trumpeting had
been won at the approaches to Brussels at least a day after
Bonaparte, by Sutton's account, had supposedly fled back to
France.

The *Morning Chronicle* rejoiced at the 'TOTAL DEFEAT
OF BONAPARTE', saying: 'We stop the press to announce
the most brilliant and complete victory ever obtained by
the Duke of Wellington, and which will forever exalt the
glory of the British name.' There followed a summary of the
Bathurst bulletin, with the French 'completely routed' after
'dreadful carnage', and a claim that this was 'entirely owing
to the intrepidity and firmness of the English'. The *Chronicle*'s leading article, after rehearsing the events described in
the dispatch, concluded with a telling expression of journal-
istic relief, pointing out that the arrival of the news 'super-
sedes the necessity of stating the various rumours that were

circulated yesterday. Many of them it proves to be false, and the rest sink to insignificance.'

While the newsboys hawked these sensational reports through the streets on Thursday morning and word spread among those Londoners who had not heard the commotions of the night before, placards were going up announcing that the victory would be formally celebrated on the evenings of Friday and Saturday, when public buildings would be illuminated. The army, however, decided not to wait. 'On this transcendentally glorious occasion', as the *St James's Chronicle* put it, the Tower guns fired a *feu de joie* and the Duke of York, as Commander-in-Chief, laid on a great display in St James's Park by all the regiments then in London. It began at 9.30 a.m., as Life Guards, Foot Guards and Oxford Blues drew up in a line that stretched, according to the *Post*, from Carlton House to Birdcage Walk. At 10 a.m. came a double salute from the guns,

> after which, the cavalry flourishing their swords, the infantry waving their caps with sprigs of oak in them, gave three hearty cheers, in which the military were joined by the acclamation of an immense concourse of people who had assembled at an early hour from all parts of the metropolis.

There followed grand manoeuvres, back and forth across the park, the cavalry demonstrating 'incredible celerity' and the bands playing rousing tunes throughout, all of this culminating in a further salute from the artillery and from the muskets of the soldiers. At this the Duke of York, who had been followed from York House to the park by an additional throng of people, took centre stage to read passages from Wellington's dispatch. Then came three more loud cheers from all present, after which the soldiery returned to barracks. It was, as one account put it, a 'joyful and truly British scene'.[1] Among those at the Duke's side, and by now satisfactorily promoted to Lieutenant-Colonel, was the Hon. Henry Percy, enjoying his moment of fame. He already knew that he would not be in London long and would leave to rejoin Wellington on the road to Paris as soon as return dispatches from various government departments were ready.

By now the *Gazette Extraordinary* was on sale, priced at sixpence, giving the full text of the dispatch elegantly printed over four pages. If any doubts remained, here was the official word, and although readers had to navigate some grim narrative before they could satisfy themselves of the victory, it was clearly found to be a worthy and indeed a noble document. And what of the City? Daniel Sutton's story on Tuesday, as we have seen, had added 1¼ points to the price of omnium, and on Wednesday Mr C's news from Ghent had added about the same again, before the market slipped back. Now, on Thursday morning, Wellington's dispatch had duly been delivered, the Lord Mayor had been officially informed and boards announcing victory decked the railings of the Mansion House. What did this do to omnium? When the exchange opened, at 10 a.m., omnium immediately leapt four points to 9 per cent premium, and it soon advanced to 10, before dipping as some traders took their profit – official news, it is clear, was worth far more than unofficial. Not that business was in any way orderly. The *Courier* reported:

> The City is a scene of complete confusion, business entirely neglected. The immortal Wellington is the universal theme, the streets and exchange are crowded to excess, all anxious to hear the details of the glorious victory obtained by our brave countrymen.

Indeed all London, as a visiting Bostonian wrote, was 'one continual scene of uproar and joy'.[2] Parliament formally deferred its celebration until Friday, but the mere announcement of this was sufficient to produce sustained cheering in both Houses. And we have another glimpse of victory fever in the recollections of the artist Benjamin Robert Haydon, who found himself unable to work:

> Sammons, my model and corporal of the Life Guards, came, and we tried to do our duty, but Sammons was in such a fidget about his regiment charging and I myself was in such a heat, I was obliged to let him go. Away he went, and I never saw him till late next day, and he then came drunk with talking. I read the *Gazette* the last thing before going to bed. I dreamt of it and was fighting all night. I got up in a steam of feeling and read the *Gazette* again, ordered a *Courier* for a month, called a confectioner's, and read all the papers till I was faint.[3]

Before long he knew the whole dispatch by heart. Others, it must be said, were slower to respond. Joseph Farington, also an artist but a rather older man, wrote in his diary:

Smirke called while I was at breakfast to speak of the glorious victory obtained by the Duke of Wellington over Bonaparte on Sunday last, the 18th inst. He had been to the park and found the people everywhere rejoicing at the intelligence recd. The Tower and Park guns were fired at 10 o'clock but I did not hear them and knew not of the victory till Smirke arrived.[4]

At Hobart House in Grosvenor Place there was a slight awkwardness to be overcome. Albinia, Dowager Countess of Buckinghamshire, was giving her annual masked *fête champêtre* in her gardens – an event attended, according to the *Morning Post*, by no fewer than six hundred 'fashionables' – and she had intended it to be the occasion for a small act of revenge. A year earlier she had held a similar event and dedicated it to the Duke of Wellington, a hero then for his Peninsular victories. Alas, he did not turn up and she was offended. On this occasion, therefore, she had decided to make a point. Between two poles in the middle of the lawn hung a banner declaring: 'This fete is given in honour of NOBODY!!!' More than that, she had employed an actor to stroll among the guests playing the part of Nobody, in which role, according to the *Post*, he was 'irresistibly comic'. The timing of this gesture was unfortunate, given that on this day the duke was more of a hero than ever, so the countess felt the need to demonstrate that there were no hard feelings. The *Post* records:

> On the health of the Duke of Wellington and
> the brave British army being drunk, the com-

pany gave three cheers, in which they were
joined by the surrounding spectators of the
scene on the neighbouring heights.

The afternoon papers reproduced the *Gazette Extraordinary* in full, plus the official bulletin and the long casualty list.
In Percy's wake, moreover, letters from Belgium written after
the battle were arriving in numbers. The *Courier* was able to
publish one, from 'an officer of high rank', that described the
duke's personal role in a manner not mentioned in the dispatch. 'No language can do justice to the extraordinary merit
and talents which the Duke displayed during the whole of
the action', it declared. He was 'all day everywhere in the
thickest of it, and his place of refuge was one of the squares
which the enemy's cavalry charged'. Another letter quoted
the duke himself as saying 'that he was never in so hard-
fought a battle, and that he was never forced to exert himself so much'.[5] How, the *Courier* asked, was it possible to do
justice to such a man? 'We throw down our pen in despair.'

That night in the theatres there were 'joyous demonstrations' and the next day, Friday, Parliament had its moment.
In the Commons it fell to Castlereagh, as Leader of the
House, to honour his friend Wellington and to measure the
scale of his triumph:

It was an achievement of such high merit, of such
pre-eminent importance, as had never perhaps graced
the annals of this or any other country till now; and when
considered, not only with a view to the immediate loss
inflicted on the enemy, but with reference to the moral

effect which it must be expected to produce on the war now commenced, in the issue of which the fate of this country, of Europe, and the world were so closely bound up, it must be felt that it opened to our view a prospect so cheering, and so transcendently bright, that no language could do justice to the feelings it must naturally inspire. He [Castlereagh] sincerely felt this to be one of those instances in which the victory gained must be depreciated by the inadequacy of language faithfully to represent the vast service performed.[6]

He praised the modesty of the dispatch, noted that Wellington, in command of an army thrown together at short notice, had defeated 'him who had been called the greatest captain of the age' and paid warm tribute to the Prussians. And then he proposed a vote of thanks to the duke for his 'consummate ability, unexampled exertion and irresistible ardour'. Hansard records: 'The motion was carried in the affirmative, *nemine contradicente*. The speech and motion were followed by loud and long cheering.'

The most noteworthy reply from the opposition benches came from Samuel Whitbread, who was an admirer, if not of Napoleon personally, then of the reforms he had brought to his country, and who had doggedly opposed the war against France since before it began in 1793. Whitbread was known both for his fairness and for his gift of oratory and so was almost always assured a respectful hearing. On this occasion he had a surprise for his listeners. He began, though, in a familiar vein:

With respect to the loss that had been sustained, and which had plunged so many illustrious families in affliction, he could not advert to that loss without dissenting from an expression used by the noble lord, and lamenting the grievous fact, that they had fallen in the prosecution of a war into which this country had neither occasion or right to enter. Neither the events of victory or defeat could alter the principle of the war, and his opinion remained unchanged upon that subject.

This much might have been expected, but Whitbread now declared that he could not sit down without discharging what he considered 'an act of duty'.

He had always been one who looked with an eye of extreme jealousy to the proceedings of ministers; but their conduct in the prosecution of this war, waiving for the moment all consideration of its necessity or policy, was such as extorted his applause; and he had no hesitation in saying, that every department of government must have exerted itself to the utmost to give that complete efficiency to all the component parts of the army, which enabled the genius of the Duke of Wellington, aided by such means, to accomplish the wonderful victory he had achieved.[7]

Here was praise not only for Wellington and his army but also for the government and its officials, and it came from their most powerful critic in Parliament. No minister could have asked for more. In the House of Lords, where Bathurst and Liverpool both spoke in similar terms to Castlereagh, nothing matched the drama of Whitbread's tribute.

That night and on Saturday night, London celebrated. Illumination – the decking of buildings with candles and lanterns of all kinds – was a popular mode of public expression of the time. Among Dorothy Boehm's social accomplishments, for example, was that when she had a party she illuminated the outside of her house in brilliant style, no doubt employing for the task some of the professionals who advertised their services in the press. Illumination could also have its sinister side: at moments of political tension Londoners were sometimes instructed to put lights in their windows to show support for a particular cause, and those who failed to obey risked having their windows broken. The two nights of Friday and Saturday, 23 and 24 June 1815, may well have seen the illuminator's art reach its peak, and newspapers devoted whole columns to describing the effects. According to the *Post*, the main streets were lit up all the way from Hyde Park to the Tower. Every public building, from the Houses of Lords and Commons to the Prince Regent's residence at Carlton House and from the Army Accounts Office to the Woods and Forests Office, was festooned with lamps, sometimes merely arranged to highlight the architecture but more often to make words such as 'Victory', 'Wellington' and occasionally 'Blücher', or in the shape of laurel wreaths, stars, crowns, palm trees, eagles and cannons. The Bank of England and the Guildhall, the homes of prominent people such as Lord Castlereagh and the Marquess of Buckingham, gentlemen's clubs such as Brooks's and White's, the great theatres at Covent Garden and Drury Lane, and insurance companies, businesses and shops of every kind – all competed to show their joy, loyalty and ingenuity. The *Chronicle* was impressed:

> Guildhall had three of the most dazzling stars we ever witnessed, in a line on the front, with a regal coronet that appeared like a piece of rich jewellery over the centre star . . .

> The Post Office exceeded every other we noticed during the night; the three principal entrances . . . were superbly ornamented with a variety of arches, stars, crowns, diamonds, festoons, G.R., G.P.R. and W. and all the avenues were lined and arched over with festoons of small lamps. The Secretary's house was one blaze of light from the base to the parapet . . .

> The Board of Ordnance – A fortification, surrounded by ten pieces of cannon, with six piles of shot, with three stars and two crowns of victory over the entrance gates.

Transparencies were popular. Rudolph Ackermann's famous print shop on the Strand displayed an illuminated scene about fifteen feet in length, showing Wellington chasing Napoleon towards Blücher, who was ready to greet him with a blunderbuss. The landlord of the Cock Tavern showed a large illumination of a game cock crowing over a fallen rival, with the legend 'England cock of the walk'.

Meanwhile Wellington's brother, the Marquess Welles-ley, displayed a triumphal arch made entirely of lanterns. Loyally, the *Post* praised Carlton House, which was usually thought a gloomy place but was now 'so thickly covered with lamps that at a distance it resembled an enchanted castle'.

To this great spectacle a vast and boisterous crowd was witness. The *St James's Chronicle* wrote:

> The streets were thronged with people beyond conception. The whole was one moving crowd, carriages going slowly and forcing their way through the populace. The fair sex were equally numerous with the male. Bands of music paraded the streets until two o'clock. Dustmen, with their bells, kept up a perpetual din. Many persons lost their shoes opposite the Admiralty and Horse Guards. The pick-pockets were very busy.

A particular highlight was the Home Office, where the cap-tured flags and eagles were on display to the public. The Bos-tonian Joseph Ballard, who generally took a dim view of the late nights and late mornings favoured by effete Londoners (he claimed to have heard two dandies greet each other with a 'Good morning' at 5 p.m.), was so caught up in the excite-ment that he stayed out both nights until 1 a.m. The crowd, he recorded, was at its thickest outside Somerset House on the Strand:

The mob would not suffer the coaches to pass, excepting the coachmen and footmen took off their hats as an acknowledgement of the favour. Squibs and crackers were plentifully distributed into the carriages, and the alarm which the ladies were consequently thrown into appeared to delight John Bull exceedingly.[8]

The *Chronicle* also noted the squibs, as well as the pistols which 'assailed the air on every side'. Despite these, and the pickpockets, and what must surely have been a serious danger of fire, the paper said it was not aware of a single serious incident on either night.

*

As London celebrated, the news was rippling out across the kingdom courtesy of the network of coach services. For decades coachmen had seen it as a proud part of their job to recount to innkeepers and customers along their routes what they knew of events in the capital. And although there were hundreds of commercial stagecoach services, it was to the mail coaches that people normally looked for authoritative information: as the official distributors of letters, parcels and newspapers, they provided a visible link to the state and to government. A few years before this the writer Thomas De Quincey had ridden on a mail coach that bore news of one of Wellington's victories in Spain, and he later described with emotion the scene at departure from outside the Post Office in Lombard Street. 'Horses, men, carriages, all are decked in laurels and flowers, oak-leaves and ribbons', he wrote. The coachmen in full livery were especially fine:

> Such a costume, and the elaborate arrangement of laurels in their hats, dilate their hearts, by giving to them openly a personal connection with the great news in which already they have the general interest of patriotism. That great national sentiment surmounts and quells all sense of ordinary distinctions . . . One heart, one pride, one glory, connects every man by the transcendent bond of his national blood. The spectators, who are numerous beyond precedent, express their sympathy with these fervent feelings by continual hurrah.[9]

Borne by the mail coaches, the news would travel westward for three hundred miles and northward for six hundred, De Quincey wrote, 'like fire racing along a train of gunpowder'. At halts along the way the heralds of victory were embraced by delighted locals. Lame men, seeing the decorated coach go by, stood erect with pride, while children waved handkerchiefs and dusters from upstairs windows in 'aerial jubilation'.

On this occasion the timing did not favour the mail coaches because it was at eight o'clock sharp every evening that they left. Percy had arrived too late for this, and so the opportunity fell first to the morning stagecoaches. Every daylight hour in London after 5 or 6 a.m. these left for Oxford, Portsmouth, Norwich, Shrewsbury, Cardiff, Manchester, Exeter, Newcastle, Edinburgh – all the great cities and towns as well as the ports for Ireland and the continent. Their starting-points were at vast inns such as the Bull and Mouth in Aldersgate Street, the Swan with Two Necks at Cheapside and the Belle Sauvage on Ludgate Hill. Since the fastest coaches managed at best eight or nine miles per hour, with half-hour meal stops and on longer trips overnight halts, informing the country in this way, however thrilling it might have been, took quite a while, but the effect when the news arrived was no less dramatic than it had been in London.

As in the capital on Wednesday, so people in the rest of the country on Thursday and afterwards were already alert to the possibility that important news was on its way. In Birmingham, one witness recalled much later,

> We were all on the tiptoe of eager expectation. On the morning of the day when decisive news was expected, many people stationed themselves far out on the London road to get the first view of the approaching mail-coach. When at last it dashed into Birmingham, covered with waving boughs of laurel, there was a great shout of joy and triumph.[10]

At the entrance to High Wycombe 'the horses were taken off and the coach drawn into the town by the populace, accompanied by a band of music, banners flying and other demonstrations of joy'.[11] Nearly a century later a writer from Aylesbury, not far from High Wycombe, repeated a story his father had told him of learning the news from a passing coachman while making hay in a meadow outside town. 'He was so overcome with joy, for he had lived his whole life in war, that he involuntarily fell down on his knees in the hayfield and thanked

God.' He then rushed into town to find the parish clerk and persuaded him to call out the bell-ringers 'to give out as hearty a peal at the church as they possibly could'.[12]

The daughter of an officer in Wellington's army recalled hearing of the victory as a young girl on the Isle of Wight:

> My brother and I, standing at the front gate of the cottage garden, were one morning attracted by the sound of music and the gaudy appearance of the coaches coming down the road, streaming with gilded flags that bore the words WELLINGTON! VICTORY! WATERLOO! These words, in printed capitals, caught our eyes. We repeated them with the passing crowd and then rushed in to my mother. 'There has been a battle,' we said; 'they have been fighting the French and we have beaten them!'[13]

In Liverpool the American writer Washington Irving had just stepped ashore after an Atlantic crossing when 'the first spectacle which met his eye was the mail-coaches coming in, decked in laurel and dashing proudly through the streets with the tidings of the battle of Waterloo and the flight of Napoleon'.[14] This was Friday morning, the 'Alexander' stagecoach having made the 205-mile journey from London to Liverpool, bearing newspapers, in what was thought an impressive twenty-seven hours.[15] Leeds, which was ten miles closer to the capital, had to wait until 9.40 that evening because of the slow running of the stagecoaches. When the 'True Briton' at last delivered the report of the victory, a Leeds paper wrote, 'it was read at the theatre amidst the loudest huzzas and *God Save the King* was sung in grand style'.[16]

In the Lake District the poet Robert Southey wrote to a friend on Saturday:

> Our bells are ringing as they ought to do, & I after a burst of exhilaration at the day's news am in a state of serious & thoughtful thankfulness, for what perhaps ought to be considered as the greatest deliverance that civilised society has experienced since the defeat of the Moors by Charles Martel.[17]

Thirty-five miles away in Sedbergh the bells were ringing too. A young Adam Sedgwick, who would go on to be one of the founding fathers of geology, heard them as he rode in from his home village of Dent to pick up the mail, and swiftly established the cause.

> After joining in the cheers and congratulations of my friends at Sedbergh, I returned to Dent with what speed I could, and such was the anxiety of the day that many scores of my brother Dalesmen met me on the way and no time was lost in our return to the market-place of Dent. They ran by my side as I urged on my horse; and then, mounting on the great blocks of black marble from the top of which my countrymen have so often heard the voice of the auctioneer and the town crier, I read, at the highest pitch of my voice, the news from the *Gazette Extraordinary* to the anxious crowd which pressed around me. After the tumultuous cheers had somewhat subsided, I said: 'Let us thank God for this great victory and let the six bells give us a merry peal.'[18]

When the coach bearing the news reached the city of Durham, a local tailor, William Robinson, took charge:

> At his own expense he decorated the coach with flags, ribbons and laurels and, purchasing a white banner, he took a prominent seat on the coach, travelled to New-castle with it, and opposite the Queen's Head Hotel, at that place, he announced the glad tidings to a large crowd.[19]

Nowhere was the excitement greater than in the Scottish capital. By chance the city's mayor, known as the Provost, was in London on Wednesday and he urgently sent word to the postmaster in Edinburgh, nearly four hundred miles away, of what he called 'the greatest intelligence that ever came to Britain'. His letter arrived on Saturday morning around 11 a.m., just in time for a late edition of the *Caledonian Mercury*, which breathlessly recorded that it had 'thrown the city into a greater state of ecstasy than we ever remember to have witnessed'. A lawyer has left us a description of what happened after a gentleman rushed into the great hall of the Edinburgh courthouse shouting 'Victory!'

> Further law proceedings were out of the question; adjournment was ruled and judges, advocates, agents and officers were speedily in the streets, already crowded by their excited and exulting townsmen. Nobody could stay at home. The schools were let loose. Business was suspended and a holiday voted by acclamation. Everybody shook hands with everybody.

As in other places, a second wave of excitement followed with the arrival of the mail coach bringing the *Gazette Extraordinary*, which set an official seal on the news:

> The streets were crowded before the post arrived. The mail-coach was descried approaching, adorned with laurel and flags, the guard waving his hat, and soon it dashed into the town amid cheers that made the welkin ring. The accounts were now official. All was confirmed, and, as early as seven o'clock, the Castle flag rose and nineteen twenty-four-pounders sounded in the ears and filled the eyes – for the effect was overpowering – of the excited throng. . . . Newspapers with the dispatches, including the list of casualties, so far as known, were snatched from the post office. They were common property, and the holder of each, whether he willed it or no, was elevated on the nearest vacant steps to read out the accounts *pro bono publico*.[20]

It was one of those occasions that stay in the memory all the way to the grave. At the very end of the nineteenth century, and even in the early years of the next, when someone died at a conspicuously advanced age, it would often be recorded in the press that he or she had witnessed the arrival of the news of Waterloo. The stories crop up in many memoirs, and many sons and daughters would later repeat the tales of coaches, flags, bells and cheering that they had heard at their parents' knees.* Inevitably the details became confused, but the spirit and mood are clear.

*

There were some, however, for whom the news was unwelcome. Wellington himself, years later, would claim that 'when the truth first came out of our having won, Lord Sefton went to Lady Jersey and said to her, "Horrible news! They have gained a great victory!"'[21] A boon for the Tories, after all, was inevitably a set-back for the Whigs, and not all in the latter party could bring themselves to match the generosity of Samuel Whitbread. But this was not merely a matter of party advantage: some people firmly believed that the people of France would be worse off, that this was a triumph for Europe's autocrats and the *ancien régime* and that the cause of reform in Britain would suffer. Among them was Lord Byron, who was at home in Piccadilly when he heard. His conversation with a young American visitor, George Ticknor, was interrupted by the announcement of an unexpected caller. Ticknor recorded:

> Sir James Bland Burges . . . came suddenly into the room and said abruptly, 'My lord, my lord, a great battle has been fought in the Low Countries and Bonaparte is

* Even two centuries later the oral tradition survives. The journalist David Benn, born in 1928, relates that his grandmother, born in 1864, had heard her grandmother describe hearing the victory bells ring in 1815, when she was eighteen years old. This was in the Glasgow area, and so loud and so long was the ringing, she said, that some people feared the day of judgement had come.

entirely defeated.' 'But is it true?' said Lord Byron, 'is it true?' 'Yes my Lord, it is certainly true; an aide de camp arrived in town last night; he has been in Downing Street this morning and I have just seen him as he was going to Lady Wellington's. He says he thinks Bonaparte is in full retreat towards Paris.' After an instant's pause Lord Byron replied, 'I am d——d sorry for it,' and then, after a short pause, he added, 'I didn't know but I might live to see Lord Castlereagh's head on a pole. But I suppose I shan't now.'[22]

Byron had sat with the Whigs in the House of Lords and spoken for Whig causes. His animus towards Castlereagh was widely shared, though few would have gone so far as to call the Foreign Secretary an 'intellectual eunuch', as he once did. Ticknor later saw Byron tackled on the same subject by the set who gathered at the offices of the publisher John Murray, a group he called 'the loungers at Murray's literary exchange':

The conversation turned upon the great victory at Waterloo, for which Lord Byron received the satirical congratulations of his ministerial [pro-government] friends with a good nature which surprised me. He did not, however, disguise his feelings or opinions at all, and maintained stoutly, to the last, that Bonaparte's case was not yet desperate.[23]

These were private conversations. There were few people brave enough to stand up openly against the tide of public

jubilation, but one who did was William Cobbett, editor
and principal author of *Cobbett's Weekly Political Register*.
In his edition of Saturday 24 June he denounced the war
as a 'crusade against France and against liberty', assailed
the leading daily papers for their role and noted coldly the
national mood.

> While this delirium continues at its height,
> it would be useless in me to attempt to bring
> the public back to reason. I might as well
> think of preaching conviction to the minds
> of the inhabitants of St Luke's [a mental hos-
> pital]; I might as well expect that a drunken
> man could discuss, with calmness and per-
> spicacity, an argument in mathematics or
> moral philosophy. That I may not, however,
> be charged with partiality, I shall here insert
> the official details which have been published
> respecting the first battle, or rather series of
> battles that have been fought for the purpose
> of determining whether France is or is not to
> be permitted to exercise the right of choosing
> her own government.

Cobbett's may have been a rare voice crying out against
the delirium, but it was not a feeble one. William Hazlitt,
writing not long after this, declared him 'unquestionably the
most powerful political writer of the present day', and his
leading articles were read – and often read aloud to large
and admiring audiences – from one end of the country to

the other.[24] Over the previous three months he had been one of those denouncing the dubious legality of the conflict, but unlike the *Morning Chronicle* he refused to bury his qualms when the fighting began. In the editions of the *Register* that followed he continued to challenge the idea that Waterloo was something to celebrate, not only because of its implications for France but also because he thought the war financially, economically and socially ruinous to Britain. His anger endured, and years later he would write that this one battle

> has produced to England more real shame, more real and substantial disgrace, more debt, more distress amongst the middle class and more misery among the working class, greater inroads upon the ancient institutions, the laws and liberties of the country, more injuries of all sorts, than the kingdom ever experienced from a hundred defeats, whether by land or by sea.[25]

Cobbett and Byron were in the minority, but how large that minority was we cannot tell.

13

Differences and Distances

The tale of the news from Waterloo, then, is a tale of four messengers. The first was Daniel Sutton, who arrived in the early hours of Tuesday. Though his news was no more than a highly misleading picture of the wrong battle, it was trumpeted as a triumph and believed even by government ministers. The second messenger was the Knight of Kerry, who followed on Tuesday evening with no word of Waterloo but with information that exposed Sutton's error. Accepted by ministers, this news was brusquely ignored by their allies in the press and thus had half the impact on the public that it should have had. The third was Mr C, who reached London during the night of Tuesday to Wednesday with the first genuine news of Bonaparte's defeat. Though his information was accurate, his word was doubted, and he was treated with the kind of scepticism that ought to have greeted Sutton. And the fourth was Henry Percy, who, after suffering every kind of delay, late on Wednesday brought an end to London's painful suspense by delivering news of victory direct from Wellington himself.

Viewed from afar, it seems a comedy of errors and misfortunes. As the *Observer* noted on Sunday 25 June, reflecting on Sutton's role:

His account only related to the engagements

of the 15th and 16th; these, however, were
magnified to important victories. Most fortunately the British public have been saved
from a grievous disappointment by the result
of the battle of the 18th.

It was indeed most fortunate. Waterloo was the narrowest
of victories, and until the last charge Napoleon had believed
he would win. Had he done so, it would have been Wellington's army that retreated, probably towards an ignominious
evacuation by sea. Such news, arriving on Wednesday night,
thirty-six hours after Sutton had raised London's hopes of
a victory, would certainly have been a grievous disappointment. But the *Observer* was unusual in drawing attention to
this. Most papers were in a hurry to forget the Sutton affair,
which did few of them credit and from which they too had
had a fortunate escape.

To the modern eye, of course, what stands out most boldly
in this tale is the slowness and the apparent fragility of the
communications. In the twenty-first century we are accustomed to following important events minute by minute as
they unfold, even when they do so thousands of miles away.
The contrast here is stark: this was sensational and momentous news that depended for its delivery on four men rowing
an open boat in the North Sea. It is tempting to believe that
our ability to discover news so much more quickly protects us
from the anxieties and misunderstandings that the Londoners of 1815 had to endure, but it is not so simple as that. Fast
communications create complications of their own, and they
are also capable of masking problems that would have been

out in the open in 1815. In our hurry today we can overlook subtleties and make mistakes. The journey made by the news from Waterloo, because it happened in what seems to us a kind of slow motion, is an opportunity not only to observe what was different in the world before fast communications, but also to identify things that have not changed. All the forces that go to work on news as it travels are plain to see.

Chief among the differences is the primacy of official information. Not only did the Regency public and press tend to believe, for good reasons, that the government would know news first, but they also placed most trust in information that came 'from authority'. Sutton's unofficial tale certainly stirred great excitement, but it was a reflex on every side to seek official confirmation of it – so much so that one was extorted or fabricated in the form of that disputed War Department bulletin. Even the most cautious editors, those who refused to accept either the bulletin or the Sutton story, continued to assert that ministers knew more than they were telling, or that only what came 'from authority' could be relied upon. And as doubt and anxiety grew, there was universal agreement on the need to have the commander's dispatch from the battlefield.

Missing from this picture is any other source of information capable of commanding general trust. Today there are independent alternatives to government – professional bodies, corporations, charities and campaign groups – which, when they speak about matters relevant to them, tend to be believed. Few of those existed in 1815. There was no Red Cross or Médecins Sans Frontières or international conflict resolution group on the battlefield to bear independent witness and report. Even more conspicuous by their absence are journalists and newspapers capable of providing reliable information on their own authority. Today, if a reputable news organisation reports a significant development, we tend to believe it. Of course there are sceptics, and of course every news organisation and every journalist gets things wrong once in a while, but unless we have particular grounds for doubt we accept. For all the reasons explored in Chapter 3 this resource was not available in 1815, and a good deal had to change, not least in the financial position of newspapers, before it would be. It is possible to detect some signs of reporting activity – the *Courier*'s coverage of Mr C, for example, and the *Caledonian Mercury*'s correspondents at work on Wednesday evening – but these were departures from a Regency norm in which, by and large, editors expected the news to come from the government or its agents, or to emerge in Parliament.

Other aspects of the story are familiar. Sutton's tale was a consequence of something timeless: the fog of war. The term was first used by that Prussian veteran of the Waterloo campaign, Carl von Clausewitz, to describe the confusions that beset commanders, but the same fog stretches out to engulf people at many removes from the battlefield. Sutton's information was incomplete and muddled partly because conflict is chaotic and tends to foster confusion. Events are difficult to interpret, people become excitable and their judgement suffers. That the fog surrounding Quatre Bras turned into a heady story of victory owes a good deal to another timeless influence on the news: official manipulation. Halted on the battlefield, the French withdrew to a safe distance to camp for the night and prepare a new assault, but a clever official in

Brussels, seeking to shore up public morale, turned this into an assertion that the French had been 'repulsed far beyond the battlefield'. Chinese whispers then transformed that into a headlong French flight across the border.

In every war in every age commanders seek control of information as it emerges from the fog, and they try to shape and frame it for the public. Wellington's dispatch did that. He alone wrote the narrative of the conflict for his government and for publication, and indeed, though he could not have known it at the time, no substantial alternative narrative would surface for many years. So effective was this that such croakers as there were had nothing to get their teeth into. The Whig journal the *Examiner* was a strong opponent of the war, but the worst it could find to say of the dispatch was that Wellington's brilliance might obscure the contribution of the ordinary British infantryman. Modern military commanders have less time than Wellington to prepare their stories, and their word is unlikely to remain unchallenged for long, but they still use every means at their disposal to ensure that their interpretation of events is the first one circulated. No less than Wellington, they want theirs to be the first draft of history.

Another familiar factor is the interplay of war news with party politics. The zealous Dr Stoddart of the *Times* found Sutton's story so perfectly in line with his political position that he could not resist it, and when first the Knight of Kerry and then Wellington's dispatch made his mistake clear, he felt no need to correct. On the other side the radical Sir Robert Wilson, who opposed the war, convinced himself on the basis of his letter from Brussels that the city must subsequently have fallen, a disaster that justified his political stance. Likewise Lord Byron grudgingly accepted the fact of Bonaparte's defeat but still insisted, because it fitted his convictions, that the emperor was not finished. Then, as now, people often make of news what suits them.

No less familiar is the exploitation of war news by financial markets – profiteering, as it would later be called. In different circumstances wars or battles may send stocks up or down, but they rarely fail to have some effect, and so it was in 1815. The government needed money to fight, and the markets lent it; investors thus had a direct stake in the outcome, and so life and death on the battlefield, or rather the news of it, readily translated into profit and loss on the trading floor. By logical extension, those with such vested interests could also be tempted to manipulate news, to bury, distort or fabricate it, which in turn created the suspicion that such distortion could be happening even when it was not. We can watch all of this playing out over those three days in June 1815, but none of it is exclusive to that era. Nor does the electronic transmission of news prevent it happening today, though it may be harder for the news consumer to detect it.

What has changed least of all is the relationship between people and news. Whether the desire to hear new information and the desire to pass it on are instinctive in human beings is a matter of debate, but those few days in June 1815 are enough to prove that they were no less strong in the age of the horse-drawn carriage than they are in the age of the electronic tablet. The scenes in the theatres and on the streets on Tuesday and Wednesday evenings vividly demonstrate the hunger to know, while there could be few better illustrations of the relish we take in spreading news than the hasty dispersal of Dorothy Boehm's guests, skipping over the cobbles of St James's Square once the dispatch has arrived. Sidmouth roused his old colleague Ellenborough out of bed to tell him, and Alvanley rushed off to Talbot's to thrill and shock the partygoers there. Such responses to news do not require the trappings of what we call our fast-moving world.

As for technology, the people of 1815 may not be quite so distant from us as we imagine. In the very same Thursday newspapers that so exuberantly reported the news brought by Henry Percy there appeared a large advertisement announcing a new service for the public:

> The Thames Steam Yacht from London to Margate starts from Wool Quay, near the Custom House, Thames Street, every Tuesday, Thursday and Saturday at eight o'clock in the morning precisely and leaves Margate on her return to London every Monday, Wednesday and Friday at the same hour.[1]

The new vessel, the advertisement continued, was rapid, capacious and splendid, and was capable of proceeding either under sail or by steam power, or by both combined. In consequence

> the public have the pleasing certainty of never being detained on the water after dark, much less one or two nights, which has frequently occurred with the old pack-

ets. Against a gale of wind, the tide, or in the most perfect calm, the passage is alike certain, and has always been achieved in a day.

What would Percy, only a day earlier, have given for a 'certain passage' from Ostend? The calm that beset HMS *Peruvian* would have been a convenience for a steamship, allowing its relentless paddles to propel the dispatch unfailingly towards its destination. His twenty-five-hour sea crossing might have been over in eleven or twelve, with no rowing necessary, and London could have begun its celebrations before Wednesday morning was out. Steam was about to begin transforming communications. It would be the early 1820s before steam-powered passages across the Channel became routine, but never again would important news from the continent be left to drift on the currents or, for that matter, be blown off its course. A new predictability, if not a certainty, arrived. On land the railways were still some way off – the Liverpool and Manchester Railway would not begin its operations until 1830 – but in 1815 Telford, McAdam and others were furiously at work on the roads, flattening, straightening, widening and hardening, and so enabling coach travel to become ever faster and more reliable.

Still more auspicious was a scientific experiment begun in that same year in a garden in Hammersmith, west of London. A young man by the name of Francis Ronalds erected two wooden frames, twenty yards apart, each frame having nineteen bars and each bar having thirty-seven hooks. Back and forth between these hooks he strung an insulated iron wire, giving him a continuous length, all within the bounds of the garden, of more than eight miles. To this wire he applied electrical impulses, satisfying himself that by such means messages could be sent over considerable distances. On 11 July 1816, his painstaking researches complete, he wrote to the First Lord of the Admiralty:

> Mr Ronalds presents his respectful compliments to Lord Melville and takes the liberty of soliciting his lordship's attention to a mode of conveying telegraphic intelligence with great rapidity, accuracy and certainty, in all states of the atmosphere, either at night or in the day, and at small expense, which has occurred to him while pursuing some electrical experiments.[2]

Barely a year after the Waterloo dispatch, Ronalds thus offered to the British Admiralty the electric telegraph, a technology that would ultimately reduce the global communication of news to a matter of seconds. Alas, this was one cultural shock that would have to wait, for the secretary to the Admiralty wrote back to say that 'telegraphs of any kind are now wholly unnecessary and that no other than the one now in use will be adopted'. Not until 1838 did the first electric telegraph enter service.

14

Afterlives

With the battle won, the affairs of Europe resolved themselves more rapidly than anyone could have expected. The day after Percy reached London, Napoleon Bonaparte signed his abdication papers in the Tuileries Palace. 'I offer myself as a sacrifice to the enemies of France,' he declared. 'May they be sincere in their declarations and only desire my person!'[1] He made for the Atlantic coast in hope of sailing to America but found his way blocked by the British navy and eventually gave himself up to the captain of HMS *Bellerophon*, beseeching Britain to treat him kindly. It did not, and soon he was on his way to exile on St Helena, 1,100 miles off the coast of Africa, where he died in 1821. The crown of France, which he had declared should go to his son, was instead returned to the unloved Louis XVIII, who at least has it to his credit that in the years that followed he made some effort to mitigate the vengeful 'white terror' that was waged against Bonapartists. Louis died in 1824. In Britain the Prince Regent succeeded his father as king in 1820 and reigned until 1830 without ever departing from the selfish and useless lifestyle he had chosen in youth. Lord Liverpool remained his prime minister until 1827, but Lord Castlereagh, considered by many to be Britain's most accomplished diplomat, took his own life in 1822 in a spasm of depression.

As for the battle, even before the fanfares of June had ech-
oed into silence Waterloo had been raised above Blenheim,
Agincourt and Crécy as the nation's greatest feat of arms on
land, and the prominent involvement of so many Scots and
Irishmen ensured that this pride was shared right across the
United Kingdom. Nor were the wounded and bereaved forgotten, for after the first flush of joy came a national surge of
determination to help. To pray for those afflicted, to organise fundraising dinners, to cheer the returning regiments, to
ensure that all involved received medals, to visit the scene
of the action – all of these became a kind of duty for those
gentlemen in England who, as Shakespeare had written of
Agincourt, thought themselves accursed they were not there.
And the famous speech from *Henry V* was brought to life in
other ways too: those that survived Waterloo and saw old age
feasted their neighbours on the anniversary, and showed their
scars and remembered 'with advantages' what they had done.
The names of the commanders – Wellington, Uxbridge, Picton, Ponsonby – also became for a time as familiar as household words, and in thousands of places were proudly given
to streets, houses, pubs, bridges and halls. There was talk of
a national monument, and public money was set aside for a
new palace worthy of the great duke, but neither materialised.
Instead England's chief memorial to the battle is Waterloo
Bridge in London, which had been under construction as
'Strand Bridge' before the campaign began but which was
relabelled and dedicated at a great opening ceremony on 18
June 1817. For years the duke resisted the writing of any
history of the Waterloo campaign, and so it was not until
the 1840s that substantial studies appeared, launching con-

troversies – for example, about how far the duke was caught by surprise and whether the Prussians received appropriate credit – that continue to this day. Nothing, however – not the end of the old rivalry with the French, nor the coming of a new one with the Germans, nor the decline of the British empire, nor the rise of European cooperation – has ever dulled the gleam of Waterloo for the British, and in particular for the British army.

The duke, for his part, swore he would never fight another battle and kept his word. He remained in France, a powerful figure, until the end of the occupation in 1818, and then returned to Britain and the life of a national hero. His flirtation with Lady Frances Wedderburn Webster, meanwhile, had provoked scandal, the *St James's Chronicle* publishing a series of sly paragraphs implying that her husband would divorce her. In the event, instead of naming the duke as her lover, Webster sued the paper, and with Wellington declaring that he 'was never in his life alone with Lady Webster', he won.[2] Since his twenties the duke had mixed politics with soldiering, and it was not long before he was a minister, and in time prime minister. Few would argue that his political abilities matched his military talents, and there were moments when his victories were forgotten and he was booed in the streets. The ultimate measure of his popular standing, however, was that after his death in 1852 more than a million people turned out to watch the funeral procession. Among his many legacies, besides boots and beef, was that for well over a century his conduct and manner defined the English gentleman for the rest of the world – courteous, elegant, unflappable, terse and detached almost to a fault. This was the man who, on hearing a brother officer exclaim in battle, 'By God I've lost my leg!', replied calmly, 'Have you, by God?'[3]

As for the less famous figures in this narrative, of Henry Percy we catch further glimpses on that busy Thursday and Friday: for example, calling on Princess Charlotte to report on the death of her uncle, Brunswick, and visiting Castlereagh at his home to pick up letters for the return journey. At the weekend he left for Brussels with his brother Charles for company, reaching Ostend early on Monday after a 'very disagreeable passage in company with Lord Alvanley' and proceeding to Brussels with all speed.[4] On this occasion he covered the distance from the coast to the Belgian capital in just fourteen hours. Pausing there only to dine, he pushed on to catch up with Wellington, deliver his dispatches and join the march on Paris. A family tradition suggests that he had suffered a wound at Waterloo and that while he was in London a musket ball was removed from his foot. A ring said to have been made from the offending metal was passed down through several generations. This does not seem likely. First, would Wellington have sent a wounded man to London when at least two fit aides-de-camp were available? Second, there is no mention of such a wound at the time in the adulatory press coverage, as surely there would have been, since it would have added further lustre to Percy's story. And third, it must be doubtful that a man recovering from an operation would have been packed off on another journey so promptly. Much more likely is that the ring related to the wound of which there is a record – the one he suffered at the time of his capture at Celorico in Portugal in 1810.[5]

Wounded or not, it is clear in retrospect that in 1815 Percy was already suffering from the illness that would prevent him achieving the eminence to which he aspired and towards which his association with the dispatch might have lifted him. When the symptoms first showed we do not know, but the previous autumn, soon after he had first joined the duke's staff in Paris, a colleague noted in a letter that 'poor Percy has been so dangerously ill'.[6] He was struck down again through much of the winter of 1815–16, taking to his bed for weeks, and again in the following spring, and yet again in the summer of 1818. In that year the same colleague wrote: 'I have long thought myself that he was in a very bad state.' What this illness was is not known: it is never named, and the only symptom we know of is a comment from his father that even after recovering from one of these bouts he was 'still suffering from violent rheumatic pains in his head'.[7] By 1818, with Wellington's mission to France complete and his personal staff broken up, Percy was back with his regiment, a change which had the unfortunate consequence that he was once again a major – his promotion in 1815 had been a 'brevet' one, valid only while he remained a staff officer. His adventure with the dispatches had none the less left him with one lasting honour, since he had been made a Companion of the Bath. Soon, after some desultory attempts to buy a better position in the army, he and his family accepted that his military career was coming to an end. 'Henry's health never will permit him to serve,' his father wrote, and he retired in 1821, aged just thirty-six.[8] By way of consolation he accepted the parliamentary seat of Bere Alston in Devon, which was in the gift of the Percy family, but in five years he never spoke

in the House of Commons and voted only once, supporting
the ministry on a matter relating to ordnance officials.[9] He
never married either, and there is no sign that Mademoi-
selle Durand ever joined him in England, but he did have
the comfort of his sons, brought up in London a short ride
from his home in Portman Square. A surviving letter from
Wellington, ending 'God bless you Percy, most truly yours',
shows that he also retained the affection, and perhaps the
sympathy, of his old chief.[10] In 1825, aged thirty-nine, Percy
suffered his final bout of illness. A niece of his would write:

> As a child of three years old I was lifted on to my uncle
> Henry's bed in Portman Square. He was then a dying
> man, and I felt very frightened, when he kissed me, at his
> very white face and black hair. He gave me a necklace,
> which he put round my throat. This necklace, alas, was
> stolen from me at Portsmouth in 1846.[11]

In his will he left all of his property in trust for his sons.
What became of the second boy is not known, but in time
young Henry proved able to fulfil the military ambitions that
his father never could. With the support of Percy's friends
he gained a commission in the army in India and there made
an illustrious career. At the time of his death in 1871 – after
a fall from an elephant – he was Major-General Sir Henry
Marion Durand.

Like Henry Percy, Daniel Sutton experienced disappointment. In one sense he had a lucky escape, for no one seems
to have reproached him for so misleading London. On the
other hand, his hopes that the publicity he had won would

boost his packet-ship business came to nothing, and in 1816 he was bankrupt. He was forced to sell his grand riverside house at Wivenhoe but managed to cling on to his post as town clerk of Colchester. According to a local historian in Essex, his brother-in-law bailed him out, and not for the first time, but by 1819 Sutton's debts were still not fully discharged and to compound his woes his ship, the *Maria*, had been wrecked. In that same year his father, the physician, died in London and perhaps as a result the family's indulgence of the feckless Daniel came to an end. They 'transported' him: he and his adult children were presented with one-way tickets to Australia. There his daughters did well – one became the wife of the Governor of New South Wales – but Sutton himself died poor in Hobart. The fate of his son Robert was more remarkable: some years later he went on an expedition to the island of New Caledonia, 'and there', in the words of the same local historian, 'fell into the hands of cannibals and was eaten by them'.[12] Unlikely as it appears, this is corroborated in an 1847 letter by a French missionary in New Caledonia, recording that the natives had killed an Englishman named Sutton 'who they claimed was very good to eat'.[13]

Among the other messengers, the eighteenth Knight of Kerry fared somewhat better, remaining a busy member of Parliament until 1831. In a venal age he stands out as a politician who adopted a position of principle and held to it despite personal cost. A Protestant and by nature a Tory, he was committed to Catholic emancipation, so denying himself lucrative positions with a long succession of Tory governments that opposed it. Through all the fierce debates on the issue and as the pressure in Catholic Ireland increased in the 1820s, he steadfastly argued the cause at Westminster and defended the extra-parliamentary activities of his fellow Kerryman Daniel O'Connell. Emancipation finally came in 1829, at the time when Wellington was Prime Minister, but the knight received scant personal reward for his perseverance, for it transpired that the newly enfranchised Catholic electors of Kerry did not want a Protestant Tory MP, and he lost his seat. Never good with money, and susceptible to expensive 'improvement' schemes for his Irish lands, he died poor and with his properties mortgaged, though respected as a man of energy and principle. The line of Knights of Kerry, the Green Knights, continues: the present holder of the title, Sir Adrian FitzGerald, is the twenty-fourth.

As for the Boehms, they continued their lively round of masquerades and routs at 16 St James's Square – on several further occasions in the company of royalty – until 1819, when disaster struck. The firm of Boehm and Taylor became entangled in a legal dispute whose results were ruinous. Edmund was forced to sell not only the house on St James's Square but also the country seat at Ottershaw and the residence in Bath. Like the Dashwoods in Austen's *Sense and Sensibility*, the Boehms were reduced to living in a cottage in Devon. After Edmund died in 1822, however, Dorothy's royal friends came to her rescue, and by 1827 she was living, attended by three servants, in a 'grace and favour' apartment in Hampton Court Palace. There she displayed on a table a gilt replica of a French Imperial eagle presented to her as a memento by the Prince Regent. In the interview of 1831 in which she described her most famous soirée she was quoted as complaining about Percy's sudden arrival – 'Never did a party, promising so much, terminate so disastrously!'[14] Perhaps things appeared that way to her after the passage of sixteen years (and the interview itself was not published until 1871), but in truth she had nothing to complain of. She could enjoy the memory of many other grand parties that suffered no such rude interruption, and after all it was this one, along with her mention in Byron's *Beppo*, that gave her a niche in history. She died in 1841. The Boehm house in St James's Square has since been merged with the building next door to provide the premises of the East India Club, but the first-floor room where Percy laid the eagles at the feet of the Prince Regent is intact.

The leading daily newspaper editors of 1815 had mixed fortunes. Dr Stoddart of the *Times* was sacked the following year, the paper's proprietor losing patience not only with his hysterical politics but also with his habit of suppressing news that did not accord with his opinions. A bitter Stoddart promptly founded a new paper called *The Day and New Times* as a platform for those opinions. Rumoured to be funded corruptly by political interests in both Britain and France, it folded after a decade, though not before 'Dr Slop' had become Sir John Stoddart. The *Times*, under the ownership of the Walter family, went on to achieve a position of brilliance and market dominance in the mid-nineteenth century that has no parallel, and the paper survives to this day. As for James Perry of the *Morning Chronicle*, whose health was already failing in 1815, he retired two years later, at the age of sixty-one, and died in 1821. His paper went on to employ both Dickens and Thackeray, but the Perry years were its pinnacle, and it ceased publication in 1862. Of the three editors it was Nicholas Byrne of the *Morning Post* whose fate was the most dramatic; indeed it is unique in Fleet Street history. As his paper later recounted, he was still in charge in the early 1830s and sitting alone at his desk on the Strand on a winter's night, when

> a man entered unchallenged from the street and made his way to his room. He wore a crepe mask and rushing upon his victim stabbed him twice with a dagger. Mr Byrne, though mortally wounded, gave the alarm and managed to follow his assailant to the street, but he escaped in the darkness of the night and was never brought to justice.[15]

According to the *Post*, Byrne died of his injuries some months later, on 27 June 1833, thirty years after he had taken charge. The paper continued in production until 1937, when it was absorbed by the *Daily Telegraph*.[16]

Lucien Bonaparte, who was once resident at Thorngrove House in Worcestershire and who had rallied to his brother's support during the Hundred Days, saw out his days quietly in Italy, but his daughter Christine-Égypte would in time return to live in England as the wife of a prominent member of Parliament. The youthful affliction that had caused her to remain behind for medical treatment left its mark, and in later years she was described as hunchbacked, but this did not stop her marrying twice. On the second occasion, in Italy in 1824, it was to a younger son of the Marquess of Bute, Lord Dudley Coutts Stuart, and it was a scandalous and farcical business. First they married secretly while the annulment of her marriage to a Norwegian count was still pending. Then, on learning that the count had died, they married again in public, only to find that he was not dead after all. Long negotiations were required to place the union on a regular footing, but eventually Dudley Stuart was able to bring the emperor's niece home to London as his bride. The couple lived with their son close to Buckingham Palace and had a country seat in Surrey. By 1840, however, Lady Dudley Stuart, as she was known, had left her husband and was living in Italy again, and there in 1847 she died.[17]

Omnium, having closed on Thursday at 8 per cent premium, reached 13 per cent the following Tuesday, the *Morning Chronicle* observing that 'the effect may be seen upon the countenances of all, both upon 'Change and in the Alley'. Such was the glee, it wrote, that 'immense purchases' were still being made 'by individuals who, having tasted the sweets of the premium in omnium, were induced to try how much farther fortune was disposed to favour them'. Alas those late investors would have their fingers burned, for omnium soon began a fall that took it back to 8 per cent within two weeks. Those who had invested early, however, generally profited handsomely. Among them was the economist and stockbroker David Ricardo, who had led the negotiations with Vansittart. In August his friend James Mill would tease him about his profits, saying, 'you are now – Bless us all! – nobody can tell *how* rich!' To which Ricardo replied that he was indeed 'sufficiently rich to satisfy all my desires, and the reasonable desires of all those about me'.[18] In fact, Ricardo sold all his omnium before the news of Waterloo arrived, parting

THE NEWS FROM WATERLOO

with the last of it on Wednesday when the price passed 5 per cent premium. No doubt his investment had been large, and he also admitted to having made some advantageous manoeuvres at the time the loan contract was struck. Certainly the profits were gratifying – 'as great an advantage as I ever expect or wish to make by a rise' – and they freed him to give up stockbroking and devote himself full-time to economics. Another of the contractors, his friend Hutches Trower, held on longer and sold at 10 per cent premium, but Trower complained to Ricardo that he was disappointed the market did not go higher than it did:

> You ask me the fate of my Omnium. I sold it at 10 and might have obtained a higher price had I not been too sanguine. I entertained a confident opinion that the result would be such as it has proved, and expected that one so glorious and important would have produced a greater effect upon the Funds. But there is no reasoning upon them, therefore the less one has to do with them the better.[19]

Also a gainer, it seems, was Nathan Rothschild. The Rothschild Archive contains a note written to him from Paris that July by a bank employee, which carried the postscript: 'I am informed by Commissary White you have done well by the early information which you had of the victory gained at Waterloo.'[20] This implies that Rothschild's letter from Ghent on the Wednesday arrived in time to permit some stock purchases before the close of trading that evening, and though he would have been buying while Ricardo was selling, there was still room for him to 'do well' from the business, albeit nowhere near as well as Hutches Trower. Confirmation of sorts that Rothschild was a buyer that day comes from the writings of a London dandy called Thomas Raikes. Looking back to that Wednesday twenty-one years later, Raikes recalled Sir Robert Wilson spreading his story of a military set-back in Belgium at a dinner in Piccadilly, and he remarked: 'I felt little alarm at his prognostics, as I had heard that Rothschild was purchasing stock largely.'[21]

This brings us back to the Rothschild–Waterloo legend, on which a few final words are required. So beset is this tale by speculation, hearsay, family lore and plain dishonesty that any credible assessment has to be firmly grounded in written records from the time – records that are unequivocally clean of contamination by ideas and suggestions that arose in subsequent years. Only two such records have come to light. First is the *Caledonian Mercury* article written that Wednesday afternoon or evening stating that Nathan Rothschild had received a letter from Ghent informing him of Wellington's victory and had reported this to the Foreign Office. And second, mentioned above, is a document from a few weeks later quoting a British government official in Paris as saying that Rothschild had 'done well' by this early intelligence. Nothing besides these two items can be trusted, and on this basis it is safe to say that Rothschild probably received early, authentic news of the victory before Percy's arrival in London, that he probably informed the government and that he was probably able to profit from Thursday morning's sharp rise in the omnium price. Beyond this, many assertions made over the years can be discarded. Rothschild was not at Waterloo.

There was no storm in the Channel. He did not establish an express courier line to Dunkirk. The news did not arrive through Amsterdam. The stock market never collapsed in the relevant days, nor did Rothschild engineer a collapse. All this can be proved. Further elements of the legend fail for want of evidence, so there are no grounds to believe that Rothschild knew about Waterloo on the Tuesday, or that he received the information by pigeon post, or that it was brought to him by a sea-captain, or that he bought shares covertly or that he made a great fortune from Waterloo transactions. In a category of its own is the commonest assertion of all: that Nathan Rothschild was the first man in London to know of the victory. While this can never be categorically disproved, there is no evidence to support it and the evidence we have points in a different direction. The first person in London who can be detected in the historical record having verifiable knowledge of the outcome of Waterloo was not Nathan Rothschild but Mr C.

Alas, even that is not the end of the matter, for there is a version of this chameleon-like legend that co-opts Mr C as a Rothschild employee, so making Nathan Rothschild the recipient of his news. Perhaps surprisingly, the chief progenitor of this appears to have been the Duke of Wellington himself, who is recorded telling the story to dinner companions on several occasions after about 1820. In Wellington's version, the messenger was a Jew who, with Rothschild, went off to the City 'and did his little business there' before informing the government.[22] There are many reasons to doubt this. First, no report of the time made this connection and the contemporaneous evidence states that Rothschild received a letter from Ghent and not a messenger. Second, from what we know, the information received by Rothschild in his letter was distinct from the information brought to London by Mr C. Third, Mr C's conduct in London was not consistent with Wellington's story, for we know that, far from keeping his news secret so he could profit from it, he shared it so freely that it was very soon in the newspapers. Fourth, since the duke was obviously not in London in June 1815, his knowledge was based on hearsay and he never identified his source. In summary, this fails the evidence test and seems to have been little more than after-dinner chatter infected by the casual anti-Semitism of the day.

Nathan Rothschild appears never to have spoken or written of Waterloo as an important event in his life, and he may never even have heard the gossip emanating from Wellington's circle. Any profits he made from stock purchases that Wednesday afternoon can only have been modest compared with those made by others who had bought into the loan earlier, and also compared with his own gains in other, well-recorded transactions. In 1834, two years before he died, he declared that 'the best business I ever did' was buying and shipping coin for the payment of Wellington's army in the Peninsula.[23] This not only set him on the path to great wealth but also won him official favour – he appears to have been offered a knighthood and to have declined it.[24] In later life he was a pioneer of international financial operations, raising loans on the London money market for overseas governments, handling large-scale foreign exchange business and buying and selling bullion. His funeral was a grand City occasion, a procession of seventy-five carriages following the coffin to the Jewish burial ground in Whitechapel, with a crowd of 10,000 in attendance. The *Times* described his death as 'one of the most important events for the City, and perhaps for Europe, which has occurred for a very long time'.[25] The *Morning Post* pronounced him 'the first merchant of the first city in the world' and said his death 'may fairly be accounted a national loss'.[26] Neither obituary made any reference to Waterloo.

A final question remains: who was 'Mr C of Dover'? Sadly we don't know. Of all the many names that have been canvassed as the first bearer of the news from Waterloo, two begin with the letter C. One is Captain Cullen, who plunges us back into the Rothschild tangle, for Nathan Rothschild employed a whole family of sea-captains called Cullen in his cross-Channel business. As we have seen, however, there are strong reasons to rule out a connection between Rothschild and Mr C, and nothing we know about the Cullens alters that. The other name to have surfaced is Cook. When *Notes and Queries* sought information on the news from Waterloo in 1858, one of the answers it received was from a correspondent identified only as L. B. L. He wrote: 'I remember perfectly well that the name of the gentleman who brought the news of Waterloo from Ghent was Cook.' L. B. L.'s credit as a witness slips a little when he goes on to claim, most improbably, that he heard the cannon-fire from Waterloo at Canterbury and had a 'mysterious feeling' straight away that there had been a great victory. Nor does L. B. L. give any details of Mr Cook. But at the risk of speculating in a field where there has been far too much of that, there was a Robert Cook, not from Dover but with family in nearby

Folkestone, who could conceivably fit the bill. He was a merchant and smuggler, part of a twilight trade that had grown up on both sides of the Channel and benefited from a measure of official tolerance. This tolerance was explicit on the French side, where the government believed that some forms of smuggling would weaken the British economy, and Robert Cook was one of a number of Channel merchants who were officially recognised by the French authorities. Though he had family both in Folkestone and London, he had been born in Dunkirk in about 1785, and there is also evidence that in 1811 he lived in the southern Dutch port of Veere and had sisters there too. Such a man might well have passed through Ghent on business in 1815, and such a man – a legitimate operator in France but rather less so in England – might also have wished to keep his name out of London newspapers. We have an idea of what became of him, for he is probably the same Robert Cook listed in the 1841 British census as a teacher of French living in Whitechapel, and in the 1851 census as a merchant's clerk in Lambeth. Both are districts of London. All of this, however, is nothing more than guesswork founded on a few flimsy associations, and there are some reasons to doubt it: for example, would a messenger with Robert Cook's credentials be described so consistently as a 'gentleman'? Until someone finds concrete evidence about Mr C we must accept that, although we know how he learned the news and how he delivered it, we cannot put a name to the first man to bring word of Waterloo to London.

My Lord

Bonaparte having collected the 1st, 2nd, 3rd, 4th and 6th Corps of the French Army and their Imperial Guards and nearly all the cavalry on the Sambre and between that River and the Meuse between the 10th and 14th of the Month advanced on the 15th and attacked the Prussian Posts at Thuin and Lobez on the Sambre at day light in the morning.

Details of the opening page of the Waterloo Dispatch in Wellington's hand (TOP) © The British Library Board, Add. 69850 f.1, and the corrected fair copy received by Lord Bathurst (BOTTOM) © National Archives.

APPENDIX I

Wellington's Waterloo Dispatch

Waterloo June 19th 1815*

My Lord,

Bonaparte, having collected the 1st, 2nd, 3rd, 4th, and 6th corps of the French army and the Imperial Guards and nearly all the cavalry on the Sambre and between that river and the Meuse between the 10th and 14th of the month, advanced on the 15th, and attacked the Prussian posts at Thuin and Lobbes on the Sambre at daylight in the morning.

I did not hear of these events till in the evening of the 15th and I immediately ordered the troops to prepare to march; and afterwards to march to their left as soon as I had intelligence from other quarters to prove that the enemy's movement upon Charleroi was the real attack.

The enemy drove the Prussian posts from the Sambre on that day; and General Ziethen who commanded the corps which had been at Charleroi retired upon Fleurus; and

* This is my transcription of the fair copy delivered by Percy to Bathurst, which is preserved at the National Archives. For ease of reading I have altered the duke's spelling of 'Bruxelles' and 'patrole', reduced some capital letters to lower case and introduced a small number of additional commas. The duke's own manuscript is in the British Library and differs from this only in minor ways – with the one exception that where the duke himself wrote of three captured eagles this was corrected in the fair copy to two. See note, p. 69.

Marshal Prince Blücher concentrated the Prussian army upon Sombref, holding the villages in front of his position of St Amand and Ligny.

The enemy continued his march along the road from Charleroi towards Brussels and on the same evening the 15th attacked a brigade of the army of the Netherlands under the Prince de Weimar posted at Frasne, and forced it back to the farmhouse on the same road called Les Quatre Bras.

The Prince of Orange immediately reinforced this brigade with another of the same division under General Perponcher, and in the morning early regained part of the ground which had been lost, so as to have the command of the communication leading from Nivelles and Brussels with Marshal Blücher's position.

In the mean time, I had directed the whole army to march upon Les Quatre Bras; and the 5th division under Lt. General Sir Thomas Picton arrived at about half past two in the day, followed by the corps of troops under the Duke of Brunswick and afterwards by the contingent of Nassau.

At this time the enemy commenced an attack upon Prince Blücher with his whole force excepting the 1st and 2nd corps and a corps of cavalry under General Kellermann, with which he attacked our post at Les Quatre Bras.

The Prussian army maintained their position with their usual gallantry and perseverance against a great disparity of numbers, as the 4th corps of their army under General Bülow had not joined; and I was not able to assist them as I wished, as I was attacked myself and the troops, the cavalry in particular, which had a long distance to march, had not arrived.

We maintained our position also, and completely defeated and repulsed all the enemy's attempts to get possession of it. The enemy repeatedly attacked us with a large body of infantry and cavalry supported by a numerous and powerful artillery. He made several charges with the cavalry upon our infantry but all were repulsed in the steadiest manner. In this affair His Royal Highness the Prince of Orange, the Duke of Brunswick, and Lieut. General Sir Thomas Picton, and Major Generals Sir James Kempt and Sir Denis Pack, who were engaged from the commencement of the enemy's attack, highly distinguished themselves, as well as Lieut. General Charles Baron Alten, Major General Sir C. Halkett, Lieut. General Cooke, and Major Generals Maitland and Byng, as they successively arrived. The troops of the 5th division and those of the Brunswick corps were long and severely engaged, and conducted themselves with the utmost gallantry. I must particularly mention the 28th, 42nd, 79th, and 92nd regiments, and the battalion of Hanoverians.

Our loss was great, as your Lordship will perceive by the enclosed return, and I have particularly to regret His Serene Highness the Duke of Brunswick, who fell fighting gallantly at the head of his troops.

Although Marshal Blücher had maintained his position at Sombref, he still found himself much weakened by the severity of the contest in which he had been engaged, and as the 4th corps had not arrived he determined to fall back and to concentrate his army upon Wavre; and he marched all the night, after the action was over.

This movement of the Marshal's rendered necessary a corresponding one upon my part; and I retired from the farm of

Quatre Bras upon Genappe and thence upon Waterloo the next morning, the 17th, at ten o'clock.

The enemy made no effort to pursue Marshal Blücher. On the contrary, a patrol which I sent to Sombref in the morning found all quiet and the enemy's vedettes fell back as the patrol advanced. Neither did he attempt to molest our march to the rear although made in the middle of the day; excepting by following, with a large body of cavalry brought from his right, the cavalry under the Earl of Uxbridge.

This gave Lord Uxbridge an opportunity of charging them with the 1st Life Guards upon their *débouché* from the village of Genappe, upon which occasion his Lordship has declared himself to be well satisfied with that regiment.

The position which I took up in front of Waterloo crossed the high roads from Charleroi and Nivelles and had its right thrown back to a ravine near Merke Braine, which was occupied, and its left extended to a height above the hamlet Ter la Haye, which was likewise occupied. In front of the right centre, and near the Nivelles road, we occupied the house and garden of Hougoumont, which covered the return of that flank; and in front of the left centre we occupied the farm of La Haye Sainte. By our left we communicated with Marshal Prince Blücher at Wavre through Ohain; and the Marshal had promised me that in case we should be attacked he would support me with one or more corps as might be necessary.

The enemy collected his army, with the exception of the 3rd corps which had been sent to observe Marshal Blücher, on a range of heights in our front in the course of the night of the 17th and yesterday morning, and at about ten o'clock he commenced a furious attack upon our post at Hougoumont. I had occupied that post with a detachment from General Byng's brigade of Guards which was in position in its rear; and it was for some time under the command of Lt. Colonel Macdonell and afterwards of Colonel Home; and I am happy to add that it was maintained throughout the day with the utmost gallantry by these brave troops, notwithstanding the repeated efforts of large bodies of the enemy to obtain possession of it.

This attack upon the right of our centre was accompanied by a very heavy cannonade upon our whole line, which was destined to support the repeated attacks of cavalry and infantry, occasionally mixed, but sometimes separate, which were made upon it. In one of these the enemy carried the farm houses of La Haye Sainte, as the detachment of the light battalion of the Legion which occupied it had expended all its ammunition and the enemy occupied the only communication there was with them.

The enemy repeatedly charged our infantry with his cavalry but these attacks were uniformly unsuccessful; and they afforded opportunities to our cavalry to charge, in one of which Lord Edward Somerset's brigade consisting of the Life Guards, the Royal Horse Guards and 1st Dragoon Guards, highly distinguished themselves as did that of Major General Sir William Ponsonby, having taken many prisoners and an eagle.

These attacks were repeated till about seven in the evening, when the enemy made a desperate effort with cavalry and infantry supported by the fire of artillery to force our left centre near the farm of La Haye Sainte, which after a severe contest was defeated; and having observed that the troops retired from this attack in great confusion and that the march of General Bülow's corps by Frischermont upon Plancenoit and La Belle Alliance had begun to take effect and as I could perceive the fire of his cannon and as Marshal Prince Blücher had joined in person with a corps of his army to the left of our line by Ohain, I determined to attack the enemy and immediately advanced the whole line of infantry supported by the cavalry and artillery. The attack succeeded in every point. The enemy was forced from his positions on the heights and fled in the utmost confusion, leaving behind him as far as I could judge 150 pieces of cannon with their ammunition, which fell into our hands. I continued the pursuit till long after dark; and then discontinued it only on account of the fatigue of our troops who had been engaged during 12 hours, and because I found myself on the same road with Marshal Blücher, who assured me of his intention to follow the enemy throughout the night. He has sent me word this morning that he had taken 60 pieces of cannon belonging to the Imperial Guard and several carriages, baggage etc. belonging to Bonaparte in Genappe.

I propose to move this morning upon Nivelles and not to discontinue my operations.

Your Lordship will observe that such a desperate action could not be fought and such advantages could not be gained without great loss, and I am sorry to add that ours has been immense. In Lieut. Genl. Sir Thomas Picton His Majesty has sustained the loss of an officer who has frequently distinguished himself in his service, and he fell gloriously leading his division to a charge with bayonets by which one of the most serious attacks made by the enemy on our position was defeated. The Earl of Uxbridge after having successfully got through this arduous day received a wound by almost the last shot fired which will I am afraid deprive His Majesty for some time of his services.

His Royal Highness the Prince of Orange distinguished himself by his gallantry and conduct till he received a wound from a musket ball through the shoulder which obliged him to quit the field.

It gives me the greatest satisfaction to assure your Lordship that the army never upon any occasion conducted itself better. The division of Guards under Lt. General Cooke, who is severely wounded, Major General Maitland and Major General Byng set an example which was followed by all and there is no officer nor description of troops that did not behave well.

I must, however, particularly mention for His Royal Highness's approbation Lt. General Sir H. Clinton, Major General Adam, Lt. General Charles Baron Alten (severely wounded), Major General Sir Colin Halkett (severely wounded), Colonel Ompteda, Colonel Mitchell (commanding a brigade of the 4th division), Major Generals Sir James Kempt and Sir Denis Pack, Major General Lambert, Major General Lord E. Somerset, Major General Sir W. Ponsonby, Major General Sir C. Grant and Major General Sir H. Vivian, Major General Sir O. Vandeleur, and Major General Count Dornberg. I am also particularly indebted to General Lord Hill for his assistance and conduct upon this, as upon all former occasions.

The engineer and artillery departments were conducted much to my satisfaction by Colonel Sir G. Wood and Colonel Smyth; and I had every reason to be satisfied with the conduct of the Adjutant General Major General Barnes, who was wounded; and of the Quarter Master General, Colonel De Lancey, who was killed by a cannon shot in the middle of the action. This officer is a serious loss to His Majesty's service, and to me at this moment.

I was likewise much indebted to the assistance of Lieut. Colonel Lord FitzRoy Somerset, who was severely wounded, and of the officers composing my personal staff who have suffered severely in this action. Lieut. Colonel the Hon. Sir Alexander Gordon, who has died of his wounds, was a most promising officer and is a serious loss to His Majesty's service.

General Kruse of the Nassau service likewise conducted himself much to my satisfaction as did General Tripp, commanding the heavy brigade of cavalry, and General Vanhope, commanding a brigade of infantry in the service of the King of the Netherlands.

General Pozzo di Borgo, General Baron Vincent, General Müffling, and General Alava were in the field during the action and rendered me every assistance in their power. Baron Vincent is wounded but I hope not severely; and General Pozzo di Borgo received a contusion.

I should not do justice to my own feelings or to Marshal Blücher and the Prussian army if I did not attribute the successful result of this arduous day to the cordial and timely assistance I received from them.

The operation of General Bülow upon the enemy's flank was a most decisive one; and, even if I had not found myself in a situation to make the attack which produced the final result it would have forced the enemy to retire if his attacks should have failed and would have prevented him from taking advantage of them if they should unfortunately have succeeded.

I send with this dispatch two eagles taken by the troops in this action which Major Percy will have the honour of laying at the feet of His Royal Highness.

I beg leave to recommend him to your Lordship's protection.

I have the honour to be your Lordship's most obedient humble servant,

Wellington

P.S.

Since writing the above, I have received a report that Major General Sir Wm. Ponsonby is killed, and in announcing this intelligence to your Lordship, I have to add the expression of my grief for the fate of an officer who had already rendered very brilliant and important services and was an ornament to his profession.

APPENDIX 2

The Price of Omnium, 19–22 June 1815

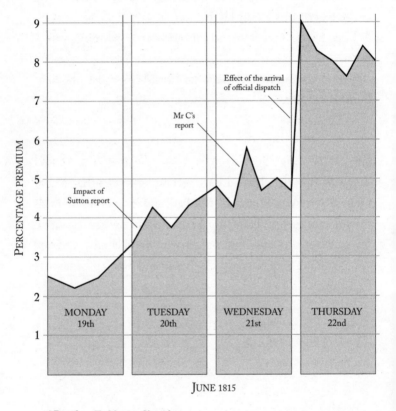

JUNE 1815

* Data from *The Morning Chronicle*

Bibliography

Newspapers have provided a great deal of the information for this book, and where quoted they are identified. The principal collections relied upon have been those of the British Library, many but by no means all of which are available at www.britishnewspaperarchive.co.uk, those of the *Times* and the *Guardian/Observer*, which have their own archive websites, and those of www.newspaperarchive.com. Journals, notably *Notes and Queries*, the *Edinburgh Review* and the *Quarterly Review*, have also been valuable sources. The following are the books and articles that have been most valuable.

Adkin, M. (2001) *The Waterloo Companion*, Aurum, London.

Alison, Sir A. (1848) *History of Europe from the Commencement of the French Revolution in 1789 to the Restoration of the Bourbons in 1815*, 7th edn, Blackwood, Edinburgh and London.

Andrews, A. (1859) *The History of British Journalism*, Bentley, London.

Aspinall, A. (1949) *Politics and the Press, 1780–1850*, Home & Van Thal, London.

Asquith, I. (1973) 'James Perry and the Morning Chronicle, 1790–1821', PhD thesis, University of London.

Austen, J. (1991) *Pride and Prejudice*, Everyman's Library edn, London.

Bagot, Lady S. L. P. (1899) 'Bygone Days', in *Blackwood's Edinburgh Magazine*, March 1899.

Bagot, Lady S. L. P. (1901) *Links with the Past*, Edward Arnold, London.

Ballard, J. (1913) *England in 1815 as Seen by a Young Boston Merchant*, Houghton Mifflin, Boston and New York.

Barbero, A. (2006) *The Battle: A New History of Waterloo*, Atlantic, London.

Barker, H. (1999) *Newspapers, Politics and English Society, 1695–1855,* Longman, London.

Benham, H. (1986) *The Smugglers' Century*, Essex Record Office, Chelmsford.

Bew, J. (2011) *Castlereagh: Enlightenment, War and Tyranny*, Quercus, London.

Bonaparte, N. (1858–69) *Correspondance de Napoléon 1er,* Dumaine, Paris.

Bonaparte, N. (2011) *Mémoires de Napoléon: de l'Elbe et les Cent-Jours,* Bonnaud, Paris.

Brownlow, Countess E. S. (1867) *Slight Reminiscences of a Septuagenarian from 1802 to 1815,* John Murray, London.

Burney, F. (1892) *The Diary and Letters of Madame d'Arblay (Frances Burney),* Warne, London.

Chandler, D. G. (1987) *Waterloo: The Hundred Days*, Philip, London.

Clark, J. W. and Hughes, T. McK (eds) (1890) *The Life and Letters of the Reverend Adam Sedgwick*, Cambridge University Press.

Cobbett, W. (1834) *History of the Regency and Reign of King George the Fourth*, Cobbett, London.

Colby, R. (1965) *The Waterloo Despatch*, HMSO, London.

Corti, Count E. C. (1928) *The Rise of the House of Rothschild*, Gollancz, London.

Cranfield, G. A. (1978) *The Press and Society from Caxton to Northcliffe,* Longman, London.

Dairnvaell, G. M. M. ('Satan') (1846) *Histoire edifiante et curieuse de Rothschild 1er, Roi des Juifs*, Paris.

Dairnvaell, G. M. M. (1846) *Jugement rendu contre Rothschild,* Paris.

Dale, J. (2006) *'Napoleon is Dead': Lord Cochrane and the Great Stock Exchange Scandal*, Sutton, Stroud.

Dallas, G. (1996) *1815: The Roads to Waterloo*, Richard Cohen, London.

Davis, R. (1983) *The English Rothschilds*, Collins, London.

Demachy, E. (1896) *Les Rothschild: une famille de financiers juifs au XIX siècle*, Paris.

Disraeli, B. (1870) *Coningsby, or The New Generation*, Longman, London.

Durand, H. M. (1883) *The Life of Major-General Sir Henry Marion Durand*, W. H. Allen, London.

Edgcumbe, R. (ed.) (1913) *The Diary of Frances Lady Shelley*, John Murray, London.

Faulks, S. (2010) *A Week in December*, Vintage, London.

Ferguson, N. (1998) *The House of Rothschild*, vol. 1, *Money's Prophets 1798–1848*, Penguin, London.

Ferguson, N. (2008) *The Ascent of Money: A Financial History of the World*, Allen Lane, London.

Fleischmann, T. (1953) *Le Roi de Gand: Louis XVIII et les émigrés français à Gand pendant les Cent Jours*, La Renaissance du Midi, Brussels.

Foster, R. E. (2014) *Wellington and Waterloo: The Duke, the Battle and Posterity, 1815–2015*, Spellmount, Stroud.

Foulkes, N. (2006) *Dancing into Battle: A Social History of the Battle of Waterloo*, Weidenfeld & Nicolson, London.

Fowler, J. K. (1898) *Records of Old Times*, Chatto and Windus, London.

Fox-Bourne, H. R. (1887) *English Newspapers: Chapters in the History of Journalism*, Chatto and Windus, London.

Fraser, E. (1991) *The War Drama of the Eagles*, Worley, Felling.

Frost, A. J. (ed.) (1880) *Catalogue of Books and Papers Relating to Electricity, Magnetism, the Electric Telegraph etc.*, Spon, London.

Gallatin, J. F. (ed.) (1914) *A Great Peace Maker: The Diary of James Gallatin, Secretary to Albert Gallatin*, Heinemann, London.

Gille, B. (1965) *Histoire de la Maison Rothschild*, vol. 1, *Des Origines à 1848*, Droz, Geneva.

Gleig, Revd G. R. (1848) *The Story of the Battle of Waterloo*, John Murray, London.

Glover, G. (ed.) (2004) *Letters from the Battle of Waterloo*, Greenhill, London.

Glover, G. (ed.) (2010) *The Waterloo Archive*, vol I: *British Sources*, Frontline, Barnsley.

Glover, G. (ed.) (2011) *The Waterloo Archive*, vol III: *British Sources*, Frontline, Barnsley.

Glover, G. (ed.) (2012) *The Waterloo Archive*, vol IV: *British Sources*, Frontline, Barnsley.

Glover, G. (ed.) (2012) *Wellington's Voice: The Candid Letters of Lt. Col. John Fremantle*, Frontline, Barnsley.

Grant, J. (1871) *The Newspaper Press: Its Origin, Progress and Present Position*, Tinsley, London.

Gray, V. and Aspey, M. (1998) *The Life and Times of N. M. Rothschild*, N. M. Rothschild & Sons, London.

Green, D. (1985) *Great Cobbett: The Noblest Agitator*, Oxford University Press, Oxford.

Greenwood, J. (1971) *Newspapers and the Post Office, 1635–1834*, Postal History Society, n.p.

Greig, J. (ed.) (1922–8) *The Farington Diary*, Doran, New York.

Greville, C. C. F. (1885) *A Journal of the Reign of Queen Victoria*, Longman, London.

Gronow, R. H. (1862) *Reminiscences of Captain Gronow*, Smith Elder, London.

Gurwood, J. (ed.,) (1837–9) *The Despatches of Field Marshal The Duke of Wellington*, John Murray, London.

Halévy, E. (1949) *England in 1815*, Ernest Benn, London.

Hamilton-Williams, D. (1995) *Waterloo: New Perspectives. The Great Battle Reappraised*, Arms and Armour, London.

Hardcastle, Mrs (ed.) (1881) *Life of John, Lord Campbell, Lord High Chancellor of Great Britain*, John Murray, London.

Hayward, A. (ed.) (1864) *Diaries of a Lady of Quality* [Frances Williams Wynn], Longman, London.

Hazlitt, W. (1821) *Table-Talk, or Original Essays*, Warren, London.

Herd, H. (1955) *Seven Editors*, Allen and Unwin, London.

Hill, B. E. (1836) *Recollections of an Artillery Officer, Including Scenes and Adventures in Ireland, America, Flanders and France*, Richard Bentley, London.

Hill, C. (ed.) (1894) *Frederic Hill: An Autobiography of Fifty Years in Times of Reform*, Bentley, London.

Houssaye, H. (1905) *1815: La Seconde Abdication et la Terreur Blanche*, Perrin, Paris.

Houssaye, H., trans. S. R. Willis (1905) *1815: Waterloo*, Franklin Hudson, Kansas City.

Ingrams, R. (2006) *The Life and Adventures of William Cobbett*, Harper, London.

Irving, P. M. (1883) *Life and Letters of Washington Irving*, Putnam, New York.

Jennings, L. J. (ed.) (1884) *The Correspondence and Diaries of the Late Right Honourable John Wilson Croker*, John Murray, London.

Jerdan, W. (1852) *The Autobiography of William Jerdan*, Hall, Virtue & Co., London.

Journals of the House of Commons (1814–15), vol. 70.

Joyce, H. (1893) *The History of the Post Office*, Bentley and Son, London.

Kaplan, H. K. (2006) *Nathan Mayer Rothschild and the Creation of a Dynasty, 1806–1816*, Stanford University Press, Stanford.

Kincaid, J. (1830) *Adventures in the Rifle Brigade in the Peninsula, France and the Netherlands*, Boone, London.

Lennox, Lord W. P. (1853) *Three Years with the Duke, or Wellington in Private Life*, Saunders and Otley, London.

Lloyd, H. E. (1830) *George IV, Memoirs of his Life and Reign*, Teruttel and Wurtz, London.

Londonderry, Marquess of (ed.) (1848–53) *Memoirs and Correspondence of Viscount Castlereagh*, Colbourn, London.

Longford, E. (1969) *Wellington: The Years of the Sword*, Weidenfeld & Nicolson, London.

Longford, E. (1972) *Wellington: Pillar of State*, Weidenfeld & Nicolson, London.

MacDonagh, M. (1913) *The Reporters' Gallery*, Hodder & Stoughton, London.

Maisonfort, Marquis de la (1998) *Mémoires d'un agent royaliste*, Mercure de France, Paris.

Mallinson, H. (2005) *Send It by Sempahore: The Old Telegraphs during the Wars with France*, Crowood Press, Ramsbury.

Malmesbury, Earl of (1870) *A Series of Letters of the First Earl of Malmesbury*, Bentley, London.

Markham, J. D. (2008) *The Road to St Helena: Napoleon after Waterloo*, Pen and Sword, Barnsley.

Mathews, C. (1822) *Sketches from Mr Mathews at Home!* Edinburgh.

Maxwell, Sir H. (ed.) (1912) *The Creevey Papers*, John Murray, London.

Mitchell, J. (1816) *A Tour through Belgium, Holland . . . in the Summer of 1816*, Longman, London.

Moore Smith, G. C. (ed.) (1903) *The Autobiography of Lieutenant-General Sir Harry Smith*, John Murray, London.

Morton, F. (1962) *The Rothschilds: A Family Portrait*, Secker and Warburg, London.

Muir, R. (1996) *Britain and the Defeat of Napoleon, 1807–1815*, Yale

University Press, New Haven and London.

Newspaper Press Fund Yearbook 1904.

Pellew, G. (1847) *The Life and Correspondence of the Rt Hon. Henry Addington, First Viscount Sidmouth*, John Murray, London.

Quincey, de, T. (1862) *The English Mail Coach and Other Writings*, Black, Edinburgh.

Raikes, T. (1858) *Portion of the Journal Kept by Thomas Raikes Esq, from 1831 to 1847*, Longman, London.

Reeves, J. (1887) *The Rothschilds: The Financial Rulers of Nations*, John Murray, London.

Robinson, M. (2010) *The Battle of Quatre Bras 1815*, Spellmount, Stroud.

Rogers, S. (1859) *Recollections*, Longman, London.

Rolfe-Smith, B. (2012) *A Gilded Cage: Lucien Bonaparte, Prisoner of War*, Stonebrook Publishing, Ludlow.

Roth, C. (ed.) (1934) *Lucien Wolf: Essays in Jewish History*, Jewish Historical Society of England, London.

Rothschild, Baron V. (1982) *The Shadow of a Great Man*, London.

Rush, R. (1833) *A Residence at the Court of London*, Bentley, London.

Sadler, T. (ed.) (1869) *Diary, Reminiscences and Correspondence of Henry Crabb Robinson*, Macmillan, London.

Savage, J. (1811) *An Account of the London Daily Newspapers, and the Manner in Which They Are Conducted*, London.

Scott, Sir W. (1816) *Paul's Letters to his Kinsfolk*, Constable, Edinburgh.

Semallé, Comte J.-R. P. de (1898) *Souvenirs du comte de Semallé*, Picard, Paris.

Siborne, H. T. (ed.) (1993) *Waterloo Letters*, Greenhill, London.

Siborne, W. (1844) *History of the War in France and Belgium, 1815*, Boone, London.

Simpson, J. (1853) *Paris after Waterloo: Notes Taken at the Time and Hitherto Unpublished*, Blackwood, Edinburgh.

Smithers, H. (1820?) *Observations Made during a Tour in 1816 and 1817*, Brussels.

Stanhope, P. H., 5th Earl (1888) *Notes of Conversations with the Duke of Wellington, 1831–1851*, John Murray, London.

Strafford, Countess A. (ed.) (1903) *Personal Reminiscences of the Duke of Wellington by Francis, the First Earl of Ellesmere*, John Murray, London.

Taylor, T. (ed.) (1853) *Life of Benjamin Robert Haydon*, Longman, London.

Thackeray, W. M. (1861) *The Four Georges*, Smith, Elder & Co., London.

Thackeray, W. M. (1998) *Vanity Fair*, Penguin, London.

Thompson, N. (1999) *Earl Bathurst and the British Empire, 1762–1834*, Cooper, Barnsley.

Ticknor, G. (1876) *Life, Letters and Journals of George Ticknor*, Houghton Mifflin, Boston.

Times (1935) *The History of the Times*: 'The Thunderer' in the Making, 1785–1841, Times, London.

Trench, Mrs R. (1862) *Remains of the Late Mrs Richard Trench*, Parker, Son and Bourn, London.

Tupper Carey, A. D. (ed.) (1899) 'Waterloo: Reminiscences of a Commisariat Officer', *Cornhill Magazine* vol. 79 (June).

Wadsworth, A. P. (1955) 'Newspaper Circulations 1800–1954', *Manchester Statistical Society Papers*, session 1954–5.

Waldie, C. A. (1817) *Narrative of a Residence in Belgium, by an Englishwoman*, John Murray, London.

Wallace, W. (1832) *Memoirs of the Life and Reign of George IV*, Longman, London.

Walters, R., Jnr (1957) 'The James Gallatin Diary: A Fraud?' *American Historical Review*, vol. LXII (July).

Ward, R. R. (ed.) (1906) *A Week at Waterloo in 1815: Lady de Lancey's Narrative*, John Murray, London.

Waresquiel, E. de. (2008) *Cent Jours: la tentation de l'impossible*, Fayard, Paris.

Weller, J. (1998) *Wellington at Waterloo*, Greenhill, London.

Wellington, Duke of (ed.) (1858–72) *Supplementary Despatches, Correspondence and Memoranda of Field Marshal Arthur, Duke of Wellington*, John Murray, London.

Wilde, E. E. (1913) *Ingatestone and the Essex Great Road with Fryerning*, Oxford University Press, Oxford.

Wilson, B. (2005) *The Laughter of Triumph*, Faber, London.

Wilson, D. (1995) *Rothschild: A Story of Wealth and Power*, revised edn, Mandarin, London.

Wilson, G. (1976) *The Old Telegraphs*, Philimore, London.

Winfield, R. F. (2005) *British Warships in the Age of Sail, 1793–1817*, Chatham, London.

Yonge, C. D. (ed.) (1868) *The Life and Administration of Robert Banks, Second Earl of Liverpool*, Macmillan, London.

Young, J. C. (1871) *A Memoir of Charles Mayne Young, Tragedian*, Macmillan, London.

References

Foreword

1 For examples, see *Notes and Queries* (27 Nov 1858), p. 434; (18
   Dec 1858), p. 502; (1 August 1868), p. 114; (19 July 1873), p. 45. Also
   Westminster Gazette (14 April 1903), p. 2, and *Manchester Mail* (22
   August 1892).
2 See, for example, Gangel, K. O., and S. A. Canine, *Communication and
   Conflict Management in Churches and Christian Organizations*, Wipf
   and Stock, Eugene, Oregon, 2002, p. 47.

1 Sunday: The News is Made

1 Strafford, p. 179.
2 Scott, p. 169.
3 Wellington to Beresford, 2 July 1815, Gurwood, vol. 12, p. 529.
4 Moore Smith, p. 271.
5 Kincaid, p. 343.
6 'À présent c'est fini; sauvons-nous.' The words were recalled by Jean-
   Baptiste de Coster, a local man acting as guide to Bonaparte. *Mercure
   Belge* [Brussels], vol. 1 (1817), p. 69.
7 Stanhope, p. 245.

2 Sunday–Monday: The Waterloo Dispatch

1 Tupper Carey, p, 735.
2 This was Col. Sir W. de Lancey. He died a few days later, but at this
   stage Wellington believed he was already dead. For his story see his
   widow's moving narrative in Ward.
3 This was Sir Harry Smith. Moore Smith, p. 291.
4 Cathcart, Sir G., 'Record of Events of My Life', in National Library
   of Scotland ACC 12686/121, fols. 75–6. By Cathcart's account it was
   Count Pozzo di Borgo who suggested a letter to Louis XVIII. See
   Chapter 4, p. 75.

5 Wellington to Earl of Beaufort, 19 June 1815, Gurwood, vol. 10, p. 489.

6 Cathcart, see Chapter 2, note 4, above.

7 Lennox, pp. 217–8.

8 The artist was his niece, Lady Burghersh. See illustration, p. 11.

9 Maxwell, p. 236n.

10 Glover, *Waterloo Archive*, vol. 1, p. 228.

11 Burney, p. 351. Her account occupies pp. 348–58.

12 Maxwell, p. 233. Creevey's account, written in 1822, occupies pp. 224–39.

13 Wellington, vol. 10, p. 531 Lord Mountnorris was the father of Lady Frances.

14 Stanhope, p. 90.

15 Stanhope, p. 145. 'Mr Quincy Adams ... declared on first reading the dispatch that it came from a defeated general, and that in real truth the Duke's army must have been annihilated at Waterloo.'

16 Wellington, vol. 10, p. 531 A third copy, only slightly amended, was sent that day to the King of the Netherlands. PRO 31/17/31.

3 Monday: London

1 See works by Mallinson and Wilson, G.

2 Austen, pp. 168–9.

3 Hardcastle, p. 29. John Campbell would go on to work as a journalist for the *Morning Chronicle* and later become Lord Chancellor.

4 Andrews, vol. 2, p. 76 The calculation was made for the year 1813.

5 Hansard, vol. 30 col. 806, Commons debate, 24 April 1815, statement by Croker.

6 *Morning Chronicle* (15 March 1815).

7 The tale of the Winchester semaphore has no foundation in evidence. Winchester was not a telegraph station, nor does it lie on any sensible news route between Belgium and London.

8 *Freeman's Journal* (15 June 1876). The film was *The House of Rothschild*, starring George Arliss as Nathan Rothschild.

9 Asquith, p. 315.

10 Rush, p. 197.

11 Both from the *Morning Chronicle* of that Monday. The court circular extract is from the same paper.

12 Savage, p. 11.

13 Savage, p. 11.

14 Jerdan, vol. 1, pp. 165–6.

15 See the official history of the *Times*, vol. 1, Chapter VII.
16 National Archives CUST 54/162, p. 83, 'Instruction for Custom House London', 13 June 1815.
17 Sadler, vol. 1, p. 288.

4 Monday: News on the Move

1 Wolfe's poem, written in 1816, achieved instant popularity through the press and was established in the canon of essential verse by the advocacy of Byron. Wolfe, an Irish rural curate, never wrote anything else that was half so popular.
2 5 November 1810. This item appeared almost word for word in a dozen newspapers around the country.
3 Gurwood, vol. 6, p. 424.
4 Third canto, verses 21 and 22. The verse that follows is 24.
5 Durand, pp. 1–2.
6 Colby, p. 12. Also, the Archives of the Duke of Northumberland at Alnwick Castle, Acc. 224/1.
7 Fraser, p. 371.
8 *Caledonian Mercury* (18 September 1815).
9 *Courier* (24 June 1815).
10 Detail of the eagle from Fraser, p. 11.
11 Captain George Barlow to his father, in Glover, *Waterloo Archive*, vol. 4, p. 157.
12 Ensign Thomas Wedgewood, in Glover, *Waterloo Archive*, vol. 1, p. 145.
13 Lt John Luard in Glover, *Waterloo Archive*, vol. 1, p. 82.
14 Glover, *Waterloo Archive*, vol. 3, p. 79.
15 Major I. B. Clarke to Carruthers family in Glover, *Waterloo Archive*, vol. 4, p. 55.
16 Earl of Uxbridge in Glover, *Waterloo Archive*, vol. 3, p. 4.
17 Captain Wodehouse to Miss Parry, in Glover, *Waterloo Archive*, vol. 1, p. 87.
18 Major-General Sir James Kempt to Major-General Sir James Willoughby Gordon, in Glover, *Waterloo Archive*, vol. 4, p. 194.
19 Captain James Nixon, in Glover, *Waterloo Archive*, vol. 1, p. 134. He refers to the battle of Leipzig, 1813.
20 Captain Courtenay Ilbert to Anne Ilbert, in Glover, *Waterloo Archive*, vol. 3, p. 198.
21 Fleischmann, p. 166.

22 Wellington to Duc de Berry, the king's nephew and the commander of his small army-in-exile, timed at 3 a.m., 18 June. Gurwood, vol. 12, pp. 466–7. This letter was delivered by Admiral Sir Pulteney Malcolm. See p. 145.

23 Semallé, pp. 255–60.

24 Maisonfort, p. 268.

25 Semallé, p. 256.

26 Maisonfort, p. 268.

27 *Le Journal Universel* (21 June 1815).

28 *Courier* (21 June 1815).

29 The later time is given in the *Sun* of 21 June.

5 Monday–Tuesday: Extraordinary Agitation

1 This pamphlet, like the nickname, was the inspiration of the radical journalist William Hone.

2 *Times*, vol. 1, p. 158.

3 See Rolfe-Smith.

4 *Times* (29 November 1814).

5 *Star* (20 June 1815).

6 *Times* (21 June 1815).

7 *Lincoln, Rutland and Stamford Mercury* (23 June 1815).

8 Wilde, p. 275. For more on Sutton's background see Benham.

9 *Courier* (21 June 1815).

10 'de le repousser jusqu'à une certaine distance': Prince of Orange to the King of the United Netherlands, 17 June 1815. Wellington, vol. 10, pp. 496–7.

11 Wellington, vol. 10, p. 495.

12 For events in Paris, see Houssaye, *La Seconde Abdication*, pp. 4–7.

6 Tuesday: An Awful Moment

1 For example, *Caledonian Mercury*.

2 Kent County Archives CKS – U269/O226/4. A time of around noon is indicated by remarks at the beginning about what 'will appear' in the evening papers and at the end showing he had seen these papers. He appears to have been writing as they arrived.

3 Disraeli, p. 72. 'In a subordinate position his meagre diligence and his frigid method might not have been without value; but the qualities that he possessed were misplaced; nor can any character be conceived

less invested with the happy properties of a leader.'

4 Gurwood, vol.12, pp. 269–70.
5 Foreign Office, 24 May 1815. *Journals of the House of Commons*, vol. 70, p. 652.
6 Liverpool to Castlereagh, 20 February 1815, Yonge, vol. 2, p. 104.
7 Castlereagh to Wellington, 26 March 1815, Londonderry, vol. 10, p. 285.
8 Hansard, vol. 31, col. 795, Commons debate, 14 June 1815.
9 Liverpool to Canning 13 June 1815, Yonge, vol. 2, pp. 178–9.
10 David Ricardo's correspondence, introduced, edited and annotated by Piero Sraffa, can be read at the Online Library of Liberty website.

7 Tuesday Evening: The Green Knight

1 Duke of Northumberland's Collections, Acc224/1.
2 Major Alexander Woodford in Glover, *Waterloo Archive*, vol. 1, p. 138.
3 Hill, B. E., vol. 2, pp. 110–11.
4 Winfield, p. 283.
5 National Archives, ADM 52/4560.
6 Houssaye, *La Seconde Abdication*, pp. 9–11.
7 Bonaparte, *Correspondance*, vol. 28, pp. 293–9.
8 Markham, p. 13.
9 This was the letter referred to on p. 77.
10 The quoted version of this appeared in *Quarterly Review*, LXXVI (June 1845), pp. 222–4. A fuller and slightly different version was published in the *Manchester Courier and Lancashire General Advertiser* of 25 September 1880.
11 The remark was made to Captain George Bowles of the Coldstream Guards. Malmesbury, vol. 2, p. 447.
12 HMS *Leveret* log, National Archives, ADM 51/2501.
13 *Morning Herald* (21 June 1815).
14 *Statesman* (21 June 1815).
15 *Morning Chronicle* (21 June 1815).
16 Cranborne can be found in the guest list of a party given in London on Friday 16th, published in the *Morning Post* on Monday 19th.
17 On the 21st.

8 Tuesday: The Rothschild Legend

1 Dairnvaell, *Histoire édifiante et curieuse*, pp.11–12.
2 *Northern Star* (5 September 1846).

3 Dairnvaell, *Jugement rendu*, p. 24.

4 See Rothschild, *Shadow of a Great Man*.

5 Demachy, pp. 65–85.

6 Reeves, p. 169–75.

7 *Newspaper Press Fund Yearbook 1904*, p. 42.

8 Wolf, p. 284. The essay in this posthumous collection is collated from newspaper articles Wolf published between 1903 and 1913.

9 Faulks, p. 152.

10 See The Rothschild Archive London, XI/112/22, May to N. M. Rothschild. May, the Ostend agent, is replying to letters from Rothschild bearing those dates. It may be significant that Rothschild has clearly written demanding information about the progress of the war.

11 The Rothschild Archive, XI/38/180, Morel to N. M. Rothschild.

12 Gallatin, p. 76.

13 Walters, pp. 878–85.

9 Wednesday Morning: A Gentleman from Ghent

1 Here too the *Times* was gilding the lily. Colchester was closer to London than the Kent ports, but the sea crossing was longer, and Colchester was a difficult port, several miles up the shallow River Colne.

2 For example, the *Times* (20 June 1815).

3 Figures from Robinson, p. 369.

4 Stanhope, p. 174.

5 Jennings, pp. 59–60.

6 See *Notes and Queries* (19 July 1873), p. 45; Hayward, pp. 157–8; *Daily Telegraph* (9 November 1962).

7 Coleridge, *The Rime of the Ancient Mariner*.

8 *Derby Mercury* (29 June 1815).

9 This distance is suggested by the *Peruvian*'s noon location, given in the ship's log as fifteen miles west of Ramsgate.

10 Wednesday Afternoon: Rumours and Letters

1 Stephen, L. (ed.) (1890), *Dictionary of National Biography*, Macmillan, London, vol. XXI, p. 204.

2 Thackeray, *The Four Georges*, p. 187.

3 Wallace, p. 297.

4 Lloyd, p. 257.

5 Weller, p. 38.

6 *London Gazette* (24 June 1815), p. 1.

7 *Haarlemsche Courant* (20 June 1815).

8 Markham, p. 23.

9 Raikes, p. 456.

10 Maxwell, p. 240.

11 Which evening paper this was is not clear, but the *Public Ledger* of the next morning reported this, only to dismiss it as 'altogether void of foundation'.

12 *Caledonian Mercury* (24 June 1815).

13 *Caledonian Mercury* (24 June).

14 Its total strength on the day was probably nearer 30,000. See Adkin, p. 70.

15 See letter, pp. 75–6.

11 Wednesday Evening: 'Victory, sir! Victory!'

1 Mathews, p. 42.

2 *Morning Chronicle, Morning Post* (22 June 1815).

3 *Beppo*, LVI.

4 *Don Juan*, Canto 11, verses 8 and 9.

5 Stanhope, 6 October 1839, p. 173.

6 Edgcumbe, vol 1, p. 87.

7 *Notes and Queries* (4 December 1858). This is a letter from Thomas Boys, who recounts that Vansittart told this story to a Revd R. L. Melville, who told it to him.

8 Colby, p. 23.

9 Stanhope, 6 Oct 1839, p. 174.

10 *Morning Chronicle* (23 June 1815). The gentleman was Sir Edwin Baynton Sandys.

11 Bennet to Creevey, July 1815, in Maxwell, pp. 240–41. 'Nothing could be more droll', wrote Bennet, who was a political ally of Wilson and Grey. 'To be sure, we are good people, but sorry prophets!'

12 Brownlow, p. 117. Her mention of three eagles rather than two was a common error in later reminiscences. See note on p. 69.

13 Young, pp. 212–3.

14 Trench, pp. 316–7.

15 Brownlow, pp. 118–9.

16 Pellew, vol 3, p. 129.

17 Raikes, vol. 1, pp. 457–8.

18 *Edinburgh Review* (April 1864), p. 331. The report of Sir Frederick Ponsonby's death was a mistake: wounded seven times and left for dead, he was eventually found on the battlefield and nursed back to health.

19 Bagot, 'Bygone Days', p. 468.

12 Thursday and Friday: The Summit of Glory

1 *Leeds Intelligencer* (26 June 1815).

2 Ballard, p. 115.

3 Taylor, vol. 1, p. 278. Haydon's recollection is discussed in *Notes and Queries* (28 Oct 1876, 10 Feb 1877).

4 Greig, pp. 11–12.

5 This appears to be Creevey's letter to Bennet. See p. 74.

6 Hansard, vol. 31, col. 980, Commons debate, 23 June 1815.

7 Hansard, vol. 31, col. 991–2, Commons debate, 23 June 1815.

8 Ballard, p. 116.

9 De Quincey, p. 311.

10 Hill, C., p. 36.

11 *Gloucester Journal* (10 July 1815).

12 Fowler, pp. 120–21.

13 Glover, *Waterloo Archive*, vol. 1, p. 170.

14 Irving, vol. 1, p. 164.

15 *Liverpool Mercury* (23 June 1815).

16 *Leeds Intelligencer* (26 June 1815).

17 http://www.rc.umd.edu/editions/southey_letters/Part_Four/HTML/letterEEd.26.2621.html.

18 Clark and Hughes, vol. 1, p. 137.

19 *Daily Gazette* [Middlesbrough] (22 May 1899), p. 22.

20 Simpson, pp. v–vi.

21 Stanhope, p. 122.

22 Ticknor, vol. 1, p. 60. Ticknor mistakenly recorded this under the date 20 June.

23 Ticknor, vol. 1, p. 62.

24 Hazlitt, p. 115.

25 Cobbett, para. 221.

13 Differences and Distances

1 It appeared in both the *Morning Chronicle* and the *Morning Post*.
2 This letter, and the reply mentioned below, are in Frost, pp. x–xi.

14 Afterlives

1 Markham, p. 35.
2 Longford, *Pillar of State*, p. 23.
3 Greville, vol. 1, p. 135.
4 Bagot, *Links with the Past*, p. 117. This was Charles's verdict, in a letter to their sister Susan. He does not say whether it was the company or the weather which made the crossing disagreeable.
5 See p. 64.
6 Glover, *Wellington's Voice*, p. 187. The subsequent quotation is p. 291.
7 Beverley to Lord Lovaine, 3 April 1816, The Archives of the Duke of Northumberland at Alnwick Castle, DNA:F/39/7.
8 Beverley to Lord Lovaine, 24 March 1821, The Archives of the Duke of Northumberland at Alnwick Castle, DNA:F/39/9.
9 http://www.historyofparliamentonline.org/volume/1820-1832/member/percy-hon-henry-1785-1825.
10 Wellington to Percy, 5 September 1819, The Archives of the Duke of Northumberland at Alnwick Castle, F/40/60a.
11 Bagot, *Links with the Past*, p. 108.
12 Wilde, p. 276.
13 18 September 1847, Fr Jérôme Grange to Fr Villerd, parish priest at Saint Jodard, near Roanne, and to Fr Nicoud, parish priest at Saint Clair, near Condrieu, in http://www.mariststudies.org/docs/Girardo661.
14 Young, p. 214.
15 *Morning Post* (2 November 1872, 28 June 1833).
16 Byrne's death, like his life, is mysterious in several respects. See 'The Strange Case of the Murdered Editor', in Herd's *Seven Editors*. Herd concludes that 'we must assume, incredible though it appears', that this attack took place.
17 http://www.historyofparliamentonline.org/volume/1820-1832/member/stuart-lord-dudley-1803-1854.
18 Letters of 23 August and 30 August 1815. http://oll.libertyfund.org/titles/ricardo-the-works-and-correspondence-of-david-ricardo-vol-6-letters-1810-1815.

19 Trower to Ricardo, 23 July 1815. Sraffa, P. (ed.) (1951), *The Works and Correspondence of David Ricardo*, Cambridge University Press, vol. 6; http://oll.libertyfund.org/titles/ricardo-the-works-and-correspondence-of-david-ricardo-vol-6-letters-1810-1815.

20 The Rothschild Archive, 112/51 and T3/341, 27 July 1815.

21 Raikes,vol. 3, p. 46.

22 Stanhope, p. 173.

23 Rothschild, p. 3.

24 James de Rothschild to Hannah Rothschild, 26 August 1815. The Rothschild Archive, T30/49/2.

25 *Times* (3 August 1836).

26 *Morning Post* (15 August 1836).

Index